PRAISE FOR SETH FERRANTI

"Seth's stories are strong and they resonate with a sense of truth that needs to be expressed." Kenneth "Supreme" McGriff, New York City Street Legend

"I'm a little biased because most of the people Seth reports on are personal friends of mine, but Seth's reporting is almost unmatched, he just doesn't copy reports, he interviews the villains, uses the reports and then weeds out the B.S. on both sides using his own battles with Uncle Sam to reveal the truth. That's why he's the best at what he does." Lamont "Fridge" Needum, author of *Straight Savage*

"Seth has written some of the most interesting biographies on urban gangsters in his Street Legends series. He is the new voice of the streets." 4Front Magazine

"Seth has the guts to tackle issues that the typical writer is either afraid of or incapable of, touching the most subtle and intricate locations in order to give readers the meat they deserve for their dedications." Walter "King Tut" Johnson, NYC Original Gangster

"Author Seth Ferranti brings his readers true crime stories from inside prison. Interviewing imprisoned gangsters and crime bosses, he manages to paint a refreshing picture of American gangland." — Gangstersinc.tripod.com

"Seth Ferranti has been busy. He is working on the next installment of his Street Legends series and other manuscripts. If that isn't enough, Seth is also a contributing writer for Don Diva, F.E.D.S. and several websites. His pen never rests." — OOSA Book Club

"With the Street Legends series in stores, an active blog at gorillaconvict. com and several regular writing gigs for Don Diva, F.E.D.S. and Get Money magazines, Seth is a candid voice that will continue to have prison administrations shook." — TheSmokingSection.com

"Ferranti is a true crime writer of note, behind bars and in the streets, and the chronicler of gangster stories that might not otherwise be told." NewCriminologist.com

"Seth has employed the power of the pen to speak for those who are slowly and painfully being digested in the belly of the beast. Through Gorilla Convict Publications he has put out the Street Legends series, which chronicles the stories of modern day urban outlaws such as Frank Matthews and Wayne Perry. His work has also appeared in long running street magazines such as F.E.D.S. and Don Diva." — PlanetIll.com

"From reading Seth's books I found him to be an intelligent and articulate writer who wraps his considerable knowledge of the street in the language of the hood. There's no doubt Seth Ferranti knows what he's talking about." — Mobwriter.blogspot.com

"Seth Ferranti is the most respected name in urban, gangster and prison literature." — Michael "Mickman" Gourdine, author *Chili Pimping in Atlantic City*

"As an accopmplished author, journalist and publisher, Seth Ferranti is most recognized for covering organized crime personalities that range from drug lords to wiseguys. He has access, on a daily basis, that few journalists can claim. The reason why he's so privy to the oft-disturbing, raw reality firsthand accounts and tales of locked up legends? Well, Ferranti himself has been incarcerated since 1993, and he's met more than a few fat cat criminals and their associates, over the last two decades, within the cold walls of Fereal institutions. Interesting thing about it... many of them respect him enough to share their stories and inside knowledge of events and people that the average citizen might otherwise only imagine as a Hollywood, unbelievable take." — MafiaLifeBlog.com

PRAISE FOR STREET LEGENDS VOL. 2

"Ferranti continues to amaze us with the most infamous OG's and their unfathomable street life." — The Source Magazine

"Street Legends delves into the legends of some of the most noted street figures of the 21st Century. Seth brings the harsh reality of America's narco history to a new generation." — Hip Hop Weekly

"Gorilla Convict is evolving into the most potent voice of the streets.

Street Legends is the apple of a street soldier's eye." — Walter "King Tut" Johnson, New York City Original Gangster

"Seth Ferranti is a gifted author that brings the realness of the street to the pages of his books. Street Legends is a classic book that should be read twice by any young hustler that's thinking about joining the game of life and death." — Freeway Ricky Ross, American Gangster

"Street Legends chronicles the life, the legend and the lore of some of the biggest names in the history of the drug game." — urbanbooksource.com

"If you haven't read Street Legends Vol. 2 by Seth Ferranti yet you ain't no reader. You talkin' about grindin' while on lock? I think Seth got me beat." — Wahida Clark, New York Times Bestselling author

"This is my first book from Seth Ferranti and I commend him for doing such a wonderful job with this book. He uses accurate points of view on each street legend. This is a must read, especially for our young generation out there in the streets. Simply though provoking." — Readers Paradise Book Club

PRAISE FOR STREET LEGENDS VOL. 1

"Seth takes readers behind the scenes in Street Legends. This isn't fiction. This is real life. Through their own words, words of those that were around at the time, the media and court records, Ferranti recounts the history of some of the most notorious." — OOSA Book Club

"Have you ever watched American Gangster on BET? Author Seth Ferranti brings American Gangster from BET to the books in Street Legends." — Rawsistaz Reviewers

"Incarcerated author Seth Ferranti has compiled a who's who of the late 20th Century's most infamous kingpins in Street Legends, a compendium series documenting crack era America's criminal enterprises. Ferranti has fashioned a rouges gallery of drug lords that is as compelling as it is concise. This is a must read for true crime enthusiasts." — Smooth Magazine

"Street Legends would be a good guide for individuals who want to know the real meaning of keepin' it gangsta. Urban fiction fans and people who indulge in crime reads will also enjoy this."

— APOOO Book Club

"In this gripping gangstaography Seth Ferranti manages to once again take you somewhere you don't want to go." — Don Diva Magazine

"You heard the songs now read the true stories of these larger than life street stars mythologized in hip-hop and gangster culture." — pulppusher.com

"While spectators wonder what really transpired between Wayne 'Silk' Perry and Alberto 'Alpo' Martinez, Seth Ferranti has actually reached out to those who knew them personally. Gorilla Convict Publications allows him to spread the knowledge via books such as his Street Legends series, which are full of street lore." — ScottsMindfield.com

"In his book Street Legends, Seth writes about hell and the devil. There is a hell on earth; it's called a supermax prison. And it's where they keep the devil. Only in this case, there's more than one devil- there's six. The stories of these street icons twirl around cocaine and heroin, money, cars and bling-bling. The merry go round turns into a Tilt-a-Whirl of violence and murder as the street hustlers ride the streets. In the end, each of the six devils profiled in this book are imprisoned in hell on earth for life." — AlvahsBooks.com

PRAISE FOR PRISON STORIES

"Prison Stories outlaw rawness mixes well with hip-hop's street essence. Fans of Iceberg Slim's pimp tales or HBO's 'OZ' series will really dig this." Elemental Magazine

"Prison Stories reveals a world of fearless convicts, inconspicuous snitches and deadly gang rivalry." The Ave Magazine

"Ferranti's details are much of what is captivating about the book- his writings about the hierarchy of the prison economy is fascinating. Prison Stories is a great read. Ferranti's voice is gritty and tough." Razorcake Magazine

"I must say Seth Ferranti is a truly wonderful storyteller, even with jail being as horrible as it is. He brought all the accounts to life as if you were there with him. It's good to see he has turned all the negatives from the beginning of his sentence to a positive." Urban Reviews

STREET LEGENDS VOL. 3

"THE MOST POTENT VOICE OF THE STREETS."

THE SUPREME TEAM

THE BIRTH OF CRACK AND HIP-HOP, PRINCE'S REIGN OF TERROR AND THE SUPREME/50 CENT BEEF EXPOSED

Gorilla Convict Publications © 2012
First Printing April 2012
ISBN 978-0-9800687-4-0   0-9800687-4-6
E-Book 978-0-9800687-5-7

Design by Matt Pramschufer of E-Moxie
Cover by Matt Pramschufer of E-Moxie

Printed in the United States of America

Published by
Gorilla Convict Publications
1019 Willott Road
St. Peters, MO 63376
www.gorillaconvict.com

FOREWORD

It is an extreme burden, yet a great honor to find myself introducing an amazing body of work by such a profound writer and friend- Seth "Soul Man" Ferranti; for what Seth has accomplished over the years in what I term an urban media analysis, is truly remarkable and cannot be easily expressed... In this information-age, where the latest gossip and misinformation is always a click of the mouse away, Seth has chosen to investigate, interview and filter the information with an unbiased eye choosing to educate his readers with truth rather than make money off of glorified lies, which countless reporters have made millions doing. For this reason, Seth has become the go-to man for many publications such as Don Diva, Street Elements, F.E.D.S., King, Slam, Urban Celebrity, 4Front, Urban Exposure and countless others. Bringing readers the truth about modern day gangsters such as Frank Matthews, Maurice "Peanut" King, Kenneth "Supreme" McGriff, Wayne Perry, Aaron Jones and Peter "Pistol Pete" Rollock – many of which he's actually done time with or befriended through mail correspondence.

I have read many books on gangsters, street kings, urban legends and mob bosses, but none with the quality or style (care for a better) that Seth brought with this Street Legends series. To quote Walter "King Tut" Johnson, "Seth takes the combination of good and evil and transforms them into a well balanced dish of (true) gangsterism." Telling the whole of the story instead of simply propagating the gore and violence. Through his style of writing, one is about to become intimate with the characters and witnesses (as well as feel) the regret or penitence in situations where such feelings are applicable. By doing so he gives the reader a full picture of the game (betrayal and long prison terms as a result) and not just the glossy Hollywood version, so readers are able to come to a better understanding of the game and make better choices concerning the game. And as I've studied his body of work I've never seen him hesitate to call a rat a rat or an informant a coward. Nor has he ever failed to expose celebrity gangsters that not only violate the street codes that they claim to live by, but also betray their supposed cohorts in light of higher record sales or more street creed. Seth is an honest and trusted voice in a game of lies and deceit. Truth, wisdom and realness have long been staples of

Seth's excellence, principals that discern him from the pack of others and make this new offering a work of journalistic art.

With Truth,
Plex (Da Ruler)

Founder of Badland Publishing and author of Boo Baby and numerous other novels.

INTRODUCTION TO STREET LEGENDS VOL. 3

Just like Hollywood catapulted the Italian Mafia into the mainstream with the Godfather movies, *New Jack City* documented the devastating crack epidemic and the drug crews that terrorized and held court in the city's projects. Nino Brown was a fictional character, as was his crew, but you didn't have to look far to find their real life counterparts who dominated the headlines of New York City's tabloid newspapers. Characters and cliques that seemed to evolve straight out of the pages of a Donald Goines novel rose to prominence, becoming larger than life figures and ghetto stars in their respective hoods.

Street tales, real life crimes, newspaper headlines, Hollywood sensationalism, and rapper's rhymes have perpetrated, promoted, and created a legend of mythical proportions that has grown exponentially over the last 20 years, keeping the Supreme Team, the most infamous crew out of the Southside of Jamaica Queens, ringing bells from coast to coast. As one of the most notorious crews from a deadly era, the team towers above its contemporaries in stature, notoriety, and infamy. But it's not all convoluted hype. Infamy has its price.

Besides Hollywood paying court to the black gangster, many rappers who were shorties in the 1980s, otherwise known as the crack era, the time of the Supreme Team's reign and dominance, have name checked the team's exploits in verse. The chosen son Nas first broadcast them to the world on 1994s *Memory Lane* and Queens native 50 Cent shouted them out on 2000s *Ghetto Qur'an*, Ja Rule and others have also celebrated the Supreme Team in their songs creating an everlasting tribute in their rhymes. With black gangsters newfound relevance in our pop culture because rappers put them on pedestals and mythologized their crime exploits in verse, a new kind of anti-hero from the inner-city is taking its place in the pantheon of outlaw heroes next to figures like John Gotti, Pablo Escobar, Billy the Kid and John Dillinger in American folklore. With magazines like Don Diva, F.E.D.S., Street Elements, 4Front and AS IS, Ethan Brown's *Queens Reigns Supreme* and BET's *American Gangster* series whetting the public's appetite for the street legends long idolized by rappers, a movement is afoot.

The Street Legends series from Gorilla Convict Publications is part of this growing movement. We are at the forefront. With Street Legends Vol. 1 we brought you the Death Before Dishonor Six- Supreme, Wayne Perry, Anthony Jones, Aaron Jones, Pistol Pete and Boy George. In Street Legends Vol. 2 we brought readers more of that real gangsta flavor with stories on Original Gangsters Frank Matthews, Peanut King, Michael Fray, The Boobie Boys, Short North Posse and New World. And now in Volume 3 of Street Legends we bring readers- The Supreme Team. Read their story and witness their rise from Baisley Projects on the Southside of Jamaica Queens. From street corner hustlers to drug barons living the fast life, their ruthless ways precipitated their downfall. But in Prince's demise, Supreme rose from the ashes and became a player in the hip-hop culture he spawned.

His resurgent rise with Murder Inc., and his conflicts with 50 Cent are revisited as are all the hoopla and controversy surrounding their beef. This book chronicles the complete story of the Supreme Team from its inception to its fall to its rise again. This legendary crew was very instrumental in the birth of hip-hop and they ushered in the crack era in New York City with devastating brutality. Their influence on hip-hop has lasted 25 years and is still going strong. This book is their story, in their words and the words of others who were there. It's brought to you straight out of the penitentiary by Gorilla Convict Publications.

AUTHOR'S NOTE

This book was years in the making. I have wanted to do it for a long time, and I finally completed it. I wanted it to be the definitive volume on the Supreme Team, but I have found out that it can never be that. There are too many stories, too many members out there, and there is no way I'll ever be able to talk to all of them. Remember that the Supreme Team is an organization that allegedly had over 200 members. I did the best job I could with the material and Supreme Team members to whom I had access, which is more access than any other true crime journalist or writer has had since I have been in prison for the last nineteen years.

By no means did I break the Supreme Team story, but I have had a hand in writing their history and I take pride in that effort. I wrote the original Supreme Team article for Don Diva magazine in Issue 23. I also wrote the Kenneth "Supreme" McGriff piece for The Good, The Bad and The Ugly issue of Don Diva, and of course I chronicled Supreme's story in Street Legends Vol. 1, the book that started my Street Legends series, of which this book represents Volume 3. I hope to keep writing and bringing readers more street stories from the chronicles of gangster lore.

I could not have done this alone though. I was lucky enough to be incarcerated with several Supreme Team members, Ronald "Tuck" Tucker and David "Bing" Robinson, whose help was invaluable to this project. Without them, this book or the previous work I have done on the Supreme Team would have not materialized. I owe a tremendous debt and thanks to them for their trust, belief, and faith in me to tell this story. But as I said, a lot of different Supreme Team members have stories to tell such as Tuck, whose forthcoming book, T*eam Player: Truths of a Southside Ambassador* will take readers places where my book could never go. Although I'd like to call my work the definitive Supreme Team book, it still only goes a little beneath the surface. Tuck and Bing were there in the midst of it all, and I know their stories can go places mine never can. I'm just giving respect where respect is due.

I have been lucky to meet stand up men like Tuck and Bing during my bid, but I also got to meet Supreme at FCI Gilmer in 2005. To meet the man that 50 Cent rapped about and who was such a towering street legend was inspiring. We talked a lot about book, movie and writing projects, and the entertainment world in general. I always told him that he needed to tell his story, but, at the time, with all the allegations surrounding himself and Murder Inc., he wasn't willing to do an interview despite getting letters every week from newspapers, magazines, and book publishers that were interested in his story.

When the Murder Inc. indictments came out and before they took him back to court, he came to me and told me that I could do the Supreme Team story, but he didn't want it to be in his words. He wanted it to be in the words of his peers, his fellow convicts, and co-defendants. He told me to holler at Tuck who was at FCI Gilmer also. I knew Tuck from being on the compound, but I didn't know that he was a Supreme Team member until Preme told me which showed what a classy and righteous dude Tuck is. He was not the type to toot his own horn or let people know he was affiliated with such a notorious crew.

Tuck and I worked on the Supreme Team piece for Don Diva shortly before he went home in 2005. And later when I transferred to FCI Loretto in October 2006, Tuck hooked me up with his co-defendant Bing, another Supreme Teamer from way back and another classy and stand-up guy. When Bing called Tuck to check out who I was, Tuck told him that I was like them, meaning a stand-up guy. Hearing what Bing said that Tuck had said about me, made me very proud because in the prison system these dudes are well known, admired, and honored for their principles and their convictions.

From these team members and Supreme, I got all of the material that I would use for the foundations of my first Street Legends Vol. 1 story on Supreme and this book. Without them it wouldn't have been possible. They gave me access to a world I had only heard about in 50 Cents and Nas' raps. These were the dudes that influenced hip-hop culture, drug war policies, and the way the dope game is played and portrayed. They were the original gangsters with the Southside flavor who have been memorialized and lauded in hip-hop's lyrical lore. Supreme told me, "I'm going to need a voice," meaning a writer to chronicle his story, and I have tried to stay true to that request by being his voice since he is buried in ADX. To me, though, the Supreme Team is more than a story.

I have been fortunate enough to call these men friends and to have had their help to put together my work on the Supreme Team. It may not be the definitive volume on the team, but it has a lot of different and diverse information gleaned from court records, newspaper articles, magazine articles, and my own interviews with the above mentioned team members, their homeboys, and others. I have gotten some inside stuff that only someone who was there would know. I believe this book is representative of the team and their history and just might be the most concise volume detailing their exploits to date. Some team members might not agree with everything in here but I can't please everybody. I have just tried to write the truth.

Just to keep it real, I'd like to say that several Supreme Team members including Tuck, Bimmy and C-Just didn't want this book to happen. For whatever reason, they voiced their displeasure with what I am doing. I have reached out to several Supreme Team members including Prince and haven't heard back from them. So what they think of this book I can't say. For whatever reason, they have chosen not to be a part of this project. I can respect that, but they have to respect my right to write and tell a story I want to tell. Other team members have stepped forward but wished to remain anonymous, so I have afforded them that luxury. Their words are in here, and anyone who was around in that era will recognize the authenticity of their stories and reflections on all that went down.

I reached out to Supreme to get his blessing, as he gave his blessing on all my previous Supreme Team projects. It took a minute for him to get back to me, since he is buried in ADX, but he gave me the greenlight. "You know I support you and your endeavor's 100 percent. You have my blessing, so do you and don't worry about anyone or anything else." Supreme wrote, giving me the approval I needed to put this book out. I stand by my work and hope you enjoy it.

Thank you.
Seth Ferranti, FCC Forrest City, December 2011

"Each generation out of relative obscurity must discover their mission, fulfill it or betray it." — Frantz Fanon, *The Wretched of the Earth*

"The majestic figure of Mephistopheles is alien to us. The devil is not loftiness- he is mediocrity and triviality." — Alexander Elchaninou

"In this country you gotta make the money first. Then when you get the money, you get the power. Then when you get the power. Then you get the women." — Tony Montana, *Scarface*

I dedicate this book to my wonderful and beautiful wife, Diane. Thank you for making all this possible. Without you Gorilla Convict Publications and all my work would never see the light of day. Behind every successful man stands a good and strong woman.

CHAPTER 1
ORIGIN OF THE TEAM

"Some fiends scream about Supreme Team/a Jamaica, Queens thing."
— **Nas, Memory Lane (Sittin' in Da Park) Illmatic 1994**

*"The Southside of Queens began making history with the birth of its
street legends and urban gangsters in the 70s and 80s."*
— **Don Diva Magazine, Issue 23**

*"Queens wasn't considered hard. The borough had tree lined streets.
Mothers and fathers raised kids together. Kids went to school and life
was simply middle class."*
— **As Is, Issue 2**

"Queens used to be a quiet little place," Lance Fuertado, a Queens
native and Seven Crowns alumni said. The working class neighborhoods
of South Jamaica, St. Albans, and Hollis lie in the 103rd Precinct, which
is a 4.8 square mile imperfect box encompassing Van Wyck Expressway
to the west, Hillside Avenue to the north, Francis Lewis Boulevard to the
east, and a jagged line that runs along 110th Avenue to the south. With
the decline of Harlem and Bedford-Stuyvesant after World War II, the
Southside of Queens became a haven for upscale blacks trying to escape
the collapse of housing stock and the rise in crime rates in the slums. St.
Albans, in particular, gained a reputation as the suburban Sugar Hill.
Such celebrities as Count Basie, Jackie Robinson, and Ella Fitzgerald
moved in. Doctors, lawyers, and successful business men followed, along
with civil servants and middle-management people. Home ownership
was common, and a dozen bus lines made the district accessible allowing
its commercial strips to thrive.

But after whites moved out in the early-60s, services began to
deteriorate. At around the same time, a powerful Harlem drug dealer

named Pops Freeman appeared on the scene, running numbers and heroin businesses. "The story I've heard is that he was sent out to Queens by Vito Genovese of the Genovese crime family," the Queens detective said. "Pop had kept his mouth shut about the family when he'd been arrested a few years before and they rewarded him with the new territory." With Freeman's arrival, the problems many tried to flee from in Harlem and other neighborhoods followed them to Queens. "When you drive around the area, you sometimes let your guard down because you see all these nice houses and quiet streets," the Queens hustler said. "But after a while you realize some of the people are doing the same shit, taking drugs and killing people that they do in neighborhoods with abandoned tenements." It was a classic case of the environment casting a seemingly innocent picture while the criminal element worked away on the fringes exploiting the pleasant, mild-mannered surroundings to their advantage, despite any perceived suburban illusions.

The subway ride from Manhattan to the 179th Street station in South Jamaica, Queens, was so long that when passengers came up the stairs and into the street, they felt as if they had jet lag. One Hundred Seventy Ninth Street was the last stop on the F line, a neighborhood so outer borough it might as well have been in another state. By heading south, across Jamaica Avenue and passing through a desolate area of abandoned buildings and trash strewn lots dubbed Bricktown by the locals, visitors arrived in one of hip-hop's fertile crescents- 134th Avenue and Guy R. Brewer Boulevard. This area also doubled as ground zero for crack. A few blocks away was Woodhull in Hollis, a middle-class oasis among the crack chaos, where Run DMC originated from. Looming over everything was Baisley Park Houses, one of the city's toughest housing projects, which spawned the notorious Supreme Team.

Queens has always been a fascinating place because it was the true immigrant borough of New York City. There were very strong immigrant areas like Jackson Heights, but at the same time, there were strong middle-class black neighborhoods like Hollis. Then at the opposite end of the scale were some very deep pockets of poverty like South Jamaica. Within the deep pockets of poverty were some extremely nasty neighborhoods that have been perpetuately nasty. These were areas that were troubled for so long that they never really turned it around the way other neighborhoods in New York City did. The whole borough wasn't doomed to a never-ending cycle of violence, but there were definitely certain areas that were very troublesome and remained high crime areas, then and now. Some parts of Queens were very rough and seemed to stay that way. The juxtaposition of the middle-class areas with private homes and tree-lined streets and the grim city housing projects provided the perfect backdrop for an emerging drug trade. With affluence on one hand and poverty on the other, it wasn't hard to foresee the consequences.

Back in the day, Queens was known as the desert, and dudes from Queens didn't have any type of reputation in the city. "They used to have a saying in New York," Bing, an original Supreme Team member says. "Manhattan make it, Queens fake it and Brooklyn take it." In the other boroughs it was imperative for hustlers to stay NYC ghetto sharp and on top of their game. The city bred a culture of respect in which god was a gun. In the criminal underworld, dudes from Queens didn't have a very high standing.

"Most men from Queens didn't have a base. They didn't have that type of name like niggas in Brooklyn or the Bronx." God B, another original Supreme Team member said. "It was only in the late-70s, 80s that niggas in Queens weren't ashamed to be from Queens." The borough was in the midst of a transformation. The climate in New York was changing, and Queens would be at the center of it.

At Rikers Island in the early-80s dudes from the city were coming through shook and scared to death. They had heard the wild ass stories. They knew who was running shit up in the island, and the wrong answer could get a dude fucked up. If someone asked a new guy where he was from, he wouldn't say Queens because Queens just wasn't considered hard. The borough had a *Mr. Rogers' Neighborhood* kind of feel. Mothers and fathers raised their children together in a *Sesame Street* environment. Kids went to school, and life was considered semi middle-class. Queens wasn't exactly on that thug-type status, especially at Rikers. Brooklyn had that thug-shit on lock back then. They had the yard, controlled the phones and mess halls, and ran the b-ball court. In Rikers the dudes from the BK held it down. There were the few and far between cats who could and would hold it down for their borough, but, for the most part, it was all Brooklyn. That was the hierarchy. But things were about to change.

Drugs had been in Queens since Pops Freeman moved his heroin operation into the area from Harlem in the 1960s. When Pops Freeman faded from the scene, a litany of other dealers sprung up to supply the developing market in the bubbling area that was earning a name for it's culture and style. Around 1981 and 1982 South Road was the drug spot. Not too far away was Jamaica Avenue, where the retail district was situated with the bus terminal, meat markets, and other stores. Mel's Diner was right there, and the numbers runners used to call in their bets at the Long Island railroad station. The bus routes crisscrossed the area while the dealers held sway on 150th Street between South Road and

107th Avenue.

On those blocks the O.G. Danny sold dope and coke. He was getting money just like the other O.G.'s Hymee and Cornbread. Everybody knew them, and everybody bought drugs from them. The ghetto was different back then before the Supreme Team and organized dealing hit the scene. This was before the violence of the crack era and before hip-hop went global. The whole Queens culture was still where it originated, in Queens, incubating, taking shape as the world force it would become. In the midst of it all were the future Supreme Team members. They were just shorties hanging out, doing what kids do, but they would play an important role in the evolution of Queens.

As Pops Freeman reached his seventies, a series of younger, more ruthless drug dealers emerged, including Ronald "Bumps" Bassett and later Lorenzo "Fat Cat" Nichols. Bassett, 36 at the time, was chosen to take over Freeman's wholesale heroin distribution around 1979 and soon achieved success comparable to that of Harlem kingpin Nicky Barnes. "Nicky was more flamboyant," the Queens hustler said, "but Ronnie was up there. Ronnie was big." Bassett had more than 100 employees running his numbers and drug rackets in at least nine outlets around Queens. He took his business to at least eight other cities around the country, forging routes to Baltimore, Detroit, and Philadelphia that later dealers would utilize. During a nine week period, federal agents traced $1.2 million worth of uncut heroin with a street value of more than $15 million back to Bumps' operation. One of the people Bassett supplied with drugs was Fat Cat, a Seven Crowns member.

According to legend, Seven Crowns started out in 1970 as a street gang of rabble rousers whose members pelted houses and threatened to burn them down. Its members grew to include the future movers and shakers of Queens, including Anthony "Pretty Tony" Feurtado, Fat Cat and James "Wall" Corley.

"Seven Crowns was way early-70s," Bing says. "I was in Seven Crowns. It was all on the Southside but different areas. It was all one gang." While the origin of the name, Seven Crowns, was unclear, two people who were arrested wore gold rings with diamonds in the shape of a seven encrusted over a crown. Each gang member was viewed as a jewel in the crown. "In the early-70s Queens had a lot of gangs," Lance said. "We were fools. We went off the chain. At one point we were 1500 members strong. That was way back in the early-70s. We were just friends. This is how everything came together. It was one love. We unified like 77-78. Our role models were guys on the street from the hood who sold drugs. Our childhood was like normal kids. We were wild, but we didn't carry any guns, we believed in a beat down."

Queens in the 70s, as in most areas where black folks settled, was filled with young people with radical leanings and no outlet. After the dismantling of black militant groups like the Black Panthers, street gangs emerged, inspired by the militancy but without the political bent. "Everybody wanted to be in a gang then," Bing says. "It wasn't wild. It was comfortable. We had little gang fights but no major killings, little brawls, shit like that, regular shit, no gunplay."

Michael Mitchell, who everyone called Mr. Black or just plain Black formed the Queens division of the Seven Crowns, a gang originally from the Bronx. His neighbors, Fat Cat and Pretty Tony, joined immediately. "We lived on the same block and we went to the same schools. We knew each other since childhood," Lance said. "We were trend setters; we would go out and steal minibikes and stuff."

Seven Crowns broke down into certain divisions and teams. There was the Seven Crowns, Big Crowns, Lil' Crowns, and Homicide Crowns. When Fat Cat and Lance first joined the Lil' Crowns, Fat Cat was quickly made war counselor. His primary duty was to represent the Crowns in any dispute requiring a one on one confrontation. "Cat was big and strong for his age," Black said. "Smart kid too, and on top of that he was good with his hands. We were the ones who gave him the name Fat Cat because of his size." In the Southside of Jamaica, Fat Cat became feared because of his fighting skills. In the ghetto tough guys were admired and respected. Violence was the currency of the streets.

"I first met Fat Cat when we went into the Forties Houses to break up the Seven Crowns. They didn't call him Fat Cat then. They called him Fat Boy. Any problem in the gang meant a call to Nichols to crush it," the Queens detective said. "There were only twelve of us in the whole task force, so you got to know the street players pretty well. The Crowns had their drugs, but it was mostly smoke and heroin. No cocaine to speak of. Certainly no crack. Only the white kids were fucking around with angel dust, the same with pills. The Crowns wouldn't screw around with pills. Fat Cat was just a kid, but he was a big kid. He had a mouth on him too. Still, he had some magnetism. You could see that. If we wanted guys to move, we'd go to Fat Cat. Once the Cat moved, they'd follow."

When Fat Cat was paroled in 1980 from Spofford, the juvenile facility where he met the young Howard "Pappy" Mason, he walked into a fertile and growing drug market on the Southside. Pretty Tony was doing his thing, so he put Fat Cat on. Fat Cat didn't just get on though, he locked it down. His ascension to the top of the Queens drug hierarchy was essentially unobstructed. By the time the Supreme Team started hustling, the landscape was changing. They would come to dominate what Pretty Tony and Fat Cat started. They would get deep in the streets and lock the area down just like Fat Cat.

The Cat moved around South Jamaica virtually untouched. He had the occasional riff with dudes from Forty Projects, but for the most part he was just about fun and money. Sixty or so thousand was an average week, and that was just off dope. Fat Cat was doing his thing. He had 20 dudes working for him, and his organization was growing. Pappy Mason held the crew down as enforcer. While everybody played their position, Cat was the shot caller. Together they moved as one, making money and partying. Everyone was styling in Queens. The names that started ringing bells in the streets of South Jamaica formed an alliance. They were all coming out of the borough that was once the place to raise a family, not duck for cover. With the coming of the young drug lords, all that would change. Forty Projects started rumbling while Baisley Projects was vibrating. The Southside was bubbling with drug crews and money. The natural order would persevere, but in the chaos of the streets anything could happen. Coke was moving, but crack was on the way, and the numbers would rise. These were the wonder years.

Rivalries had existed between the loosely organized hustlers of Hollis and South Jamaica, but the balance of power had never tipped in any one direction until 1981 when ex-con and former Seven Crowns' member Fat Cat set up shop on 150th Street near 107th Avenue. The block was ideal for drug dealing as it forked off from Sutphin Boulevard, making it easier to conduct deals with a sense of privacy, and Fat Cat's heroin and cocaine business took off almost immediately. The 150th Street and 107th Avenue site was also just ten blocks away from the Corley family's Forty Projects base. Hustlers from every part of the Southside were shocked by Fat Cat's boldness. It didn't help that Cat wasn't a local since he was raised in the Ozone Park section of Queens, nor that his background was in armed robbery, not drugs. Still Fat Cat did what Fat Cat wanted. Word of the bustling drug trade on 150th Street made it a magnet for both upandcoming entrepreneurs like the Supreme Team and seasoned tough guys like Fat Cat. "Cat was down there, other crews," Bing says. "It was where niggas hustled at. It was the turf of Seven Crowns." They called it the block, 150th Street and Sutphin Boulevard.

The Southside of Queens began making history in the late 1970s and 1980s as their street legends and urban gangsters gained a measure of fame. Ronnie Bumps, Cornbread, Hymee, Danny, Pretty Tony, Wall Corley, and Fat Cat were the pioneers. They played a big role in the way things were. "The Southside mentality. That stigma of the Southside just imposes its will on the people who live there," Lance said. That mentality was shaped by the gangsters in power, but it was taken public by hip-hop. Rap culture blew Queens up, and the force behind hip-hop was the hustlers on the block. The music brought pride and enjoyment to the youth, but the gangsters gave them that "get money" mentality. As dudes on the street tried to one up each other, their swagger became more outrageous, and the flashy materialism of bling-bling would come to dominate. About 62 percent of the population in Queens was black while 18.5 percent was Hispanic. The median income was about $35,000. With stable homes, the kids had time to explore hip-hop, and the freedom to try getting money. Hip-hop and hustling became the two biggest pastime in the borough. The youth of Queens became enamored with hip-hop and the dope game. It was the best of both worlds. This contrast mirrored their environment. "The neighborhood is like a residential neighborhood but these projects are right there," a Supreme Team member says. "The elevated train, Long Island Railroad, a train track, went right by the projects." The Baisley Park Houses at Guy R. Brewer Boulevard and 116th Avenue was one of the largest public housing developments in Queens County. Thousands of hardworking families lived in and around the development. "If drugs weren't in the community Jamaica Queens could have been a beautiful place to live," Tuck, a Supreme Team member says. "Not everyone from my hood sold drugs. Drugs weren't the only opportunity to get money. Drugs were easy and fast money." And the youth of Queens was susceptible to the trappings of the life.

"Hollis was about heroin dealing and numbers running," the Queens hustler said, "while South Jamaica was into organized cocaine dealing." Traditionally, the area was home to many blue collar families. Infected by the age of materialism, the individual was born. A lavish lifestyle emerged, impacted by gang culture and rap music. "We had better living," Bing says, "B-ball tournaments, cookouts; it was a nice place to live for a hood. I love where I grew up at. We had big front yards and back yards for parties and all that." Queens was a community, and in that community hip-hop exploded. There were hip-hop parties everywhere. In the beginning the music wasn't violent. It was about talking shit and getting people together; it was about music and having fun. It was about black people celebrating something that was their own, something that they had created and could hold claim to.

Run DMC repped with the Adidas, fat chains and leather suits, setting a standard in the rap game that others watched and emulated. But Run DMC was just copying the guys on the streets, the hustlers up on 150th

Street. They took the music and gave it a street vibe. Rap music was always street music, but before Run DMC, rappers looked more like disco holdovers. The groups from the Bronx resembled the Village People. They were still into that 70s style. Run DMC, by popularizing the b-boy style, moved hip-hop forward. They dressed like cats on the block with Kangols, black Lee jeans, fly eyeglasses like Cazales and shell toe Adidas. Run DMC weren't gangsters by any means, still they looked like street thugs. They represented that Queens style and attitude, showing what street culture was all about.

Queens was a Mecca for drug lords and hip-hop, but first came the gangs. Sevens Crowns was the dominant gang, but others played a factor in Queens while one in particular would prove instrumental in the Supreme Team's formation. "Everybody was in a gang before they started selling drugs," Bing says, "Seven Crowns, Savage Skulls, Savage Nomads, Ghetto Boys, and Five Percenters." Two of these groups would merge to form the nucleus of the Supreme Team. The Seven Crowns with Fat Cat and Pretty Tony would lead the way, but most of the Supreme Team started out as Five Percenters. They would embrace the ideology that started on New York's streets and make it their own, creating a unique hybrid of hip-hop and hustling.

Five Percenters were an offshoot of the Nation of Islam, which started on Harlem streets in 1964 under the leadership of Clarence 13X Smith, a Korean War veteran and former member of the NOI's elite Fruit of Islam security force. Smith, aka Pudding, was expelled from the NOI's Harlem mosque Number 7 in 1963 by Malcolm X, reputedly because he refused to forgo his fondness for dice games. The Five Percent Nation considered itself a religious and cultural movement directed toward young blacks, aiming to teach them the correct ways of Islamic life. Its name derived from the members belief that ten percent of humanity (the devils) controlled and exploited 85 percent of the poor and uninformed who hadn't received knowledge. The remaining five percent were those "civilized people, also known as Muslims and Muslims' sons," whose task was to educate fellow blacks in their true religion.

The fiery teachings came slamming off the radio and boom boxes in the 1960s. It was hip-hop before hip-hop. The messages were delivered in a staccato street rap that mesmerized New York City youth. "The black man is god," Clarence 13X told his people with a rhetoric that was something they had never heard before. His followers called him Father Allah and rejected the belief that NOI founder Wallace Fard was God. They were the five percent; they were the righteous, and they enacted a cultural movement for their people. There was no easier way to offend

Five Percenters than to call them a gang. But the Five Percenters were labeled a gang from the jump, viewed originally as an outgrowth of the Blood Brothers and other old fashioned fighting gangs. In the late 1970s and 1980s, Five Percenters were like the Bloods and Crips are now. "They were a religious thing that got labeled as a gang," Bing says. "They were very big in the city and Queens." The group espoused a black supremacist ideology and held the belief that five percent of all men were enlightened and became Gods. Five Percenters countered the senseless violence of gang life with a message of unity and respect. But since many adherents were from prison, there was a crossover.

"When a Five Percenter goes among the 85 percent, one of two things happens. Either the 85 percent start acting like the Five Percenter or the Five Percenter starts acting like the 85 percent," the Queens Five Percenter said. Some Five Percenters, empowered by the black man's divinity, used the knowledge to uplift themselves and their communities, while others abused the notion of Godhood to justify criminal behavior. Joe Clark, who was immortalized by Morgan Freeman in *Lean on Me* remarked, "I am at war with the Five Percenters. It fills me with sadness and chagrin that this band of hoodlums and thugs could capture the minds of hundreds of teenagers." The principal couldn't cope with them at his school.

By taking names such as King, Justice, Knowledge, and Divine, the Gods were empowering themselves in an environment that was hostile to them. The movement was classified at the time by authorities as a cult, a fad, and a jailhouse religion. They didn't think it would last. It was linked with gang fights and killings but was also praised for turning delinquents into serious law-abiding students. In Queens, God B and his brother First Born Prince were two of the first Gods who influenced Supreme and the rest of the youth that would become the Supreme Team. "We were the Five Percent. We weren't known to deal in drugs, it was kind of a religious taboo," God B said. But the prisons were a stronghold for the group, a recruiting ground for the Five Percenters, and when prisoners were released, they brought their prior vocations with them.

About getting into the drug game, T, a friend of Supreme's relates, "What probably influenced him getting into the life was becoming a Five Percenter. With most of them coming out of prison, it had to influence his decisions." The prison system provided valuable new recruits who weren't afraid to stand up. The Five Percenters knew that prison was an important conduit for their message. With social outcasts, misfits, and disaffected youth rising to their banner, there was no reason to discount former felons and ex-convicts, as they fit right in. When Supreme discovered the teachings of the Five Percenters, he began envisioning himself differently. "Supreme got his name in 1971 from his affiliation with the Five Percent Nation," Lance said. Supreme got a name and a way of life. He didn't smoke, drink, or eat red meat in accordance with Five Percenter beliefs. He held to the other tenets of the faith in his own fashion, manipulating them to suit his circumstances.

"The brother Supreme grew up partly in the 60s and 70s when guys in the life had a semblance of principles," explains T. "He tries to stay true to his word as a man. Even as a kid he was sharp enough to put things into place." Preme had a stellar reputation as one of South Jamaica's best and brightest. He was a talented student, an avid football player, and a welcome presence in his Queens neighborhood. Preme developed into a very intellectual and culturally aware young man. He came from a two parent home where both parents were employed as transit workers. He went to PS 140, the public junior high in Rochdale Village, and discovered the Five Percent Nation at an early age. "I don't think he graduated from high school," the Queens hustler said, "but he definitely graduated from the streets." By the end of high school in the late-70s, while his friends were preparing for college, Preme was immersing himself in the streets. "His pops was ex-military, a marine or something, a very strictdisciplinarian," the Supreme Team member says. "He lived right across the street from the Baisley Projects in a house. Preme grew up on Foch Boulevard and the Guy R. Brewer intersection in South Jamaica, Queens." Preme had a couple of sisters and brothers, all older. One of his sisters was Prince's mom. Preme and Prince were around the same age and were raised like brothers. "Preme is only two years older than Prince," an original Supreme Team member says. "They grew up together."

In the working class environment of South Jamaica, Preme lived in a stable household. "His whole family is square," T says. "All his brothers are professional people in their own lives. His brothers and sisters were way older than him. Brothers like ten years older." Preme was always a bright kid and his embrace of Five Percenter ideology at the age of ten made him different than most. Even though he wasn't the tallest dude growing up at five-foot-five, trim and slightly built, he was a natural born leader.

Preme and his crew were known as the Peace Gods. They were always down on Linden Boulevard. Dudes in the hood called them the Peace Gods because that was how they greeted people, "Peace God." The exiled Dumar Complete was believed to have given the knowledge of self to Supreme, who in turn gave it to his crew. They embraced Five Percenter ideology less as a religion and more as a rebellious pose. With their unique way of thinking and religious ideals they made themselves out to be more than just drug dealers. On the block they stuck out. With Supreme leading the way, they followed. "Preme's greatest leadership quality was his ability to lead men," the original member says.

He took to heart the Five Percenters tenet that said blacks were supreme beings. With his quiet demeanor and pale green eyes, he seemed far from a typical thug. His power was never physical; rather it came from street wits, charisma, and the implication of danger. "He gets along with everyone," a convict who was in prison with Preme says. "All different nationalities and geographical locations embrace him." It was really about respect with Supreme. "If he don't really know you, he don't fuck with you," Bing says. "He's very careful about what he says." Preme was guarded when he had to be and outspoken when necessary. He always seemed to know the right way to act or the correct thing to say, and he had perfect timing when it came to violence. He made his moves when it would have the biggest impact. Call him calculating, calm, collected, and precise; Supreme was all these things. He mastered the ability to affect other people at a young age. In 1979 Preme was 20 years old.

"I came home in 79," First Born Prince said. "I started hanging on 150th Street with the Crowns. They said go get some of your friends to help you out. To help you do what you're doing." First Born Prince was never officially a member of what would become known as the Supreme Team, but he played a role in their formation. "He was around more in our Five Percenter days when we were active with that," the original member says. But First Born Prince introduced them to hustling. Going to the block with First Born Prince indoctrinated the Five Percenters into the life.

"It really started with the Five Percenters. Preme and them were Godbodies. That's like 1980," Bing says. "They wasn't really selling drugs at that time. It was a religious thing." With Preme embracing the movement, he used his influence to get other youngsters like his nephew Prince involved. "Although God B and his brother First Born Prince recruited and organized us within the Five Percenter Nation, Preme created an underground economy for us to thrive and flourish off," Prince said. As street dudes came home from prison they showed Preme the principles of the drug game, and Preme combined their knowledge with his Five Percenter ideology.

He went back to his Peace Gods crew and told God B, "We have an opportunity to make some money. They getting money. We ain't getting nothing. Can you support me?" God B agreed, "He wanted me to tell all the Gods it was all right for him to go down on the block and get us started." He was Supreme's right hand man and personal bodyguard. He was instrumental in orchestrating the deal with the Seven Crowns gang which allowed Supreme to get paid on the block and organize the Supreme Team. "The deal with God B was simply this," the original member says. "He was a man's man, a gangster's gangster, and he did not take shit from anyone including Preme. God B and Supreme were the most respected. We all grew up together." Supreme took over the oldest gang in Queens, the Five Percenters, dubbed himself Supreme in Five Percenter tradition and called his crew the Supreme Team. The grandiose sounding name was typical Five Percenter hyperbole and in another nod to Five Percenter ideology the first members of the crew even called themselves the original seed. "Supreme was the originator of the team. He brought it into existence," Tuck comments.

"He started that like 1983. A bunch of dudes that were Five Percenters started getting into the drug game on 150th Street and Sutphin Boulevard. Baisely was a hangout then," Bing says. Supreme's crew was emulating the established hustlers that were already up on the block at 150th Street. With Supreme's connection to the Seven Crowns through God B and First Born Prince, he made inroads on the hustling strip with his own crew. "I was a little guy," Lightskin Knowledge, a Supreme Team member said. "I wanted to emulate the dudes on the block." Preme's much feared crew, the Peace Gods, transformed into the Supreme Team. They adopted the crime habits of Queens' outlaws and villains and Supreme became the main character of this saga.

"It wasn't no official shit," Bing says. "It was a loose affiliation of friends and businessmen trying to come up. It took us a while to get on the map to get respect in the city." But there was a no more deserving character than Supreme who could negotiate his way through the tribal ganglands.

Preme and his group of hustling Five Percenters started their own small operation down on the block where selling drugs was more of a movement than a business or game. But Preme's clique was conflicted about embracing both the Five Percenter ideology and the Queens under world mentality. "A lot of the brothers and sisters didn't like the idea that we hustled, because it was contrary to the lessons," remembered Lightskin Knowledge. But the drug money in the early 1980s proved irresistible, and the crew began growing into its grandiose moniker.

The ideology Preme and his crew embraced influenced a lot of New York's inner-city youth. They were mostly black and came from all five boroughs, but the Supreme Team was unique in what they were and what they became. Still they were similar in other ways. That was reflected in hip-hop, where many artists who came of age in the 1980s, used

Five Percenter imagery or lyrics in their music. They gave knowledge, and dropped jewels and science in ciphers. They used Alphabets and Mathematics as secret codes to pass messages or inspire loyalty and rebellion. "Being a Five Percenter was nothing more than a license to be brutal," LL Cool J said. The rap icon who flirted with Five Percenter ideals as a teenager conceded that his experience didn't reflect the true nature of the teachings. "At its core there is a strict religious doctrine, but we weren't following that. We were just using the Five Percent label as a shield to do our dirty work, fighting and eventually robbing." In the case of the Supreme Team, selling drugs was their business.

Preme and company loved the nation, but they were out there hustling. They combined the two ideologies creating a unique hybrid. Their influence on the other hustlers and on hip-hop in Queens was undeniable. As a culture and way of life, the Godbodies emerged and presented themselves to youngsters at the same time hip-hop was in its infancy. "When the gangs I hung out with in the early-70s gave way to 80s hip-hop culture, it was the street language, style, and consciousness of the Five Percent Nation that served as a bridge," Russell Simmons said. Youngsters took the Supreme Team's Five Percenter ideology to heart which showed in the music of Rakim, Big Daddy Kane, A Tribe Called Quest, Busta Rhymes, the Wu Tang Clan, and others. The idea of being a Five Percenter and hustling was very tightly entwined. The Supreme Team brought this juxtaposition into fashion. As Preme got acclimated on the block, he fell right in with the Seven Crowns alumni.

"Supreme met Tony and Cat before me," God B said. "Preme, Cat, and Pretty Tony would be at the Pink Shade. The library on Jamaica Avenue was the hang out. Before that the Seven Crowns beefed with the Five Percenters in Queens in the early-70s." Fat Cat had beef with Allah Supreme God dating back to 1972. Allah Supreme God had convinced his brother Supreme Master Allah to quit the Seven Crowns. One night the Seven Crowns, led by Mr. Black, attempted to rob a pizza shop and got chased out by the owner. Allah Supreme God witnessed the fiasco and offered to help. "Give me the gun," he told Mr. Black, "and I'll rob the store." Mr. Black handed over his gun, and Allah Supreme God managed to slip away with a free pistol. The humiliated Crowns threatened revenge, so Allah Supreme God drummed up support. The Five Percenters ran up on the Crowns and challenged them, but the beef was squashed.

With Supreme, one of the most influential Five Percenters, hanging out with Fat Cat and Pretty Tony, a union was formed between the Seven Crowns and Five Percenters. "That was the beginning of the Seven Crowns and Gods relationship. We decided we don't fight among ourselves," Bing says. "We never beefed with each other like that. No heavy shit. We came together against outsiders."

The outsiders were numerous, with gangs like the Savage Skulls, Ghetto Boys, Savage Nomads, Latin Soul Brothers, and Sex Boys all fighting for territory in Queens. "The gangs were very territorial," the Queens detective said. "The Seven Crowns weren't allowed up on Hillside and Parsons. The Latin Soul Brothers weren't allowed to go down past South Road. Shit like that. The blacks weren't allowed to go over 102nd Avenue where the Sex Boys were. The Sex Boys were white guys. The big thing back then was wearing colors. Nobody really had guns yet. The fighting was mostly hand to hand stuff. Occasionally you'd see a knife or homemade zip gun." It was Gangs of New York-type action, a far cry from the New Jack City gunplay it would become.

"The Five Percenters and the Seven Crowns were the two most prominent movements in Queens that changed Queens," God B commented. "Originally we started out as kids. We went from robberies to selling drugs to stealing cars to everything." The neighborhood cliques honed their skills growing up on the streets of South Jamaica. Eventually they all got heavy in the drug game but the first one to test the waters was Pretty Tony, a Spanish cat getting money, with a good head on his shoulders who knew how to move. "The birth of Queens was under Pretty Tony," God B said. "Pretty Tony supersedes Bump. Everybody thinks it all started with Cat and Bump. Ask anybody from the neighborhood; Pretty Tony was the dude and Cat, Preme and all the rest were bonded by the Crowns like brothers." They became the three amigos.

Because Fat Cat could whip most dudes, he stayed in trouble. He was the fighter of the group. Pretty Tony was more behind the scenes. "Pretty Tony avoided the limelight," the Queens insider says. "Tony was not with putting himself out there like all the rest of the fools. He was very discreet and did not take unnecessary chances by overexposing himself and business. He did not attend any major nor minor social events. He allowed Lance and Todd, his brothers, to do any partying for the Fuertado faction. Overall Tony was one hell of a dude. Very good dude." Preme was the third amigo of the group, and he combined both Pretty Tony's cunning and Cats' ferocity. He was breaking bread with them but in infamy he would eventually surpass them both.

The Seven Crowns/Five Percenter connection played a major part in the formation of the Supreme Team. With Preme embracing both groups, it was only a matter of time before he did his own thing, combining the best elements of both movements. With his Five Percenter foundation and indoctrination into the game under Fat Cat and Pretty Tony, Preme put his own twist on the game and brought into being the Supreme Team, the hustling Peace Gods with that hip-hop swagger. Cats and Pretty Tony's influence was apparent, but Preme stood on his own platform, juxtaposing what he picked up from them with his own idealogy. The end product of Supreme's conclusions and ideas were his own. Everything around him impacted him in some way, but he digested it all and formulated his own plan based on all the knowledge he had taken in.

"I been knowing Preme since 79 when I was supposed to be in high school," Bing says. "I knew him from playing in the different b-ball tournaments. I met him on the block on 150th Street. I was supposed to be in high school, but I was hustling." Supreme was like a magnet to other inner-city youth. He attracted them with his words, style, and presence. "My uncle is an exceptional and natural born leader," Prince said. "Ever since I can remember Preme exemplified the qualities of a true gangsta with a capital G, a general who could muster his troops within minutes and be on the battlefield himself." Preme was a battle tested soldier and thinker who could outfox any opponents or rivals. Supreme carefully studied the work of the older, more experienced Southside Queens hustlers, and in his apprenticeship he offered to take on some of the most dangerous and risky tasks for his bosses, such as guarding drugs and cash at Southside stash houses. Preme was no street fighter himself, but he could turn to his crew, the much feared Supreme Team, when trouble arose. They were more than willing and ready to handle or deal with any situation or problem that occurred.

He paid his dues by working as a stash house guard for Ronnie Bumps and helping with Pretty Tony and Cat's operations. But his greatest asset was his diplomacy. "Preme is a dude who will rationalize, talk it out. He's very diplomatic and humble when necessary," Tuck says. "I remember Supreme as someone who always was spoken highly of. I don't know if it was out of fear or respect. But usually when people spoke that name, they were speaking of something greater than themselves." Preme was a throwback gangster, but then again he was so much more. "Preme was a better boss than most because he did not have to be bossy," the Queens insider says. "Dudes for some reason wanted Preme to boss them, even when they were down with other crews." Preme wasn't a loose cannon-type of dude, but he had the "go and get it" mentality that success embodied. He combined ruthlessness with unchecked diplomacy, forcefulness with mercy and generosity, and cunning with street smarts and intelligence.

"He's very intellectual and culturally conscious. Not bias or racial," T says, painting the picture of a gentleman gangster who upheld the virtues of honor, integrity and loyalty. "He's not flamboyant and he's highly intelligent. Ain't nothing slow about him." Preme used this intelligence to build his team around him, a team that was loyal and brutal, and a team that would follow his orders without hesitation. "I remember him saying that he didn't want to be the boss. That he was chosen only because he was best qualified at the time." T says. "Supreme is respected because whatever he's gonna do he's gonna do it 150 percent. The most brutal individual on the planet will work with you if he respects you." And Supreme attracted some vicious dudes as part of his crew.

Following Pretty Tony, Ronnie Bumps, and Fat Cat's lead, Supreme rallied his crew and installed in them the codes he had learned and lived by. He also saw people's potential and encouraged them to live up to it. "Preme was a master of the build up," the original member says. "That's what he was capable of doing. Building dudes up to a certain level or aura and having them live up to it." Preme taught his crew respect, loyalty, and honor. He treated them as individuals and with appreciation. The Supreme Team reflected Supreme in all facets. "We respected people, we wanted people to respect us too, even if it meant going to war," Bing says. "But the neighborhood loved us. We took care of the neighborhood." Supreme became a ghetto strongman that roamed the streets and became revered locally as a Robin Hood figure. His command of the criminal group was absolute as he played out a role in a gangster movie.

What became known as the Supreme Team was a crew organized in the early 1980s in the vicinity of the Baisley Park Houses in Jamaica, Queens, New York, by a group of teenagers who were members of a quasi-religious sect known as the Five Percenters. Under the leadership of Kenneth "Supreme" McGriff and Gerald "Prince" Miller, his nephew, as second in command, the gang concentrated its criminal efforts on wide spread drug distribution. "Preme basically taught Prince everything he knows about the game," the Queens insider says. The dynamic between Preme and Prince was one of big brother/little brother, with Preme being the older sibling. Even though Prince was Preme's nephew, Preme was only two years older, so in effect they grew up as brothers with Supreme leading the way. Where Preme went Prince followed.

First they went into the Five Precenters and then into the streets together. Preme attracted a lot of dedicated followers, but Prince was his most steadfast and diehard supporter, always at his side and watching his back. With a master's degree in the drug game acquired under the tutelage of Ronnie Bumps, Pretty Tony, and Fat Cat, Preme's game point average (G.P.A.) was off the charts. Using this knowledge, Preme moved his crew off the block and into Baisley Projects. "Preme and them were from Baisley," Bing says. So it was only logical that Baisley Projects would become their headquarters.

Cocaine had found a boom market in Queens. Colombian drug dealers were pouring into Jackson Heights, killing people by the dozens. When Ronnie Bumps, who was buying kilos directly from the Colombians, was arrested for drug trafficking in Baltimore, Fat Cat took over. Cat figured with so much profit to be made there was no sense dying in a drug war. Cat called a meeting with some of the other dealers in the area, namely the Corley Brothers, Claude Skinner, Supreme, Prince, Tommy Montana and Cornbread. After a night of partying in Fat Cat's clubhouse, a grocery store called Big Macs at the corner of 106th and 150th Street, the area was split up. The Corley Brothers were given control of Forty Projects. The Supreme Team got Baisley Projects. Tommy Montana got Lauralton and Hollis. Prince and Skinner were made enforcers. Cornbread remained hidden, handling distribution. Everyone answered to Fat Cat. This was the Round Table, and Fat Cat was King Arthur at least he was for the time being. "It wasn't like they sat down and divided it," Bing says. "They had respect for different dudes' areas, where they grew up. That was theirs."

At the same time that Preme was getting his crew situated at Baisley Projects, a movie came out that impacted him and all of the young drug dealers of the era. "In the early-80s when *Scarface* came out, all the young cats wanted to be like that," Lance said. *Scarface* was a movie about them and for them. The Supreme Team embraced the gun culture promoted by the movie. Firearms became a must have fashion accessory. A "shoot or be shot" mentality emerged. The guns gave them a feeling of having juice or power over their rivals.

"It made all of the youngsters dream. All the youngsters wanted to be drug dealers. It gave us a dream," Antoine Clark from F.E.D.S. magazine said. "This was the bible. It was inspirational. Had people taking risks. Doing crazy shit. Glamorizing sex, guns and drugs." And as big of an impact as it had on the drug world, its effect was equally important on hip-hop culture.

"They saw his come up. To the people in the hood it was a way to get on. Nino was working *Scarface* in *New Jack City*. It made niggas want to get money. It's the classic hustler movie. They went crazy with *Scarface*," Antoine said. "None of us thought we could be *Scarface*, but we could have that mentality of taking over wherever we went. He gave us that mentality." *Scarface* made selling drugs seem cool and lucrative. It romanticized the dope game while glamorizing it and led a whole generation of youth astray. In reality that movie corrupted the black community. It made dudes want to be hustlers and get money by any means necessary. Supreme was one of those who took the *Scarface* mentality to heart.

He dressed in expensive white suits with the crisp white shirt open just like Tony Montana. He embraced the swagger and adopted the fictional gangster's style. He carried himself with the class of an older, more established hustler even when he wasn't. His debonair appearance and demeanor was what made the Supreme Team willing to go to war for Preme. It was his presence, his class. Preme was the epitome of gangster cool. "He's very charismatic, he can be the perfect gentleman, but he wants to win at all costs," T says. "He is not an abrasive dude. He's a good hearted individual." Behind the ghetto glitz and kind heart was a seriousness about hustling that elevated Preme above his many peers on the streets.

"Back then the game was the game. Everybody stood by the rules. Soldiers were soldiers," Bing says. This was the era from which Preme and the team emerged. It was a time when men were men, and the consequences of snitching were clear. In Queens snitching was forbidden. It was embedded in the youngster's DNA. Omerta played a powerful role in shaping the lost generation in terms of how they saw the world. Nobody took liberties and keeping your mouth shut became a sign of a go hard gangster.

"Not all gangsters are outlaws and not all outlaws are gangsters," Prince said. "Stand up people do not fold or run when faced with difficulty. We analyze and determine the best course of action, holding firm to the principle of never harm another to save yourself. We understand that every action we choose has consequences. Therefore, before we act, we first settle within our hearts and minds that we can handle the consequences, whether it be beneficial or detrimental to ourselves and the lives of those we risk our life and freedom for." These were the ideals Preme embedded in the team, and this was an era when a man had to be verified by someone who was qualified in order to be certified.

There were rules in the dope game and prospective dealers or wanna be gangsters had to prove their mettle to the hierarchy of already established hustlers in their hood. They were tested before they were allowed to put a foot in the door. Not just anybody was allowed to be a player in the game. Dudes like Preme had to pay their dues, as did all the members of the Supreme Team. "Niggas was always hustling before they was selling drugs," Bing says. "They were robbing banks, burglarizing, shooting dice, robbing, sticking dudes up, gambling. The team did banks and shit. That's how they started in 1982. We always had our hustles before we started dealing drugs and we were gangbanging." Down on the block the team learned the ropes of the game.

The O.G.'s taught them to follow a time honored tradition. Bing explains, "Death before dishonor. You get arrested, you closed your mouth and kept it shut and went to jail. That was installed in me as a kid by older guys who I came up under in the streets. The way I grew up and the people I looked up to showed me morals and principles. They told me that when you go out to hustle, you hold your own." The streets were vicious and the most important lesson was to trust no man. Tuck explains, "Trust no man was the most important lesson I ever learned. The only thing was I learned it too late. There are no rules to that life. No loyalty, no love just the street code, no snitching." The criminal intention was to defeat the system. That was why the street code was so important. It held that the authorities were the pre-eminent enemies, above all else. A true gangster wouldn't rat out his worst enemy, even on his deathbed.

"When we was coming up there was a code of conduct," Supreme said. By following this code of conduct the team gained power and respect. "We followed the old school street code. No rape, stealing from each other. No shit like that," Bing said. "We respected people, people respected us or else." Because in the streets that was how dudes got their props, by instantaneous violence. That was how hustlers acquired that gangster pedigree. When it jumped off, the drama got thick with the quickness. It could get hectic in a New York minute. Still, there was another angle to it, the way the Mafia did things.

True professional criminals who chose to traffic on the dark side of American society didn't seek public acclaim. "A heavy handed gangsta lives in the shadow of death," the Queens hustler said. Being the man behind the man implied an inner confidence that allowed others to assert themselves in the arena of public aggrandizement, while knowing all along that the real power resided offstage in the hands of the marionette. That was how organized crime worked. That was the model the Supreme Team followed, but they put their twist on it. They weren't the Italian Mob. They were young and black; they were the hip-hop Mafia, and kings of the inner-city.

The flashy hustlers set the standard and became role models for the neighborhood, flaunting their alluring lifestyle, which was well beyond the reach of working class Queens. "Ronnie Bumps, the Corleys, Pretty Tony on Liberty Avenue, Tommy Mickens on Rockaway, these were the niggas we looked up to. These were the niggas that set shit up for us," Bing said. These were the youngsters who came together to form the Supreme Team, who grew up under these hood stars and learned the game from them. "That was our real life, how we came up," Bing said. "You see it all in hip-hop, but back then that was the streets." The youngsters got their style and swagger from these ghetto celebrities and rocked it.

"The team was the flyest crew in Queens," the original member says. They talked the talk and walked the walk, becoming lords of the ghetto in the process. The young drug dealers and hip-hop scene that would sweep the nation in the 1990s and popularize Queens' culture owed a debt to these icons. Dripping in gold and carrying guns, with neat clothes and flash cars they popularized thug culture.

"Dudes from Queens always stayed fly," Bing says, "Queens was always fly niggas, getting money niggas. We had to prove ourselves though." The Supreme Team had a reputation to earn, a reputation to uphold. A legacy was born, and they embraced and adopted it. That reputation earned Queens a place in the power struggles of the streets and in the rap world. Queens became hip-hop, and the Supreme Team epitomized Queens. Not surprisingly, the moment Run DMC started making noise in hip-hop in the early-80s was also when the real street thugs started making inroads into the business. Street life's growing intersection with rap and the music world would impact both deeply. There were six degrees of separation between hip-hop stars and the criminals they emulated which would affect Supreme much later.

Queens became where it was at, and dudes from the borough started to stick their chests out. It was a drug game thing; it was a hip-hop thing; it was a Queens thing. It was a growing mentality and attitude that they developed, nurtured, and created. All the neighborhoods in Queens were now being heard together with one defiant voice. Respect was what that voice demanded, and dudes from all parts of the city knew that Queens' hustlers were getting theirs. Queens went from faking it to running it. They were getting their respect in the streets, in the prisons and in hip-hop. "It was the niggas from Queens making all the noise," Bing says. "We started all this gangster shit." With his team supporting his moves, Preme's power on the streets of South Jamaica grew. The Southside was gradually coming under the sway of the team. "From 81-85 everybody was home," Bing says. "The team was in full effect and dominated the streets." As they became more entrenched in the drug game, dudes got busted, cases would come and go, and they would lose members to the criminal justice system. But their first run was uninterrupted, and during this time they forged their legend in the hood.

At the same time, hip-hop was evolving and becoming a force in the inner-city. It was still New York street music, but hip-hop was growing and getting bigger. It was becoming a culture that would dominate the nation just as the Supreme Team dominated the Southside, the same hoods that the rappers grew up and congregated in. Run DMC would drive through the ghetto, back and forth, hanging out. They were everywhere, very present and accounted for on the streets. They looked and dressed like the guys from around the way, like the dudes playing basketball in the parks, the fly guys hanging around the clubs and projects. The hustlers in Queens embraced Run DMC long before they were stars when hip-hop was nothing.

Shakim Bio Chemical explains, "Rap game put in work, dope game put in work. I come from an era where hip-hop wasn't on vinyl yet. The music was being played in the purest form in the parks which caused a reaction everywhere it vibed. Growing up, there weren't too many heroes to look up to. My era produced the graffiti artist, the break dancers, DJ's, the MC's and shit like that. People claimed that these kids weren't doing nothing but making a lot of fucking noise, now those kids and millions after them are what's up. I used to go to high school spitting the illest shit ever and crushing niggas in rap battles, but music didn't appear to be the future back then. I became a product of my environment, and I began to hustle."

The culture of Queens clashed as the dope game and hip-hop strove for prominence. The drug dealers became street legends that were lionized in hip-hop's lyrical lore and the chronicles of gangster infamy. By the mid-80s hip-hop was pushing boundaries in the musical world, and major labels started signing rappers to deals. But the street vibe and influence of drug dealing organizations like the Supreme Team were at the forefront of the genre. The lasting impression they left, which forged the flashy arrogance of 80s hip-hop, wasn't a coincidence. Hip-hop and hustling were closely related as were the people who resided jointly in both worlds. The links between the growing hip-hop nation and the new-style, organized crime networks would prove resilient.

CHAPTER 2
THE PLAYERS

"You know how them niggas do/Hymee, Cornbread and Supreme, niggas that were getting money/that I was growing up trying to be like/word up to all them gangster niggas."
— **Capone-N-Noreaga**

"In the 80s the mindset was get mine or be mine and the rumor has it nobody embodied this attitude more than a crew out of the Southside of Queens, New York, who have become known as the Supreme Team, the most legendary street gang of its time."
— **Don Diva Magazine, Issue 23**

"Handsome, charming and rich beyond the imagination of anyone in southeast Queens, McGriff was to borrow Queens rapper Nas's memorable phrase a 'hood movie star.'"
— **New York Magazine**

"It was about getting money and staying fly, about who had the baddest broads," Bing says of the dope game. That was the inspiration behind getting in the life. That was the gangster etiquette. Supreme and the other Five Percenters wanted that, and their vices transferred to the burgeoning hip-hop world. The up and coming rappers wanted those same things-the flash, the glitz, the bling-bling- that the Queens hustlers brought into prominence. "Anchor chains was a trend about who could get the biggest one with the most diamonds," Bing says. "We had all that shit before Run DMC had it. We wore all that shit way before." The hustlers in Queens were the trendsetters. Their style became so in vogue that dudes from all five boroughs started biting. "When they saw how fly we be they were coming out from all the boroughs," Bing says. "It wasn't what they thought it was about. Queens was changing, getting that rep in the city."

Still, in the dawn of the hip-hop age, rappers like KRS-One tried to keep the old stereotypes alive. In *The Bridge is Over* he rhymed, *Manhattan keeps making it, Brooklyn keeps taking it, Bronx keeps creating it, and Queens keeps on faking it.* But Queens wasn't faking shit. The Supreme Team put a stop to all that. The borough became synonymous for hustling, getting money, and the dope game. The Supreme Team raised the stakes considerably. Their position in the hood and the life was strong. Their tactics changed the game. They made it about a culture; it became a movement for their people; the impoverished, the downtrodden, the fringe players. It was about more than just selling drugs. To them it was about hip-hop, the youth and the lifestyle they created.

"It was DJ battles in the park," Bing says. "Break dancing was early-80s. We could relate to what they were doing. They were representing us." But the rap guys didn't have anything the street guys wanted because hip-hop wasn't really there yet. MC's were flowing free style, battle rapping on the block. It was a neighborhood thing. It was in the street, in its infancy. There was no money or fame at that point. It was just a copy of drug dealer style and flash with the beats and rhymes thrown in for the entertainment aspect. Rappers took hustlers' fashion and made it popular. The big ballers adorned themselves in 80s style bling, borrowing from both pimps and hustlers. The roughneck, gold chain look adopted by Run DMC was what dudes on the block were sporting. The player look, popular in Queens at the time, was also coming into fashion with LL Cool J and Big Daddy Kane, representing for the ladies.

That was all for show, what dudes saw on the street and in the hood. They were styling and profiling, creating a culture. Like Tupac, they came up from the gutter. This was a time before studio gangsters. There was no faking it. Still there were choices. "No one is born to be involved in the street life. I chose to make the streets a part of my life," Tuck says. "I believe one's environment has a lot to do with how one will turn out." Though Queens was a predominantly middle-class area, the pockets of poverty existed, and the youth from these areas, like Baisley Projects, lacked guidance, so they looked to the streets for the love which they couldn't find at home. And they found Supreme, a smooth, charismatic young G who preached Five Percenter ideology and showed the youngsters a way to get money. "I was influenced to head for the streets after working at a job that paid minimum wage," Tuck says. "I also lacked guidance in the form of a father figure so I looked to the streets for that." In the streets Tuck found the Supreme Team.

"Our views are not puritan views," T says. "The average individuals, give them a decent job, and they'll work forever. They aren't criminals. You got to be ready to rumble." The core of Preme's followers, the original seed that formed the Supreme Team, was definitely ready to rumble. Supreme could call on his henchmen to solve the business problems his various criminal enterprises encountered. His foot soldiers were more than ready to indulge in any gangland dramas that were necessary to increase the team's prestige.

"I haven't grown out of the street life or the game as it is often referred to. I've evolved into it," Prince said. "What we call the game really isn't a game at all. Although we play by set rules, the breaking of those rules aren't like other games, in which the penalties may be softened, like giving the other team possession of the ball, loss of yardage, suspension or fines. Rather in the game of life there's a much greater sense of personal accountability for each choice we make. One bad choice may lead to someone else's demise or your very own. So there isn't any room for error in today's game. The stakes are just too high." But even referring to the drug life as a game is an oxymoron.

"I don't agree that dealing drugs and murdering human beings is a game. It's just chasing money and power," Tuck says. It's a vicious attempt to come up by any means necessary. It's trying to get what capitalism offers and finding a place in the street hierarchy. In the street they call it, "Getting in where you fit in" and "Playing your position." But really it's a matter of survival. By finding a niche, hustlers could survive and even prosper in the brutal drug trade that dominated the Southside of Queens. Shit was rough in the hood, and often the choice of right now was all people could see. These were the choices the Supreme Team made, and their decisions would leave them facing harrowing consequences.

As Preme got deeper into the game, one of his main dudes was Fat Cat. "Him and Preme were real close," Bing says. "They started fucking with each other. Preme was more with Fat Cat at the time. They were good friends." In the early-80s, in Queens, Cat was the HNIC. "Fat Cat was a legend from our hood," Bing says. "He was a major figure." Cat and Pretty Tony were the dudes making things happen in the hood, and Preme was down with both of them. "Cat was the man. He was the dude to see. He made the Corley's, Pretty Tony put Fat Cat on. Fat Cat helped a lot of people out," Bing says. Supreme and the team were one of the beneficiaries. "Supreme was always his own man, and he started out as an independent who knew how to network very well," The Queens insider says. "Once he networked and became strong enough, he planted his own flag and took it from there." Through intimidation and a gangster man largesse, Supreme carved his niche in Queens where violence was a part of the social fabric of the hood.

Preme watched, studied, and then applied what he learned to his own plans with the Supreme Team at Baisley Projects. He saw Cat open a deli on 150th Street and 107th Avenue, called Big Mac's Deli that doubled as Cat's headquarters. He saw Cat's crew hold it down on the block, 150th Street. That was the strip in Queens where all the hustlers held court and plied their trade, but Cat made it his own. Preme saw the value of having your own real estate, and he followed Cat's cue by setting up shop at Baisely Projects. "Cat had already started getting money," Spoon, a dude from Cat's crew said. "He was pushing a 98, wearing Adidas, and had a lot of fat jewels. He weighed a good 300 pounds, and he would be on the block with mopeds lined up for his people." By getting the 411 from Fat Cat, Ronnie Bumps, and Pretty Tony, Preme put together the plan that led the Supreme Team to fame and fortune.

"At one time they were rivals," T says of Cat and Preme. This was due to the Seven Crowns/Five Percenter rivalry. "But a mutual friend, between them both, settled the rivalry, and they became alright." This led to an influx of Five Percenters into the Seven Crowns, so that the two groups became synonymous with each other. In the catalog of hustlers, drug dealers and gangland brutality Cat and Preme were big time cocaine gangsters. "Preme's relationship with Cat was one of mutual respect and admiration. Cat and Preme were like brothers. Cat would do almost anything for Preme," the Queens insider says. "Preme and Pretty Tony were cool with each other. They totally respected each other, but their relationship was mostly based around business. Cat was a real money getter and he was completely about his business, just as Preme was." The drug trade was so lucrative that rather than competition between crews, the money was spread around. Preme saw the advantages of networking with bigger dealers. He didn't mind playing his position. He gained insight, knowledge, and solid connections. He knew his time would come. Prince downplays the Fat Cat connection though.

"The Supreme Team stood on its own legs, business, muscle, or otherwise," Prince said. "The fact that my uncle and Cat were cool in 1984 didn't change that." But Cat was one of the original ghetto dons involved in narcotics trafficking. He supplied a lot of dudes and gave several of the Queens dealers their start. Speculation suggests that Preme was under Cat for a time but team members digress.

Bing agrees with Prince, "We were never getting shit from Fat Cat. There were a lot of different people we were buying coke from. I had like three or four connects." Regardless Supreme was pumping guns, cocaine and money into Baisley Projects, despite of who he was getting it from. The original member says, "Supreme was never under Fat Cat nor anyone for that matter, but Cat loved and admired Preme. He admired Preme cause he was a witness to Preme's rise from out of the dust. But Cat had a little jealousness for Preme cause he knew Preme was better than him at the boss game, and Cat is a very bad loser. Cat knew he had more money than Preme, but he also knew that his money was no match in comparison to Preme's allure of being a supreme leader. On his wits alone Preme commanded way more men than Cat. Cat could not purchase the amount of admiration that dudes had for Preme and not just men. Preme had more broads vying for his attention than any other boss in New York State. Preme gave the dudes some game and gave the women basically hard dick and bubble gum."

Preme and his Five Percenter crew were hustling packages of coke and heroin in hand to hand sales on the street and in the projects. "We were selling heroin and coke like 1983, 1984, selling drugs, doing our regular," Bing says. "We were selling drugs on the block, in Baisley, in the park on Sutphin, 118th on New York Boulevard." The Supreme Team was spreading their wings, but Fat Cat was still the man. He respected Preme and the team, but they weren't on his level. "One of the best money earners in the early years of the team was Melson. He used to get so much money for the team that Fat Cat offered Preme quite a chunk of money to take Melson away from Preme. Preme respectfully declined. In the early years Melson was simply an incredible money getter and the fiends loved him," the original member says.

The team was out there getting money, grinding while Preme was setting the stage for the Supreme Team's ascension. He was becoming a star in Queens. His name was ringing in the streets loud and clear. When he stepped out on the block, dudes took notice as did all the females who clamored to get down with Supreme, Prince, and the team. It was not only because of their big boy status but because of their style and influence in the hood. Preme had witnessed the party, and not only did he want to join the party, he wanted to become the party.

"Back in the day the team was the greatest show on earth," the original member says. "We did not have the money that Cat had or the Corley Brothers. In fact, we did not have the type of money that most of the major crews had. But what we had, none of the other crews had. We had the complete admiration from the world at large; our swag was on one million. We had so many broads sweating us that we could have started our very own women's league. Preme had bitches that looked so good that when he would cut the fine broad off, and she would be crying and shit for Preme to give her a second chance, I would cry with the bitch and tell her if you give me some pussy at least you'll see Preme once in a while." Being with Preme and the team was one big party. Regardless of his partying, Preme used his intelligence as well.

The Supreme Team did something that the other crews of the era didn't do. They successfully merged blacks and Latinos into one crew. Under Preme they unified, something that was unheard of before in the hood. With his charisma, influence, and Five Percenter hyperbole, Supreme gained support from all angles. All of Baisley Projects youth flocked to Preme's banner. Puerto Rican Righteous was one of Preme's top recruits and became a main lieutenant on the team, ensuring the future participation of Latinos in the Supreme Team and, more importantly, helping the team to gain a foothold in the Latino dominated world of cocaine distribution.

"Righteous was from Hillside," Bing says. "They were all together. They grew up together and became Five Percenters." A Latino face in the Supreme Team camp enabled Preme to gain access to Colombians, who were weary of dealing directly with blacks. With the language and cultural barriers, Supreme's inclusion of Latinos in the team was a major coup. The Colombians controlled the cocaine trade and moved weight at wholesale prices. With his Spanish members, Preme could make the right connections and deal directly with the Colombians, bypassing dealers like Fat Cat and Pretty Tony. Preme was a student of narcotics, and he had learned his lessons well. Every play he made was well thought out and calculated.

As the Supreme Team started grinding and getting their hustle on in the Southside of Queens, they were only little fish in a big pond. There were much bigger names in the underworld of the Queens drug trade. "In every hood people made a name for themselves," Bing says. "It goes with the territory." Fat Cat, Pappy Mason, Tommy Montana, the Corley Brothers, the Feurtado Brothers, and Hymee all hailed from the Southside. "Preme was fucking with all those dudes back then," Bing says. All of those notorious drug lords grew up in the 103rd Precinct and built up multimillion dollar drug territories, which they guarded ruthlessly with reckless abandon. Drug game era politics weren't pretty.

"Cat and the Corley Brothers were down on the block across from Linden Boulevard," Bing says. "Pretty Tony was on the block. Skinner, Danny, Early, different muthafuckas down there selling drugs." All of them had big names in the hood and were well established when the Supreme Team started gaining notoriety for their hip-hop and street exploits. "The Corley Brothers were street legends in South Jamaica, they ran Forty Projects," Bing says. "Pappy Mason was a real thorough dude. He was from Brooklyn though, Crown Heights, not Queens." But

Queens was where Pappy made his name as an enforcer for Fat Cat. Cat was the center of all the activities in Queens back then and all the players who later became infamous circled around him. "Fat Cat had a store, a poolroom, a hangout spot, dudes he knew, different people hung out," Bing says. And in the streets Fat Cat created order.

"Jamaica had a little order," a Bebos member from Pappy Mason's crew says. "There was Cat, Supreme, Pap, Corley. They had a thing called the Round Table. They all had rings. They were all together. Whenever there was a beef among crews, they'd come down to the Round Table to settle it, so everyone wasn't at each others necks. That was Fat Cat's idea. We were security for Cat, an extension of him. Even the Supreme Team, we were all down together. Wall Corley was different. It was like open season on them. But he was still a board member on the Round Table. But Supreme and them, we never had a problem with them. Cat started all of them. He put them all on except Wall. He put Preme on, and then Preme went on his own."

The Queens insider disagrees and tries to separate fact from fiction. "That Round Table shit with Fat Cat was some non-existent shit, never happened, straight make believe," he offers. Still the legend persists. In the beginning, the drug trade revolved around Queens reigning star Fat Cat, but he wouldn't shine forever. In the constellation of Queens' drug lords, Fat Cat was the biggest star, but his time was getting short, as Supreme would soon eclipse him. When Cat's star fell, the Supreme Team took over as new kings of the street.

"Prince came home in '84," Bing says. "Prince went to jail for some cat burglar shit. He wasn't even selling drugs. He started that after he came home. As soon as Prince hit the streets, Preme put him on. He had his own crew, his own thing and blew up. Ghostbuster was the name of his dope." Prince was a contrast to the always serene Preme. He was more of a hothead and strategist than an outright charismatic leader like Preme. "They were like night and day, but they were bonded by blood," the Supreme Team member says. Where Preme was diplomatic, Prince was more military like. He enforced his leadership with extreme violence. Members of the team quickly learned not to incur Prince's wrath. "Prince was the quintessential chess player," The Queens hustler says. With Prince supporting his every move, Preme was indeed formidable. In a way Prince was Preme's psychotic alter ego. He spoke with the roar of gunfire and the finality of death. He was Preme's avenging angel.

"Prince was real calm, in control of everything," The Supreme Team member says. "He was a general. He demanded respect." Prince also wanted out of his uncle's shadow. It was only logical that eventually

Prince would want to step out of his uncle's presence as he gained more insight and knowledge about the drug game into which Preme brought all of his disciples. Prince sought to carve his own niche, so to speak, to set himself aside from Supreme and to differentiate himself from his uncle. Prince did this with violence. His answer to everything became the unhesitating use of violence. By doing this, he added a facet to Preme's aura and arsenal that wasn't already there. Prince would become the dark side of the Supreme Team. And knowing the drug game like he did, Supreme didn't mind. His love and trust for his nephew was absolute.

"Prince's whole thing was the fact that he was hell-bent on proving himself to Preme," The Queens insider says. "Something that was completely not necessary. No matter what Prince did, it would never change Preme's opinion of his nephew. Prince wanted so much to raise his G.P.A. in Preme's eyes that he blinded himself to the fact that Preme's love for him was unconditional and without question." Whatever Prince's need to prove himself, his business acumen was unquestionable. "Prince was a very good person when it came to taking care of business," The Queens insider says. "He was the ultimate businessman. He was so on point concerning business it was unreal. I don't know why he didn't go into the legal or finance world. He was a real genius concerning matters of making different ways to sell work."

Despite his genius, Prince was the firecracker to Preme's statesman. With Prince, it was on and popping at any time. He gravitated toward other wild, crazy-type dudes like Pappy Mason while Supreme was more comfortable with innovators like Fat Cat and Pretty Tony. "Prince and his crew were not directly under Preme," the original member says. "They were by way of Prince being Preme's nephew and Prince being the absolute next in line for the throne of the team if something would have happened to Preme, but when we were all out there in the game at the time, Preme and us and Prince and his crew, when we went to party and stuff like that, Prince would be on some other shit. When we would be partying every night, Prince and his crew would be making money, scouting out other business ventures. Once in a while Prince would roll with us. Preme would make Prince come out and party. But he was not with the nightlife like we were." Still Prince's loyalty to his uncle was never in doubt.

"Preme told me something about his nephew Prince," the Queens insider says. "He said that he knows without any question that Prince would die and go to hell for him and that he never had to worry about his nephew betraying him, which I already had figured out to be a fact of life, but he also knew that Prince was bound to do crazy shit based on his need to be violent. Prince was always trying to show Preme that he was all about his business and how different and better he was in comparison to the rest of Preme's seconds-in-command. Prince and his crew did not roll like Preme and us as far as partying and just hanging out." Despite the differences, Prince and Preme were family and as they say, "Blood is thicker than water."

"The first person I met from Cat's crew when I came home from state prison on July 1, 1984 was Pap. Pap was Cat's strength in the streets," Prince said. Similarly, Prince would go on to become Preme's strength and the Supreme Team's security director. "Prince was about that real gun smoke," Bing says. "Prince was about that gunplay. People fear that gun smoke. The streets feared Prince." In the growing drug and hip-hop worlds, all these names would become cemented in street legend. These were the dudes that the rappers hung around on the block and tried to be like. "The Feurtado Brothers, the Corley's, Fat Cat, Supreme- those were the biggest dudes in Queens at the time," Bing says. And those were the dudes that would gain infamy in hip-hop's lyrical lore. It was the flash and style that Preme and his entourage exhibited on the blocks and the clubs, juxtaposed with the viciousness and violence of Prince and his crew, that led to the mystique of the crew collectively known as the Supreme Team in the streets of Queens during the early to mid-80s. But there were other players besides Preme and Prince who were just as vital to the team and to its legend.

Preme broke the team into four crews that were organized under members of the original seed. The four dudes under him calling the shots were his nephew Prince, Black Justice, Babywise, and Bimmy. Along with God B, First Born Prince, Green Eyed Born, Serious, Puerto Rican Righteous, Dahlu, and Melson, they composed the original seed. "The originals were God B, Dahlu, Preme, Babywise and Green Eyed Born," the Southside player says. The original member disputes this though. "Neither Bimmy nor Black Just were original members of the team; they were second generation so to speak. Black Just originally started out as Babywise's worker, and Bimmy came about due to the fact that he knew how to network. The original seed was Dahlu, Babywise, Green Eyed Born, Melson, Preme, Prince, God B, Mo Dog aka Deemo, and Bing. Black Just and Bimmy were second wave. All other members derived from the original team members." Still legend holds.

"They were Godbodies," Bing says. "Righteous was always there. They were all together. Serious grew up with them too. They grew up together. Serious was a Five Percenter. He was a bank robber, never a drug seller. A lot of the original seed were into banks. They were always around."

But Preme didn't just recruit Five Percenters. "We were from different parts of Queens," Bing says. "They was from Baisley. They branched out so much they had muthafuckas I didn't even know about. There was no crew bigger than ours."

Puerto Rican Righteous was said to be genuinely fearless. While some Supreme Team members caved in to law enforcement pressure when they landed in jail, Righteous would hold his own, do his time, and carry the weight. "Preme knew that Righteous was not all he was cracked up to be or what he was trying to perpetrate," The Queens insider says. "Righteous was nothing more than one of Preme's creations." But to the streets Righteous was a killer who was unafraid to get his hands dirty, executing rivals and dumping the bodies in the outlying wooded areas of Southside Queens that Supreme Team members dubbed "the burial grounds." Righteous and Prince formed a deadly duo that Preme called on to handle team business, but one of the most vicious and feared Supreme Team members was C-Justice. He had an impeccable reputation in the streets as a dude who wasn't afraid to put in work or take care of things for the team. With this cadre of young killers, Preme and the team were a brutal force to be reckoned with.

Everyone on the team answered to Preme, as he was at the top of the pyramid. Everything that happened was under his banner. At Baisley, team members would talk about Preme as if he were God himself. Dudes like Bimmy were known to punctuate every sentence with "Word to Preme." Just like "Word to mother," this became a catch phrase in South Jamaica. Supreme was known to different people as the Chief or the Chosen One. On the streets of the Southside of Queens, Preme was a respected businessman, a ladies man, and a ghetto superstar. He ran the team. He collected a group of hustlers, players, thugs, criminals, and killers from the Southside of Jamaica, Queens, and molded them into the Supreme Team. They were a group of diverse personalities and loyalties. There were crews inside of crews. Infighting and jealousies occurred as in all families, but all answered to Preme. Some held more juice than others.

"God B was the only person alive that could tell Preme to go fuck himself, and Preme would not take it as disrespect," The Queens insider says. "God B could tell Preme all types of shit, and it did not matter who was around. And trust me, we had so many dick riders around us it was unbelievable. But if anyone ever questioned why God B had talked to Preme like that, their days around us became non-existent. No one could question Preme about God B's conduct on any level. Preme once told me that the person that brings him anything about God B was not fit to live and that they were not going to stay among the living. God B lived by his own rules, and no one could alter the way he went about his business. No one." God B was down since the jump, and out of all the original seeds, Preme respected him the most.

"God B taught everyone how to basically fight," the original member says. "We would have boxing matches. The only time Prince played with his hands was when him and Preme would box each other. Prince and Preme were both very skilled in boxing for dudes that never had any formal boxing training." The whole team was ready to go at a moment's notice.

"Dudes say all types of shit about the team in very low tones a million miles away from us, but in our presence it's all love and respect even if they hated us," the original member says. "If the team was up in the Bronx partying, and a beef broke out someone would always manage to get a message to Prince about it, no matter how small, and he would be on his way. Sometimes we would cold crush some dudes, and when we got back, Prince and his crew would be in front of Baisely on the ready, ready to go to wherever we just came from and tear shit down. Preme would calm Prince down by telling him how we already handled our business. Most of the time when Prince and his crew would be out partying with us, it would be for a reason, say if we had gotten into some beef with another crew from say Brooklyn or the Bronx or from wherever at some club in another borough. When it was time to go straighten the beef, make no mistake about it, Prince and his crew were rolling with us. If something went down and Prince felt like whoever was with Preme should have went to the next level and didn't Prince would let you know about your mistake and how that mistake was not to ever happen again. He did not play when it concerned Preme's well being."

Preme was the boss. He was the center of the universe for all things Supreme Team. Everyone catered and bowed down to him. His word was law and everything was under his banner. Even though he had different relationships with all the members under him, everyone on the team wanted to be around him. Whomever he showed favor to was looked on with envy by the other members. Prince could be especially jealous. Growing up it was always him and Preme, but as the team multiplied and grew, a lot of dudes wanted Preme's favor. Consequently Prince was jealous of any other team members that took up Preme's time. It also led to a competitive factor between the crews as all of them were seeking Preme's approval. Preme had the charisma and personality to stroke everybody's egos, but still there grew to be an undercurrent of resentment, especially on Prince's part, toward some team members who monopolized and held Preme's attention.

"Outside of Preme's immediate family there were only two people who I know without a doubt that Preme had more love for than me," the original member says. "Those two people are Prince and God B in that order." Supreme showed love for his whole crew like a benevolent godfather. He had favorites, but he didn't play favorites.

Other members grew close to Preme as they advanced in the hierarchy. "My stature was high up there in this organization. I was right up under them," Bing says. "I was considered the money man. But don't get it twisted, we were always armed and dangerous out there. We did shit a certain way, so we could get away with it. We'd be real incognito about how we did shit."

Prince was always coming up with ideas for the Supreme Team concerning drug sales, spots, security, or whatever, and most of the time Supreme had Prince implement his ideas as policy or working principles for the team. Prince was forever trying to prove his worth to the team to show that he just wasn't Preme's nephew. He was always trying to impose his authority also, but dudes on the team weren't having it. They answered to Preme and Preme only. But Prince's crew was loyal to him first. He had his own faction, still Supreme Team but different. "Prince and his crew were not flashy like Preme and us," the original member says. "Prince did not allow his crew to resemble team members. He wanted himself and his soldiers to have a complete different style then anyone who was directly under Preme's orders. Prince did not splurge. He was not flashy like Preme. Prince would be looking for angles on everything." Prince's policies had a big impact on the Supreme Team's legend, almost as much as Supreme's.

"Prince was not into politicking," the Queens insider says. "If someone violated, that was their ass, ain't nothing to talk about. If someone got out of line with Preme and it got to Prince, they had better had all their insurance paid up." When Prince brought violence into the equation, even among team members, a lot of dudes were frightened. Violence against outsiders, rivals or opponents was one thing, but violence against team members was something totally different. Preme mediated as much as he could, but when it came down to it, Prince was his nephew, and he viewed him as a necessary evil. As was Prince's crew that existed within the structure of the team and was loyal to Prince and to Prince only. All of the counter surveillance and security measures came from Prince as did the color coded vials for the different crews. Prince wanted to show Preme that his crew was not only the most violent but the best earners also.

The team used the color coded scheme for their distribution system.

Each color signified which crew the cocaine belonged to. Each recognized crew leader had his own color for the vials of cocaine and heroin and had his own distinct spot. "That color code system is what Prince came up with," the Queens insider says. "To be honest it was designed to differentiate who was selling what, so Preme would know Prince's crew sold more product than Black Just and Bimmy. Preme made everyone go along with it. Prince used to come up with all types of innovative ideas to show Preme who the best earner was. Prince was in competition with Black Just, Bimmy, and Babywise, because they were more successful than Prince in regards to business and due to the fact that they did not draw the type of attention to themselves in the way Prince did. Yeah, they used to floss a lot and get themselves noticed but not in the manner that Prince got himself extra attention. His solution to everything was violence and downright murder." Before the violence, the wonder years were marked by united legions of black and Latino street soldiers in matching red jackets with Supreme emblazoned across the back. With his team united, Preme came to rule Baisley Projects. "There was never no Supreme Team jackets for me," Bing says. "Babywise's crew had that shit."

Using building tops as surveillance towers, the team's watchmen encoded their walkie-talkie communications with the Supreme Alphabet and Mathematics from Five Percenter science. Leaders used the Five Percenter code to plan "assaults, intimidation, extortion and drug dealing," law enforcement officials said. All the mystique and mythology that surrounded the team was real, and it reverberated throughout South Jamaica and into street lore. One legend that held true through the years was the one that said Supreme had Sabrina Jackson, a Supreme Team member, killed in 1984 after she fucked up some money. Sabrina was the mother of Curtis Jackson, the future 50 Cent. "She was dead for days before they found her," 50 Cent said. "When they found her, her body was fucked up. Someone put something in her drink and turned the gas on." This rumor would come back to haunt Preme, but at the time it was just another random murder in the hood. Other team members have spawned their own legends as well, becoming equally famous in hip-hop lore.

James "Bimmy" Antney's crew held it down for the blue vials. Bimmy was down from the jump. He was one of Preme's original guys. Photos from the era show a light skinned, serious looking brother that liked to have fun. Bimmy was from Hollis, and he liked to profile and shine. He drove BMW's and sported the latest fashions. Dudes from the era said he was down with Run DMC before they became rap stars. Bimmy was immersed in the hip-hop culture from day one. A lot of the styles the rap group adopted they got from Bimmy and his crew. It's said Bimmy was highly devoted to Preme and the team. A South Jamaican loyalist, he had a number of lieutenants and soldiers that worked for him. "He grew up with LL Cool J," the Queens insider says. "Bimmy had a three to life bid before he came home and started messing with the team. He had gotten some type of record label deal with 3 to Life Entertainment. Bimmy is like family to Russell Simmons and that whole Run DMC crew. He also executive produced at least some of LL Cool J's albums. Bimmy is the most well connected member of the team in the entertainment business bar none."

Bimmy was known to step on the set with all the rappers of the day, promoting the music and culture before it even went main stream, when it was still just a New York underground fad. This was when Russell Simmons was just coming out with Curtis Blow and everybody listened to DJ's like Marley Marl and Mr. Magic. "Dudes been out there forever," the Supreme Team member says. "He was like Preme's son. Preme was like a God to him. Bimmy came about by idolizing Preme and having hip-hop connections. Bimmy's crew was Shaheer, Doe Dee, Lil' Charlie and Big John aka BJ." And Bimmy represented for Supreme and the team. He was a good earner and always had Preme's back.

"Babywise's crew was bubbling," Bing says. His color was red. Troy "Babywise" Jones was known as a ladies man with brown skin and waves in his hair. He was a major league criminal and one of the city's premier black drug dealers and urban legends. "He was a party animal, a dancing fool. Never been to jail. He did like a deuce, he ducked the big cases, did two or three years. One time Preme and Green Eyed Born got in a scuffle and Babywise shot Green Eyed Born," the Southside player says. "That Green Eyed Born shit stems from his stealing some jewelry from Preme. Preme had so much jewelry that he did not realize it was missing until he wanted to wear some particular pieces and could not find them. The fool Green Eyed Born had stolen them, and the dumbass tried to sell them to Chaz Williams, like Chaz was not going to let Preme know that Born was trying to sell him Preme's jewelry." Babywise was fiercely loyal to Preme, so when Preme confronted Born and the altercation started, Babywise shot Born. They called him the Baby in the street because he had a baby face. He looked like a little kid, but he wasn't. He was a gangster. He was Supreme Team to the core and represented to the max.

"Babywise did not give a fuck," the Queens insider says. "His loyalty was to Supreme and Supreme alone. Babywise was one of the best thinkers amongst the entire team, bar none, in regards to handling business. The only person Babywise ever trusted was and is hisself. He is one of the most honorable men I've ever known, and his word has always been his bond. Babywise never took phone calls. He would not talk on the phone before *Goodfellas* and long before *The Wire*. His business was always his business. He was never a part of the broadcast business. Babywise didn't take photos either. He was very cautious. His style irritated a lot of people including Preme and triple that on Prince. But it was uniquely his own, and he played the game by his own rules. He did not tolerate any disrespect from anyone, but sometimes he could not do anything about the disrespect. Babywise had a right-hand man named Iron Horse. He was killed in the late-80s. Babywise is simply the smartest member of the whole team. Very low key. Me mentioning him is totally too much for how he moves and against all his rules."

Orange caps were controlled by Colbert "Black Justice" Johnson. He was Preme's main man. Black Just used to stay uptown in Harlem with rappers always hanging around him. "Black Just was from Harlem, but he moved to Queens; he was a big gambler. He was sniffing that heroin," the Southside player says. He was a visible dude in the hip-hop community. From its inception he was a big part of that world. "Black Just started off being Babywise's worker, and then Preme took him from Babywise. Basically he and Bimmy were second tier team members," The Queens insider says. "I'm not saying Black Just and Bimmy did not earn their positions because they did. In fact they surpassed expectations. They were very good earners."

Black Just and the orange caps have gone down in legend. "Black Just was down with a lot of dudes from uptown," Bing says. "They'd come to the project side to hang with the team." Alpo, Rich Porter, AZ- Black Just would be with all of them, hanging out at Carmichael's Diner, right next to Baisley, where all the hustlers ate breakfast. Black Just was flashy, looking like he just walked off the set of *Belly*, he was one of the original hip-hop hustlers.

"He was in Harlem a lot at the Rooftop. They'd be up there gambling. Just would lose like 30 g's at a time," the Southside player says. "Black Just was Rich Porter's man. He used to come uptown, and Rich would come out to Baisley Park and play ball. Bimmy and Black Just would go to Harlem all the time to hang out with Rich and Alpo. Black Just was driving Rich's Porsche 944 one time, and the police pulled Just over and seized Rich's car." The smooth, dark skinned African looking brother would become Preme's favorite. He kept a big bank, stayed fresh in the latest hip-hop gear, and always drove flashy cars.

Prince controlled the yellow top vials of cocaine and heroin that were sold out of Baisley. "Prince had it where all of Baisley was all his work," the Southside player says. "If anyone else sold work they were hit." Being Preme's nephew, Prince was given prime retail locations or drug spots, and he held them down fiercely.

"Most of Prince's crew were very dangerous men. Their thinking abilities were borderline crazy. But overall very good dudes," the original member says. "Prince and his crew did not hang out with the team. Meaning Preme, Dahlu, Babywise, Black Just and Bimmy. He was quite uncomfortable to have to be in Preme's presence and be totally under Preme's command. Prince's faction of the team was 10 times more violent and dangerous than us. Whereas we would stomp some dudes ears between their heads, Prince and his crew would just remove their heads. He was about his work." Prince had a reputation in the streets as a killer, and along with Puerto Rican Righteous and C-Just, he worked as an enforcer for the team, handling all problems and disputes. If Preme gave the word, then Puerto Rican Righteous, C-Justice and Prince put in work.

"Prince was the most feared member period," the Queens insider says. "His faction was the most dangerous and most lethal." Prince's crew included Trent "Serious" Morris, Hobie "Robo Justice" Townsend, Peter "Knowledge" Jimenez, and Shannon Jimenez. These dudes were gunslingers straight out of a gangsta rap song. Their proclivity for violence eclipsed their status on the team.

"Robo Justice was down with Prince for the most part. He was not really around for the team's wonder year. When the team was at its height he was in jail. When he got out of jail the team was on its way to jail. He was able to run around with Prince for a minute, but then he caught a body out in Far Rockaway somewhere and got 25 to life for it," the original member says. "Both C-Just and Righteous are Puerto Rican. Shannon and his brother Knowledge are not. Shannon is a very good dude. He was about his business. He was super loyal to Prince, even to a fault. Knowledge is a good dude too, loyal and very dangerous, but a drug addict. All were part of Prince's faction of the team." They mostly dealt with security matters, but Prince had a whole retail side also.

Prince's retail operation was booming. The yellow top vials were known as a top seller back in the day. "Prince had a drug spot that was making crazy money and what made it crazy was the fact that the police would raid his spot two or three times a day," the Queens hustler says. "And never catch anyone of Prince's workers selling his work. He took an old garage and had it renovated into a spot for him to hustle out of. In the front of the spot he had roll up security gates installed, but the thing was they were not just your everyday regular security store gates. Prince had them particularly designed so that when the police would come to bust his place, whoever was inside would roll up with the security gates; they would literally be rolled up in the gate. The police would bust the outside locks on the gates and rush inside, and no one would be there for them to arrest. The police would go crazy trying to figure out how whoever was selling the work had gotten out. The spot was built just like a cell, only one way in.

"The police would bring in rams to bang on the walls and floors thinking there was a hidden exit and never find nothing, no work, no seller, period. We would all be posted up across the street watching the police raiding Prince's spot, and we'd be laughing at the police making fools of themselves. One time we watched them set up a post right in front of Prince's spot for 72 hours, and they still did not get anything. Prince would open back up when they left and go right back to work. The police would come back a minute later thinking they were going to catch someone and still nothing. It would be slapstick funny."

All the crews were bringing in crazy money. And Preme was the man in command of all four crews. He was the top dog, so most of the money made its way to him. Preme also set rules such as the infamous, "No singles, no shorts," policy that Supreme Team members would chant like a slogan. It meant no dollar bills and don't come short with the money. With all the crews, the enforcers, and the drug flow, Preme was in control and making serious money.

"Preme and Prince rarely occupied the side of the projects were drugs were being sold," the Southside player says. "They were the bosses. They didn't fuck around with the product." Hand to hand was for the workers and low level soldiers of the team. Back in the 80s when dudes rolled up to Baisley to see Prince or Preme, they would see kids on top of the buildings talking into the big walkie-talkies. By the time they got to the courtyard on the Guy R. Brewer side of the projects where the brain trust of the Supreme Team held court, there'd be a group of soldiers waiting for them. The more important Supreme Team members would be playing a dice game or chess, but there'd be a crew of younger guys standing around them like bodyguards. That was how the original seed got down. They started that whole entourage shit.

Another prominent team member in the early years was Nathan "Green Eyed Born" May. "Green Eyed Born was the corniest member of the team," the original member says. "Green Eyed Born's eyes are not green. They are blue. He was totally jealous of Preme, and every chance he thought he had, he would try to challenge Preme. He wanted to have the swag and respect that Preme had. Born always resented the fact that he was not the boss of the team. He is like a year older than Preme and back in the days, in our early years as Five Percenters, Born was a bank robber. Him and Serious robbed banks in the early days. He did a bid in the feds way before any of us experienced jail period." With Supreme, either it was dudes hated him or they did their best not to let it show because despite how anyone felt, everybody wanted to be a part of the Supreme Team show.

"Green Eyed Born's second hustle was clownism," the original member says. "He was the king of the used car lot. He always thought that he was his own entity apart from the team. Preme tolerated him because we all grew up together, and Preme has a soft spot for dudes he grew up with especially if they were around before the emergence of the team. But every chance Born got, he would try to undermine Preme. He hated the fact that he had to abide by Preme's rules since he felt that he was out there before we were. Green Eyed Born did not have a good rapport with any of the other lieutenants- Dahlu, Babywise, God B, or Melson. Him and Prince was cool because he was scared of Prince.

"Green Eyed Born had a little brother named Bossman. Back in the day he stole some drugs and money from Prince and his crew. Prince had Bossman's fingers cut off. Really, his fingers got cut completely off. Born would try to poison Preme about everyone on the team except Prince and God B. Prince was Preme's blood so there was no way Born could poison Preme about him. Back then Black Just and Bimmy had just gotten down with the team, and they were leery of Green Eyed Born, so he didn't see them as a problem. Everything Preme did Born would try to emulate in a better way. Preme only tolerated him because we all grew up together in the Five Percent Nation." Preme held his crew to a high standard, and respect was paramount, but he was still loyal to those he grew up with.

"The streets will always respect Preme for who he is," Bing says. "Everybody had their good ways and bad ways to them, but Preme set it all in motion." The respect level for Preme was on one million. In the streets he was highly regarded. The loyalty and devotion Preme inspired was legendary in its own right. With his charisma, he charmed men and women alike. He was a walking, talking, original gangster; a legend in his own time that controlled killers, drug dealers, cutthroats, thieves, thugs, and the criminal underworld elite as easily as he got the ladies into bed.

Supreme had worked his way up from hustling on the block to the CEO of the biggest crew in Queens. By the fall of 1985 the Supreme Team was finally coming into its own. "The Supreme Team literally took over Baisley Projects during the 1980s," the Queens hustler says. "They actually controlled lobbies, walkways in some of the apartments." It was just like *New Jack City* and The Carter. The team didn't fuck around. A lot of people said the Wesley Snipes film was based on the Supreme Team and Baisley Projects. It's been called the Hollywood version of the Supreme Team story. Truth or not, the Supreme Team's legend is up there with John Gotti's and Pablo Escobar in true-crime popular culture tales.

CHAPTER 3
THE COME UP

"One of the most notorious crews from a deadly era, the team towers above its contemporaries in stature, notoriety and infamy."
— **Don Diva Magazine, Issue 23**

"When you hear talk of the Southside/you hear talk of the team/ see niggas feared Prince and respected Preme/for all you slow muthafuckas I'm gonna break it down iller/see Preme was the businessman and Prince was the killer."
— **50 Cent, Ghetto Qur'an (Forgive Me)**
Guess Who's Back (2000)

"Cracks arrival in 1985 leveled the playing field between established hustlers and ambitious new jacks, throwing the rhythms of the street trade into chaos."
— **Vibe Magazine**

Fat Cat was the king, but the Supreme Team's time was coming. "Supreme had his own crew. He was what he was, he had his crew. He made his money. He was a figure in Queens," Spoon said. Supreme would become more than a figure; he would become the man. The Supreme Team didn't play. They locked their territory down. They were young, up and coming, and ready to pounce like wolves. "The Supreme Team was a completely different animal from any other crew out of South Jamaica, Queens," the Queens insider says. The team was willing to pay the price to wear the crown. They were violent gangsters who thought they were in some kind of Sopranos like show. In a Machiavellian world where the hustlers had to keep it one hundred.

"Our areas was 118th and Baisley," Bing says, "but the team had shit I didn't even know about in the Bronx and in Queensbridge, Rockaway,

Merrick Boulevard." The Supreme Team was locking down anything that wasn't claimed by the Round Table. "A house on 116th Drive off Sutphin Boulevard, a private house," Bing says. "One hundred eighteenth and 153rd- Baisley Park, where team members hustled behind the handball court. Cedar Manor- two buildings, a co-op next to Baisley Projects, adjacent to it." The team knew territory was the important thing and they were putting in bids. Supreme knew that was the key to running a successful drug operation. Real estate was the end all and be all for a drug tycoon. Preme knew that Baisley Projects was a gold mine, and he urged the team to protect the home turf. He enforced his will, but he worked as an imparter of knowledge also. He was the wise one, the exalted one, the supreme one. He didn't give orders. He guided men and let them make their own decisions. "Preme knew how to separate family from business, friend from foe. Preme did not allow his emotions to make any of his decisions," the Queens insider says. Most importantly Preme knew how to make money. His know how and guidance led the team to crazy wealth. Supreme tried his hand at several legitimate business ventures also. He knew to succeed totally he had to go legit. The drug game only held death and prison in the cards.

"Back in 1994, Preme wanted his own cab service that catered mainly to people from the underworld," the Queens hustler says. "So what he did was he purchased about 25 Lincoln Continental Town Cars to use as cabs for the service. In the beginning the service did well until the guy from whom Preme used to purchase the cars decided he did not like how Preme was running the cab service, and the cars started disappearing. What the dude was doing was stealing the cars whenever he saw one parked and taking the cars down south where he started his own cab service. You see, it was easy for him to do and get away with because all the cars were in his name, and he had keys for every car. He knew that his only problem would be if Preme and the team ever found out where he was at. When the cars first started to go missing, Preme did not even suspect that he was behind all this."

Supreme also invested and owned a satellite business. The original team member remembers, "Back in 84 Preme also owned a satellite business. We were literally selling satellite dishes, big ones that get placed on top of office buildings. Shit was crazy. The only problem was the buildings where we sold the satellite dishes became like a hotel for us. I used to take girls there and fuck them literally on top of the dishes." Supreme and the team were trying to invest the drug money they made into legal ventures and flip it. Everything was looking kosher until crack hit.

"The popular history of the era is that nothing existed before crack, and suddenly everyone's just driving a Mercedes," Ethan Brown, the author of *Queens Reigns Supreme* said. "Actually it was totally the opposite. Fat Cat had this unbelievable multimillion dollar organization in the early-80s. Think about how much money that is. Way before crack. Crack killed them all off. Most of the people in the crew became addicted to crack." Law enforcement also moved in on Cat. A bust at his headquarters at Big Mac's Deli, where drugs and guns were seized, signaled the beginning of the end for Cat. With Fat Cat's demise, opportunity beckoned in the Southside of Queens. To that point Cat's organization had dominated the retail drug markets in South Jamaica, but when the NYPD shut the block at 150th Street down, the Supreme Team, with all four of their crews organized and in place at Baisley Projects, took advantage of the drug traffic coming through the area. Their ascendance was immediate. Around the same time crack hit the scene. Just like the Italian Mafia used prohibition to get money and power, the Supreme Team would use crack. Supreme saw the advantages of selling the drug and soon had all four of his crews pumping crack out of Baisley Projects. The Supreme Team didn't just sell out of Baisley, it took over. The Supreme Team would go down in infamy and make plenty of paper in the coming crack era, but it would also turn down a dark road from which they could never return.

"Crack hit. That shit was big. That shit was 84-85," Bing says. The emergence of crack cocaine sparked a phenomenal crime wave in the 103rd, and nowhere did criminals more boldly seize upon the opportunities that the emergence of crack afforded those willing to break the law, than in Queens. South Jamaica became ground zero in the city's crack epidemic. Crack changed Queens just like it did everywhere else. "The game got messed up," the Bebo member says. "We didn't sell to pregnant women, kids, old ladies. Crack fucked the game up, but it made people rich too. Pappy taught us to have honor. A lot of people didn't have no honor. In New York, crack stared like 84-85. What happened was, you had a lot of people start getting money that never got money. With crack there was more crews, more money, more guns. People who never got money all of a sudden, they getting money. So there was beef."

Prior to the explosion Queens had known violence, but not to the degree that it would. "The violence became crazy. They had to fight off all the new crews. The new crews had no sense of how to run things and were killing each other," Ethan Brown said. From the old school dealers rose the new- the A-Team, the Bebos, and the Supreme Team. The lure of the potential money making made dudes on the block reinvent themselves. They became much more aggressive. "The crack era was instant rich overnight," the Queens hustler says. Recognizing this fact, the Supreme Team jumped in. Not realizing the collateral damage that the crack game would create. "We started selling crack," Bing says, and the rest was history. A grim legion of crack addicts were served at Baisley day and night. For those entrusted with keeping the killing fields of New York's outer borough streets crime free during the mid-80s, the new crack gangs were lethal.

"Crack was the first out drug. Guys on the street sold crack, standing in the doorways. Back in the day dealers would never think of selling drugs in the open," Barry Michael Cooper, the screenwriter of *New Jack City* said. "I think crack became so widespread because it didn't involve needles. With crack you smoked it, and it was an immediate high. Even people who weren't getting high off crack felt the cultural effect it brought. That drug changed hip-hop. This is gonna sound freaky, but crack made hip-hop corporate because the guys who emulated the crack dealers became rap stars. They wanted to be tough like them and wanted to floss. Crack made hip-hop corporate. It took it beyond break dancing, graffiti, and the South Bronx."

Crack cocaine gave ruthless gangs like the Supreme Team maximum power and unlimited resources. Without the birth of crack in the inner-city during the mid-80s, the Supreme Team wouldn't have reached the heights in the street hierarchy that it did. But due to crack cocaine's emergence it flourished. It would also lead to the team's demise. What crack giveth, crack taketh away.

Crack was cheap and easy to manufacture. It expanded the drug trade and decentralized it. Crack got its name from the distinctive crackling sound a cocaine rock makes when it's ignited. The highly addictive cocaine distiller could be produced cheaply and easily with just a pair of coffee pots, a hot plate, a little coke scale, and baking soda. Introduced on the streets of the Southside sometime in the mid-80s, crack instantaneously flattened the bottom lines of the drug organizations. It also created a whole new set of problems, from rampant drug addictions to low level hustlers suddenly being thrust into the position of street CEO's.

"Crack started with the Dominicans who were the retailers between the street guys and the Colombian suppliers," the Queens detective said. "They were very smart marketers and knew their product would sell." When crews like the Supreme Team saw the effect of the powerful new drug on users, they streamlined their own operation to serve crack only. They franchised like McDonald's. With their organization already set up to mass market retail amounts of narcotics, it was easy to change the game up and switch their operations to exclusively sell crack. Makeshift drug labs sprung up in project apartments, crack dens overflowed to capacity with zombied-out baseheads, and Baisley Projects became Crack Cocaine Central.

As in other areas across the country, crack took hold quickly in the Southside of Queens. Because of its accessibility, crack encumbered the drug trade with hundreds of new dealers setting up shop with operations small enough to elude law enforcement's attention. Blocks near Sutphin Boulevard and Farmers Boulevard that once had moderate cocaine and heroin traffic were now full of young dealers selling crack for as little as five to ten dollars a vial. New dealers with names like Wise and Young Allah began to dominate the streets, replacing Fat Cat and Ronnie Bumps who were serving time. "We'd done a good job locking up the big guys like Fat Cat and Ronnie in 85," the Queens detective said. "But by 86 there was a whole new crew on the streets with crack. When the warm weather came, it was unreal how many there were." Young black and Latino males with crack, guns, and swagger filled the streets, recreating the image of the young urban male into that of the ultimate hip-hop hustler.

"The privates became generals. You had guys on the streets that had only experienced the drugs and the easy cash but had never feared any consequences for their behavior," Spoon said. "Crack came out full scale. It came out a little bit before we got busted, but 90 days after, it was rapid. Like once they closed 150th Street after our arrest, you got offshoots shooting up all over the place, and it's not organized; it's just niggas out there doing their thing. They just out there now. Every corner is a drug area now with a lot of money floating around because you had like a million or two million coming through the area." The money that was going into Fat Cat's pockets became fair game. It was there for anyone who had the balls to grab it, and the Supreme Team grabbed it with both hands. In the process the members became the image of the new era young black gangster that would come to dominate the drug game and hip-hop.

Crack spread like wildfire due to the notorious dealers and crews like Alpo, Pappy Mason and the Supreme Team. Former b-boys and alpha males became street generals and traded in hip-hop for a shot at being the next Tony Montana. Crack brought on a terrifying new kind of violence. Once, the cocaine business was dominated by old fashioned dealers who were tough young men who could start small and build a structured empire which used fear and sophisticated connections. The prohibitive cost and effort of getting large amounts of cocaine and heroin limited the number of major dealers in the area. But crack and the Colombians changed all that. It became the deadliest, most profitable drug trend to hit the ghettos since heroin in the early-70s, during the Nicky Barnes and

Frank Lucas era.

The cartels had Americanized themselves by the mid-80s at about the same time crack hit. Queens became the East Coast headquarters of the Colombians. They were buying into local businesses, perfecting both their smuggling operations and distribution efforts. With the ability to offer lucrative jobs, cocaine at wholesale rates, and a code of silence enforced through murder and kidnapping,- all tools perfected by the Italian Mafia- the Colombians won a solid lock on the Queens region. With their Spanish members the Supreme Team had the ability to deal directly with the Colombians in comfort, fueling their take over of Queens from retail to wholesale distribution. They regulated the ghetto with bloody duels, Wild West gunfights, and drive-bys to win street corner supremacy. It was war on the Southside, and the NYPD had a front row seat.

The South Jamaica streets were boiling with fury and malice, the crack vial being at the epicenter of all the action and reaction. Bubbling right alongside the crack industry was hip-hop, and the two would quickly find themselves on a collision course. At first, in the summer of 1985, everyone wanted to believe crack was another faddish drug. They hoped it would go the way of acid mescaline and angel dust. But the drug quickly turned into an epidemic. On November 19, 1985, four months after the word crack first appeared in the *New York Post*, *The New York Times* finally got around to writing about the drug. The headline read *A new Purified Form of Cocaine Causes Alarm as Abuse Increases*.

In the streets it was chaos. Crack replaced powdered cocaine as the drug of choice. So sudden was crack's arrival that it caught the Queens narcotics cops off guard. "We'd arrest somebody on the street and say, 'What's this shit?'" The Queens detective said. "And they'd say, 'That's the new shit they're selling, crack.'" Dealers sprung up on every corner. Everyone started to sell crack. It became more fashionable to be a crack dealer than to have a real job. Crack was a phenomenon that would change the face of police work, organized crime, and hip-hop all at once. Nothing infuriated the law abiding populace more than the image of the millionaire crack dealer. The media jumped on the story portraying crack dealing as one of the most profitable jobs in America.

"Crack is a cottage industry," Sterling Johnson, the city's special narcotics prosecutor, said. "Anybody who's got a little coke, bicarbonate of soda, and some balls thinks they can be an entrepreneur now. With the way it's made, if you have 20 grand worth of coke, you can sell 80 grand worth of crack. There's a new generation of kids selling out there who we don't even know about. A lot of them are in their late teens or early 20s. They're a less mature, more primitive group than the older dealers like Fat

Cat who they're up against. They're reckless, and they don't care about the future. They do their talking with guns." And these were the youth that ended up swelling the ranks of the Supreme Team.

Crack's arrival leveled the playing field between established hustlers and ambitious new jacks. At first established drug lords like Fat Cat resisted the lure of crack. "Cat never wanted to sell crack. He thought it brought way too much heat to the business," Bobo, a Fat Cat lieutenant, said. "We didn't need crack because we were making crack money before there was even crack." But after Cat and his crew went down in a succession of raids and cases that Queens County prosecutors brought against them in 1985, the new jacks, namely the Supreme Team took over. Crack was a godsend for the lower level hand to hand dealers grinding on the streets. Crack democratized the drug trade, and Supreme was the ultimate politician. With the streets swarming with naïve, inexperienced hustlers, Supreme started recruiting, building an army.

The Supreme Team was in effect. Canvassing the streets like four corner hustlers and ghetto politicians, their numbers grew. They had that *Terminator*-type of feel. Nothing could stand in their way. They were bigger and badder and stronger and tougher. They were the number one dominator. They were bold in their audacity, and fearless in their attempt to come up. "They're right in your face," said the Reverend Floyd Flake. "I was taking a church group around South Jamaica when we ran into a bunch of them out on the street. They were completely brazen. They just stood there and taunted us. When they finally did move, it was just down the block to keep selling. The whole neighborhood turned to crack overnight. This was a nice neighborhood. White people from outside began driving in buying and leaving. It destroyed the community."

The Supreme Team had the game on lock. They were the undisputed kings. Fat Cat had missed the boat and with him locked up, his crew was getting weaker. His enforcer, Pappy Mason, joined Cat in the Queens House of Detention, charged with murder and a weapons violation. That was a death knell for the Cat organization. Their reign was almost finished. One afternoon in November 1985, Fat Cat was sitting in the prison dayroom and called his sister, Viola. "Hey, Busy," Viola said. "That new stuff people is wild for it," She told him, referring to the new drug.

"What stuff is that?" Fat Cat asked.

"The stuff they be calling crack," Viola answered. "It comes in a vial, and the homeboys is going crazy for it."

Queens was about to enter a dark age as the crack wars jumped off. But one crew would put their gorilla act down and claim the title of boss crew on the streets. They would show their goon hand and get paid. There was a lot of money available, and crews like the Supreme Team did what was necessary to get it. The streets of the Southside were about to get bloody. In 1985 there were 186 homicides in Queens. In the first quarter of 1986 that number grew to 242. Queens became one of crack cocaine's earliest and most active hotbeds. A new cadre of gun thugs were going hard and getting paid. They were putting down their stamp as NBK's- Natural Born Killers. And their guns didn't discriminate.

"A lot of the young crack guys out there will shoot anybody who gets in their way, and they don't worry about the consequences," the Queens detective said. It was a "get mine or be mine" mentality, and the Supreme Team epitomized the "shoot first, ask questions later" mindset. Supreme's nephew Prince especially embraced this philosophy. He quickly gained a reputation in the hood as a man who wasn't afraid to pull the trigger, even in broad daylight.

"Most of the shit Prince was doing was based on Prince's need to prove to Preme how competent he was. Prince was a very good earner, but his violent nature prevented him from seeing the bigger picture; it's always business and never personal. Prince allowed his emotions to consume him," the Queens insider says. "If Prince would not have been so violent, he would have been more successful than Preme from a business standpoint. Prince was about his business. He was not about being fly and flashy. If you fucked with his business the end game would be the end for you. Prince did not take any shorts where business was concerned. If he gave someone some work at a particular price for it, that is what he expected, not one penny short. On the other hand Preme was a whole lot more tolerant about his money business. Dudes still owe Preme money from the early-80s that could easily exceed a few million dollars including every member of the team, and that is up to this very day."

The criminal underworld and drug game were entering a much more lethal era of organized crime, the likes of which the NYPD had never seen. And hip-hop was primed to get sucked in along with it. Queens became the deadly courtyard of the Supreme Team, where violence and chaos ruled and ran recklessly. Numerous members of the team would find fame in the crack era, but the team's two leaders were held in high regard; they were living and breathing legends. Still, they were on opposite ends of the spectrum. Supreme's name was spoken in reverence while Prince's name was whispered in fear.

Law enforcement officials said older dealers like Fat Cat continued to control part of the cocaine and heroin trade from jail, but young crack sellers cut into his areas and profits. "Why pay $20 to $30 for a bag of heroin when you can get just as intense a high from a $5 crack vial?" The Queens detective asked. In 1985, 350 cocaine arrests were made in Queens. In the first three months of 1986, 572 crack arrests were made. A lot of the guys arrested were young kids with no criminal history. Some would hold to the street code, but others would try to minimize their activity telling the cops, "I'm not a big guy like Fat Cat. I'm just selling some drugs to take care of my children."

The old criminal code of no snitching was deteriorating with younger and younger dealers that had never been initiated into the game. The rules were changing. Still, the Supreme Team stuck to the code. The cops were frenzied with crack's arrival. The Police Department added 60 cops to its Queens Narcotics Bureau and created a new city wide unit to handle crack arrests. "We had some impact," the Queens detective said. "But we haven't run out of people who are selling. We may arrest a guy but there's always someone to take their place. It's where the money is."

With their quick draw mentality, flamboyant demeanor, and get money philosophy, the Supreme Team made Fat Cat look outdated, an older dealer whose time had expired. They were like N.W.A. to Fat Cat's Big Daddy Kane, bolder, more violent, and just as slick and deadly. The torch had passed, and as hip-hop gained national prominence, so did the crack era drug crews. Ethan Brown explains, "I think the crack era was influential in a couple of ways. Hip-hop guys came of age during that moment, so it was by nature influential for them. It was a movement when the streets truly had money and power, so it affected not just the hip-hop community but the entire country as well."

The Supreme Team represented the new breed of criminal, the ones who the hip-hop world embraced and emulated, turning Queens' culture into a national trend even as they devastated the streets and neighborhoods they grew up in. "Everybody knew us everywhere we went. That's how well known the team was," Bing says. "There's always been a whole lot of us." Under Supreme the team was said to number over 200. They had their picks, though. Dudes just couldn't join up, even if that's all they wanted. A lot of people wanted to be down with the movement.

"You had to be thorough to be on the team," Bing says. "A lot of dudes wanted to be on the team, but they couldn't cut it." It was a vicious era and only the strong survived. The team became masters of crack selling and protection rackets. They were the new drug kings of the inner-city."That was an extremely serious time in history, and the team definitely made an impression on New York City with their many activities and unity," the Queens hustler says. "When the Supreme Team rolled into the club, you definitely knew it." The team became identified with the inner-city thug life from which movies like *Belly* and *Menace II Society* would take their cue.

"Before Supreme entered the crack business, dealers were free agents. Supreme consolidated disparate dealers, putting together nine or ten sales locations around the Southside of Queens, which included Baisley Park and Sutphin Boulevard," the Queens detective said. "It's possible that the Supreme Team was the first ever crack organization." Supreme was, to borrow Queens' rapper Nas's memorable phrase, a hood movie star. "The team had that shit bubbling," the Queens hustler says. In the streets of South Jamaica, the Supreme Team reigned king. They taxed the streets just as it was in the tale of Robin Hood. The have nots taking from the haves.

"Back when he was younger, he fucked with Fat Cat and started getting money," the Southside player says. "But then he went out on his own and blew the fuck up." The Supreme Team ruled the streets, and when hip-hop exploded nationally, they would gain a special place in pop culture. "When you see *New Jack City*, it was just like that," the Queens hustler says. "Once you crossed the tracks into the Baisley Projects, it was a warzone." Preme and a fellow crew member, Crusher, would cruise the area surrounding Baisley in a black Mercedes, flashing the muzzles of high powered automatic weapons and waving thick wads of cash out of their car windows to the awe struck residents of the neighborhood. This showy demeanor translated to hip-hop where boasting of the finer things in life was the norm. Gucci, Prada, Louis Vuitton, Mercedes and BMW's- the trappings of capitalism became the currency of hip-hop. The Supreme Team perpetuated this trend. They were street stars and hood icons who encouraged and promoted this type of lifestyle. "I was jive crazy then," Supreme says. "Getting a lot of money. Real wild with the team." The Supreme Team patrolled the streets in bulletproof, armor-plated vehicles, wore bulletproof baseball caps and coats, used counter surveillance measures to thwart police, and issued instructional manuals on criminal activity to members.

Under the red brick towers of Baisley Projects, an around the clock crack cocaine trade that operated more like a corporation than a drug outfit prospered, selling 25,000 crack vials a week and earning $200,000 a day. "They controlled everything in Jamaica," Tuck says. "From Liberty Avenue and 171, even Hollis where Irv Gotti is from to Sutphin Boulevard, from 121 to Linden, which is 10 blocks. It was crazy. All the way to 205th and Hollis where Jam Master Jay and Run DMC are from." To be affiliated with the team provided props in the ghetto. One team member, Big Just, had a sign outside of his apartment building on Foch

Boulevard reading, *Big Just, Preme Team,* representing to the world his criminal associations.

But it wasn't all smooth sailing; nothing in the drug world was. "One time they got beat for $500,000 on a coke deal," the Southside player says. "Preme was fucked up. He sent some dudes down to Florida, and the deal went bad, and they lost the money."

The Queens insider clarifies and gives some more insight into the deal gone bad, "One time back in the day, 1985, we went to Miami to get 500 birds, and we got beat. The shit was straight garbage. We made our money, and that was about it. We had to sell it to the snorters and shooters because it would not cook up to make crack. Preme was pissed." In the drug trade, shit happened but Preme kept it rolling.

"Another time when they robbed Preme's stash house, Prince was gonna get the perpetrators, but Ronnie Bumps stopped it and said, 'You can't get them until 12:01 a.m. on the new year.' So Prince waited," the Southside player says. There was respect in the drug trade especially for the O.G.'s, but mostly it was larceny. With the money came the power, but greed would ultimately cause betrayal even within the loyal ranks of the team. Despite all the glamour, a lot of infighting occurred. The team was divided into factions, but Preme held it together through his strength of personality.

"They were the bad dudes in my hood, the heroic villains of urban folklore, the first hip-hop styled, gangsta conglomerate to hit the big time," Derek Parker, the hip-hop cop said. "You'd see them driving around the boulevard in their late model expensive cars. In the neighborhood, I'd hear guys talking about the Supreme Team's reputation, homicides they supposedly committed, how and where they were selling drugs, where the bodies might be buried." For the team a couple of days receipts could bring in $500,000. With this type of money being generated, turf wars resulted. "The dealers in South Jamaica were particularly territorial," the Queens detective said. As a bloodbath ensued, the team remained the image of ghetto success. In the most violent epoch of New York's history, the Supreme Team stood alone as victor in the crack wars. Blood was running along the sidewalks of Queens as hustlers fought for position and recruited soldiers for those lost in battle. Hundreds joined the team to answer the call.

"Always dudes were trying to get down with the team, join up," Bing says. "If a person who had good credibility wanted to get down, they were put through a little test. I was put through a test. Every individual should have been put through a test." The team placed a premium on loyalty. If it wasn't "Word to Preme," than the team wasn't having it. If dudes got out of line, skulls got peeled. That's how it went down. They kept the whole area in check not only through violence, but also through the respect and loyalty that Supreme inspired. "Supreme was held in a high standard. He was a major figure," Bing says. "Preme was on in 84 and 85 and before that."

Supreme wasn't known for his brutality, but he wasn't above ordering swat-styled raids on rival dealers in which team members stormed their homes in vans with automatic weapons on execution missions. Any infraction or slight against the team elicited a brutal, clear cut response. "They were the best, real people and very thorough. They worked their muscle hard. They had the cars. Everything you could think of, they had," the Queens hustler says.

In the dawn of the hip-hop age, the team was bling-blinging. "Nineteen eighty-four and 1985 was the years we were making a lot of money," Bing says. With the Colombian hookup for cocaine and the retail crack spots, the Supreme Team was balling. "That shit was nothing," Bing says. "We had access to 300-400 kilos. That shit would be around in duffel bags; we had rooms full of that shit."

Fifty of 500 was what Supreme Team workers made. There was no free styling either. Dealers were either down with the team or else. "The Supreme Team has really perfected the street distribution system. They had the people out there selling. They had the people preparing the drugs," the Queens detective said. The packaging locations were crowded with dozens of baggers who were forced to work in the nude. Preme didn't take any chances with his product. This visual image was later used in numerous movies about the crack era. Just as the rappers bit the Supreme Team's style, so did Hollywood.

"They had a seven by 24 operation, which means seven days a week, 24 hours a day," The Queens detective said. "They were certainly if not the top, one of the top groups throughout the city, not just in Queens. And I think they had the arrests and the body count that would indicate that." By compartmentalizing the organization's structure, Supreme sought to ensure his safety from arrest and keep the rest of the team on a need to know basis. The competition between crews also increased sales and the money coming into Preme's pockets. With strict rules and operating procedures, the team's retail sales flourished.

"I started off selling hand to hand to the crack heads," Tuck says. Tuck was caged in by the handball court at Baisley Park. As soon as the crack heads got in the park, they would yell the colors out; like "yellow, yellow" to signify whose crack they wanted. There were strict rules. There was a line on the handball court, and workers couldn't cross that line to make sales. They had to wait for the crack heads to come to them. And they couldn't knock somebody else's customer out of the box. If the crack head wanted yellow then yellow it was. They followed Preme's policy down to the letter.

"The Supreme Team was the most feared organization in Queens," Bing says. And the teams reach was far and wide. Stickup kids were crazy to try to rob the team. "We had some shit at this dude's house, and these girls had little cousins from Hollis who envied us," Bing says. "The dude held drugs and money in his crib. They wanted to burglarize this kid. We had to go to Hollis and find these kids, and this dude got the shit back. They got wind we were looking for them, and they left town. We never saw them again; that's how scared they were." Crossing the team was a big no-no and a sure invitation to death. Anybody who crossed the team was surely suicidal. With trigger happy enforcers like Prince, Puerto Rican Righteous, and C-Justice, death wishes were granted with impunity. Perilous murder missions were the norm. "Murder was a joke for Prince and most of the dudes in his crew, the exception being C-Just," the Queens insider says. The Supreme Team guarded their territories and markets ruthlessly. They spread terror with drive-by shootings on the Southside. The sound of gunfire on the streets of Queens became commonplace as the Supreme Team regulated the area. But it wasn't all work and no play.

"I watch all these rappers videos with all the bling," First Born Prince said. "We were doing that 20 years ago. My man Preme had an apartment on Queens Boulevard with a VIP room, girls banging on the glass doors to get in like groupies." With Preme it was always MOB or TOB, team over bitches.Overall the whole team had its way with the ladies. "We had a hotel that we used back in the day named The Jade East," the original member says. "We damn near owned that joint, fucking all types of broads there. The managers did not give a shit what we did in there, going from room to room, getting sniffed up on coke." Preme never used drugs, never ever, and neither did Prince or C-Justice. But everybody else on the team got their snort on one time or another. With the team, though, the main thing was girls.

"With the broads we had nobody could touch the team," the original member says. "You know how many of the other boss's wives was trying to fuck Preme? It was ridiculous, and when another boss's girl came to give Preme some pussy, she always brought some of her girlfriends, and you know how it goes, a boss's girl's girlfriends are always not as good looking as the boss's girl. I fucked a lot of ugly bitches back in the day. I remember one time me and Preme was in the same hotel room with these two broads. Preme's girl was beautiful. My girl looked like a cross between ugly and uglier. I'm fucking her, and she is fucking me back so good I get ready to bust, and I jump up in mid-stroke and say to Preme who is right in the next bed giving it to his girl, 'Preme you've got to try my girl, her stuff is really, really good.' Preme said, 'Nigga, you crazy. I'm not sticking my dick in that ugly bitch.' My bitch was not even offended. She was so happy to be able to fuck a team member."

Basketball was big on the Southside too. Harlem had the Rucker, but Queens had the SNIFF tournament at Baisley. Officially SNIFF stood for Supreme's Nite Invitational Fastbreak Festival, but to all the hustlers who sponsored the teams, it was known as the cocaine league, hence the SNIFF moniker. For kicks Preme ran the league. "All the games took place over here at night and they were big money games," Lance said. "First game started off at 20-25 g's. But by the end of the first quarter, it was up to 75 g's. Almost three thousand people would be watching the games." All the big dealers would show up to support their teams and place bets- Pretty Tony, Wall Corley, Tommy Mickens and a representative for Fat Cat. And of course the man who ran the league would be there, Supreme, in all his glory, holding court with his ghetto fabulousness. Team members and crew leaders Prince, Bimmy, Babywise, and Black Just would be flossing and profiling, making their bets, and cheering on their teams. "The SNIFF tournament was like that," the Southside player says. "Mark Jackson, Rod Strickland, Pearl Washington played, and Preme ran with them." It was the Supreme Team show at its best.

"The team had our own basketball tournament," the original member says. "We had some of the best pro ball players on our team and on other teams that were participants of the tournament. We had Chris Mullin, Walter Berry, and Mark Jackson out there on the basketball court in Baisley Park, the project park at that. Lloyd Daniels was like an unofficial member of the team at the same time he signed with the San Antonio Spurs. Those NBA players were in complete awe of how we were living. They were literally our very own fans. They'd be on the ball court playing in our tournament at the same time we would be conducting all kinds of illegal shit. I mean they loved us, and they wanted to be around us more than anything, but most of them wised up and got away from us, due to the fact that gunplay was just as common to us as basketball was to them. And most of the time when someone sustained an injury playing the game that we played, rehab was not even an option unless they did rehab in the morgue."

At one of the games, Gregory Vaughn, a 33-year-old gym teacher at Public School 140 and former head coach of Medgar Evers College, was asked to referee a summer league game. The teams were playing for high stakes, supposedly 50 grand in prize money, not including the side bets which were in the 100k range. Vaughn, the husband of a cop, had a reputation for getting kids off the playground and into schools. He made a controversial call at the end of the game and was beaten to death, allegedly by members of the team. No one was ever charged, as witnesses never stepped forward, but the whole crowd saw. The SNIFF tournament was quickly disbanded. Overall, despite the violence that came along with the crack trade, the crews were having fun. "Preme is not the bad guy he is made out to be," Teddy, a Supreme Team member said. "He owned businesses before dudes were ever thinking about it. He used to own a neighborhood store. He gave away more food and diapers then he sold. People always hear the bad, but the good is never mentioned." On the Southside, Preme was a revered figure. He had icon like status in the streets of South Jamaica.

"We could get into a big fight in a club and dude would fight with us and we did not even know dude but after it was over the dude would be like, 'I'm down with the team.' Didn't nobody fuck with us," the original member says. Being down with the Supreme Team was a status thing. It was about reputation and getting money. They attracted all types of hustlers. Not just the gun thugs from Baisley. "I grew up in a good house," Teddy said. "I was just attracted to that lifestyle, and it was something I wanted to do. I just wanted to be down. I made more money before I got down with the team then when I got down. It was a movement that I wanted to be a part of. There was a level of respect that the team commanded and that the team earned that was intoxicating."

In Queens, the Supreme Team was gangster royalty. All the hot young ladies were trying to get down with team members. "Most crews were paying for their broads to be with them," the original member says. "Preme would take care of his broads like most bosses did but he did not have to. Most of his broads would give their lives just for a minute of Preme's time. Preme had broads in all 50 states and the UK. Preme had broads of every race and nationality. Preme had a broad that did not speak any English, fine as a muthafucka. We had to get an interpreter. She was some type of Asian broad. One time Preme let me see her while she was naked in the shower. She was beautiful. This broad looking like something out of a dream, and she did not phase Preme one bit. She was just another broad to Preme. When Preme cut one of his broads off, she would be so sad. You would have thought someone in her family had passed away. I've done twisted my foot in quite a few of Preme's fool ass whores, but he did have some that were untouchable and that he was genuine about." It was a popularity type of thing. The Supreme Team was the Jay-Z's of the day. They held court at Baisley and partied at all the hot spots in the town.

"We had parties at the Roller Dome, Disco Fever in the Bronx where DJ Starchild routinely saluted the crew by shouting, 'Queens in the house,' Empire Roller skating rink in Brooklyn, Latin Quarter and the Red Parot in Manhattan," Bing says. "Somebody would have a party; throw a party for certain individuals. Curtis Blow might come out and rap. It was crazy, dudes free styling, battle rapping." In the era of turntables, graffiti and MC's battling freestyle just to see who could get the most props; it was a good time for all. Hip-hop events were different back then. They were all about the DJ's scratching skills and dance music like Lisa Lisa and the Cult Jam, Shannon, and Grandmaster Flash, flossing, stunting, and shining at Bentley's, the Palladium and the Roxy were the norm.

The team would be combat ready when they went out to the rough and tumble b-boy spots like Union Square and the Latin Quarter. It was an era of drink tossing, shoving matches, and fist fights. Hip-hop was about to go mainstream, but crews like the Supreme Team savored their moments as they witnessed the beginning of something big. But the team didn't just witness the evolution of hip-hop; they were a part of it. They partied at the clubs, knew the artists, and helped to set the styles and trends. They helped to make hip-hop dangerous and give it that edge. "If a fight broke out to a record you know you had a hit on your hands," the Queens hustler said. And that was the era. The Supreme Team showed hip-hop culture how to party. Infamous and extravagant parties became the norm.

"The Olympic Palace party was for Preme and James Wall Corley's birthdays," the Queens insider says. "Their birthdays are like a day apart. The only party that was bigger than that was Fat Cat's birthday. It was in 1984." At the Olympic Palace party photos and images of all of the young drug lords were captured- Preme, Wall Corley, and Fat Cat included-showing their jewels, their money and stunting for all they were worth.

The images from the era show the Queens gangsters having fun and enjoying life before crack hit, the murders started, and all the cases imprisoned them. At that time, it was about showing off what you had. When the team came through, it was like a car show. "Dudes would rock the Oldsmobile 98, Delta 88's, Saab 929, Audi's, BMW 325, M3 Mercedes Benz. BMW was the top car we were driving," Bing says. The Supreme Team did everything in style and combined street politics with flash, and gutternomics with glamour. That was just how they carried it. "Before Preme got his first state bid he was driving a Benz and quite a few

BMW's," the original member says. Preme would drive down the block in front of Baisley Projects showing all the youngsters the illicit trappings of being a hood star. He was a living testament to the life he was living.

"The media tries to portray like they had the projects held hostage," the Southside player says. "But things were done for the residents of the community that wouldn't have been done by the city. In any neighborhood where there's an influx of drugs, you're going to have neighbors who like you cause you're paying their bills or whatever, and you're going to have neighbors who don't like you because they feel you're destroying the community." According to many of the residents they were being protected and held down by the team. Even as Supreme pushed drugs in the projects, he tried to help the downtrodden and despair-ridden in his Southside Queens neighborhood.

A.U. Hogan, Baisley Park Housing President, recounted how individuals like Preme and Prince sponsored sports programs for the neighborhood kids and helped many of the community residents out when they were in financial trouble. Other neighbors relayed stories of the Supreme Team funding turkey giveaways and bus trips for kids to amusement parks.

"The team paid rents, bought people food. Prince himself would take $3000 in dollar bills every week and give them out," Teddy said. "We were like family to the people in the projects. We stayed there so much that we related to everyone. No other crew would come in and do anything stupid. We treated the residents with respect. Innocent people weren't getting hurt. You couldn't come over here to Baisley and fire shots or do no dumb shit. That type of shit just didn't happen. The residents knew if we were out there, there was order." The team controlled and maintained the area. Savoring their hood's love and playing the Robin Hood role. "The neighborhood loved us," Bing says. "We took care of the neighborhood. I wouldn't trade it for nothing in the world. I got no complaints about it."

CHAPTER 4
SUPREME'S INCARCERATION

"New York is split into two periods: BC and AC, before crack and after crack. There was a profound change when that drug hit New York. Crack was destroying neighborhoods but it was also making people rich."
— **Barry Michael Cooper, Stop Smiling Magazine**

"By the summer of 1986, the city had seemed consumed by crack. The drug had created a cottage industry of dealers. Anyone with a bag of pure cocaine, frying pan, stove and baking soda could get into the act."
— **Copshot by Mike McAlary**

"Crack changed Queens just as it had all over. Prior to the explosion Queens had known of violence but not to the degree of its own demise."
— **As Is Magazine, Issue 2**

"In 1985 Supreme had a state case. Bing was on it too. They got arrested in a house with drugs," Tuck says. Preme's arrest was surprising but not unexpected. "I went to jail in 85 with Preme," Bing says. "I was his right hand man at this time. We were like brothers. I was with him all the time." The team was attracting a lot of attention from law enforcement. Street dealers and couriers were getting busted due to all the drug traffic. As members got arrested some broke the code of the street. "Different stories about how it unfolded," Bing says. "You had guys getting arrested, going to the precinct, ending up right back on the street. So they were giving info about us. We had cabdrivers working for us. One cabbie got caught with guns, supposedly gave up info on our whereabouts, certain cribs where we got guns, coke, money."

For several months prior to September 1985, Officer Myron Cherry of the 113th Precinct Robbery Unit had been receiving information from a confidential informant. Although he was Officer Cherry's informant, Officer Cherry regularly passed along tips provided by him to other policeman, including Sergeant Clyde Foster. Sergeant Foster also briefly met and spoke with the informant on at least a few occasions when the informant tried to reach Officer Cherry. Sergeant Foster started utilizing the informant in narcotics investigations. The informant's information unveiled a lot of illegal activity revolving around the Supreme Team.

Police found out that a homicide at 144-15 Guy R. Brewer Boulevard was in some way connected to an alleged $80,000 cocaine and currency robbery at 116-66 231st Street in Queens during the week of July 4, 1985. The 231st Street stash house belonged to the Supreme Team. They didn't take it kindly when they got robbed. They found out some dudes from Hollis executed the heist and acted accordingly. Street justice was a bitch. It was a dog eat dog world in the Southside of Jamaica, and karma was paid back in full. What came around went around; still lessons were learned. Preme started rotating his stash houses to deter future robbery attempts.

The team had a second stash house at 155-47 116th Avenue. Officer Cherry got a tip from his informant on September 10, 1985, that sometime later that day, there would be narcotics delivery at 231st Street or 116th Avenue. Officer Cherry relayed this information to Sergeant McKeon of the Narcotics Unit who in turn relayed it to Sergeant Foster at about 6:15 p.m. Foster telephoned Queens Criminal Court Judge Steven Fisher seeking search warrants for both 166-16 231st Street and 155-47 116th Avenue. "I received information that allegedly a location at 231st Street and Linden Boulevard had been robbed of approximately $80,000 in U.S. currency and narcotics and this was property that belonged to the Supreme Team," Foster explained to Judge Fisher, who immediately granted his request.

"Be careful," said the judge to Foster. "There's an excellent chance that Supreme will be present in the apartment." Queens police were on the trail of the Supreme Team's namesake like a junkie on a search for smack. This wouldn't be an opportunity to miss, and they knew it.

"They set up surveillance on us and got a no knock search warrant from the judge that they executed. These search warrants led me and Preme to get arrested in September 1985 at an apartment in Cambry Heights," Bing says. At the first location, 155-47 116th Avenue, seven people were arrested and misdemeanor quantities of drugs as well as several rifles were found. The search on the 116-66 231st Street residence led to the arrest of five people and the seizure of eight pounds of drugs, eight handguns, and over $35,000 in cash. "They confiscated guns, coke, money, counting machines, assault rifles, vests, counterfeit money and bulletproof shirts, jackets and coats, that's when I got that case," Bing says.

When Foster's unit raided the Supreme Team base at 231st Street just after 9 p.m. on September 10, 1985, they caught Preme with four others in the act. As Queens' narcotics cops descended on the stash house, its door and windows slammed shut. One occupant peered out the window, looked into Foster's eyes, and closed the blinds. Foster later found out that those pale green eyes belonged to Preme. "Police," Foster shouted at the door. There was no response. "At which point I hit the door with the ram." Heroin and coke littered the tables in different stages of packaging. Foster had busted Supreme red handed. Preme and Bing were hit with drug and weapon charges by the city's special prosecutor. But that didn't stop the team. They moved on multiple levels.

In 1985 while incarcerated at Rikers Island, the ladies man Supreme seduced a female guard. "In 85, Preme was fucking with a C/O from Rikers Island. She used to spend the night with him. He made the Supreme Team buy her a BMW," the Southside player says. The guard was very instrumental for Supreme, as he used her to send out orders, bring him drugs, other contraband, and for various other purposes. It was Preme's first experience of working and manipulating the system in prison, a trait he would perfect.

"We were the first crew in New York to be arrested by TNT (Tactical Narcotics Unit)," the original member says. "In fact TNT was designed and targeted for us, the team, and other crews out of Southside Queens. The case that Preme and Bing had was the first arrest in New York City for the TNT unit. Eighteen members of the team were arrested in a joint raid on two different locations. Out of the eighteen, at least ten members had the charges dropped due to lack of evidence. Bing, Preme, Born, Brett, and a couple of others got convicted on that case. Bimmy and Dahlu were also arrested on that case but had the charges dropped."

On May 19, 1986, Supreme pled guilty to count twelve of the New York County indictment, criminal possession of a controlled substance in the first degree. "In 1985, NYPD Task Force executed a warrant for a house we had," Supreme said. "I was arrested and sentenced to nine years to life." Bing got six to life, Brett four to life, Michael "Born" Timmons six to life, and Eric three to life. The sentences were pursuant to the draconian Rockefeller drug laws. New York State didn't play when it came to drugs. Some missed the party though.

"Some individuals got released, dismissed off the case for no apparent reason," Bing says. "Probably gave some info." The streets said that prominent Supreme Team member Bimmy was the informant, but Bing corrects that, "I never saw nothing with Bimmy's name on it."

The Queens insider concurs, "I've never seen any paperwork on Bimmy and neither has anyone else. That whole lie was conjured up by haters. Some dudes were totally jealous of anyone they felt was getting too much props from Preme. They felt that would be taking away from them, never stopping to realize that Preme had love for everyone on the team." Still, the rumors swirled in the streets, and certain Supreme Team members picked up on them. The bust didn't stop the team at all, as it was set up like the Mafia, so with Preme in prison, Prince stepped in.

"Whenever Preme went to prison, Prince was the boss. It's that simple," Tuck says. After Preme's arrest and conviction, he was out on bail before starting his state sentence. He planned a big party, a going away event for him that doubled as Prince's twenty-second birthday.

"Olympic Palace in 1985, was a club in Queens at Hillside. That joint was for Preme and Prince," Bing says. The entire Supreme Team gathered to toast the aspiring kingpin Prince and say a final goodbye to Preme. The party was packed with A-list hustlers like James "Wall" Corley, and photos from that night feature members of South Jamaica, Queens, most prominent crews posing with piles of cash. Supreme Team lieutenants Bimmy, Black Just, and Babywise all mugged for snapshots, but the most memorable picture to emerge from the party featured Prince holding a thick wad of cash over the head of a child.

Preme did it big and spared no expense. His parties were always extravagant and featured hip-hop artists booked by Preme's pal, Russell Simmons of Def Jam fame. "Preme and Russell Simmons were cool," the Queens insider says. "But it was not like they had what you'd call a friendship. But understand this, Preme respected all of his peers. If fact Preme respected everyone, but his respect had many different facets. Like the respect Preme had for his elements (street dudes) was not the same respect he had for no industry dude. If a dude was a street boss, Preme would deal with them on equal footing, but some fly by the night-type industry square ass dude would be made to understand who was the true big dog." So in reality Simmons was riding Supreme's coattails.

"Preme used to book Run DMC, the Beastie Boys, LL Cool J," Simmons said. "They would have big parties, every rapper played and he'd give every rapper one thousand dollars." The Supreme Team supported hip-hop when it was just considered a fad. And the rappers learned to make it rain by watching the Supreme Team. Team members tossed stacks of money into the air and showed off glistening rocks of cocaine all night. Lil' Wayne and Cash Money have nothing on the Supreme Team. Their videos are just a reflection of the team's real life.

The less connected members of the Supreme Team were furious when Preme handed over leadership of the team and a prime drug dealing spot to his nephew. And outrage grew when Prince used this status to begin assembling a sub-organization of his own. He already had his crew, but now his numbers multiplied. Nobody could stop him though. Prince was the heir apparent. By the time Preme was in prison, Prince had assumed leadership of the team. Prince ruled the team through fear and intimidation. From that point on Prince was the leader of the Supreme Team. "Prince wanted to prove to his uncle that he could lead just as good as Preme and that was one of his gravest mistakes in his super short reign, Prince did not know how to distinguish leadership from guidance," the Queens insider says. "Dudes on the team were hating on Black Just, Prince, and Bimmy because of their success and their ability to think for themselves. Some team members wanted them to fail in an effort to make Preme think that Black Just, Prince, and Bimmy needed Preme to guide them." Preme and Prince's leadership tactics differed also.

Whereas Preme was generous and diplomatic, Prince was trigger happy. "A lot of people would rather have Prince on their team rather than opposing them," Tuck says. And under Prince's leadership the Supreme Team was about to enter a dark age. Under Preme it was about styling and profiling, hip-hop and money making, uplifting the community and giving back. Team members from the first run call them "the wonder years." But under Prince it would turn into murder and chaos, betrayal and death. The Supreme Team's fortunes were about to take a brutal and deadly turn. "Paranoia keeps a drug dealer alive," the Southside player says. "On the streets it was crazy. It was some Tony Montana/*Scarface* shit for real." And like Tony Montana and his fictional descent into hell, Prince would follow, the devil be damned.

Like his uncle, Prince recruited Latinos in order to boost his connections to the Colombians moving weight. He hired brothers Knowledge and Shannon, who grew up in Baisley, as his lieutenants and appointed Puerto Rican Righteous as one of his top enforcers. "Preme was locked up when Puerto Rican Righteous was home running with Prince," the Queens insider says. C-Just, Big C, Pookie, Ace and Shannon formed the security team. The security team had a well deserved reputation in the hood when they got geared up for battle. The army fatigue look was a Supreme Team signature. Their war gear was black fatigues and jackets, bulletproof vests, black Timbs, and hats, the drawstring joints or baseball caps. And their weaponry consisted of AR-15s, Mac 10s, Nines, 45s, 357s, techs; they had it all. They were as vicious as a pack of hungry rottweilers. When they were on a mission, shit got crazy. They would jump out of minivans like black ops. When dudes on the block saw them, they'd start running and scrambling, praying the gun thugs weren't coming for them.

"Preme did not grant Prince authority over any official team members-Dahlu, Babywise, Black Just, Bimmy," the Queens insider says. "They all had their own crews. Preme was in jail. But Black Just and Bimmy were still out there making plenty of money, but their loyalty was to Supreme and only Supreme. Some of the team members hated Prince's security team. Their problem with the security team was the fact that since they were under Prince, they thought they could bully other team members. Once word got to Preme about Prince's security team running roughshod, Preme would send word for Prince to raise them the fuck off team members. Some members had problems with Babywise too, because Babywise was and still is his own man. This divided the team into factions; there were crews inside of crews. Nobody fucked with God B though, as he was still well respected. God B did not tolerate any bullshit from anyone and that included Preme, Prince and on down the line." The security team's tactics divided the team and led to all the other higher ups getting bodyguards.

"We all had a security team," Bing says. "Everybody had their own security guys. Everybody was trained to go at any minute. So many ruthless individuals were down with the team. You had individuals who had no regard for the law." If the security team was in the projects, it was all good, as that was their home. But if they were spotted across town, it could only mean one thing- that they were on a mission, and motherfuckers had better get the hell out of Dodge.

"Imagine muthafuckas jumping out of minivans like a taskforce," the Queens insider says. "The security team had muthafuckas shook. The team changed dramatically under Prince. Preme is a dude who will rationalize and talk it out. Prince is vicious. He doesn't believe in talking. Prince was big on counter surveillance. He was way beyond his time. If the police were following him, he would follow them and take their license plates. We'd go to Radio Shack, get the walkie-talkies, and the radios with earbuds going to your ears."

When cops seized thirteen grand of Supreme Team cash from longtime member Serious, Prince marched over to the precinct house and got the name and phone number of the arresting officer and the voucher number for the seized cash in hopes that he could retrieve it. Prince would also demand that Supreme Team members forcibly take over housing project apartments or even entire floors of the building to use as a base to sell drugs. "Take the third floor," Prince ordered security team member Pookie. "Make that home." Prince was referring to 116-80 Guy R. Brewer Boulevard in Baisley Park Houses, the Supreme Team's home base since their formation.

Under Prince, Baisley became a high rise crackhouse. Not only were the residents using, but now members of the team were too. A lot of the security team was allegedly smoking crack. But with the team's reputation in the streets sky high, Colombians were actually approaching Prince with offers to do business. One Colombian dealer, Gus Rivera, begged Prince to go into business with him, offering to slash his prices and even suggesting that they rob rival dealers together. Prince accepted the offer and made Rivera a member of the Supreme Team. "I'm a true product of the streets," Prince said. "It shaped me into the man I am today. The streets nurtured me into the next level of consciousness that's needed to understand and accept, to play the hand I've been dealt."

The Supreme Team's name was ringing loudly on the Southside. They had the security force, the retail spots, and stash houses which stored and processed their drugs. They were moving weight and selling retail. Prince rewarded those under him accordingly. Dudes who stood strong and held their tongue were given more responsibility. Those who didn't were eliminated, like they said, "Snitches get stitches." Prince was the general and had a strict chain of command. His tactics and management policies alienated some of the older team members. The team under Prince split into factions as a result. It wasn't the same as with Supreme. It was more cutthroat and brutal. Plus with the security team and other team members smoking crack, shit got shady. "Prince did not know how to guide," the Queens insider says. "He didn't do things how Preme did them and this upset a lot of dudes. He was all for his crew and let dudes know that was how he felt. This alienated him from a lot of the other team leaders."

With Supreme in prison, not all of the original seed rode with Prince. Babywise, Bimmy, and Black Just did their own thing. They let Prince do him while they stayed grinding themselves, backing off from the heir apparent and his homicidal security team. "They was afraid of getting robbed," the Southside player says. "With those dudes on crack, anything was possible." They still had their spots and crews, but Prince controlled the Supreme Team assets outright. The drug spots and Baisley were his as were the connections and security force. That didn't stop dudes hustling; the original seed still got down. Prince gave them that respect, but that was the only concession he made. "Prince wanted to mirror Preme so much that it consumed him," the original member says. "What he failed to realize was the fact that Preme was a great leader, and all great leaders have a number of different facets to their leadership abilities." A lot of the original team resented Prince, but he still had those loyal to him.

C-Justice was one of Prince's main dudes. The trusted enforcer was known as a thorough and feared member of the team. He was said to be very quiet, a soft spoken dude who never raised his voice. "Dude was like that for real," the Southside player says. "Wasn't nobody trying to fuck with C-Just. He made the other killers like Puerto Rican Righteous and Prince seem nice." Big C was Prince's bodyguard, a very serious and intimidating cat who had dreads, sported dark glasses, and wore tank tops that showed off his chiseled physique. Pookie was a gunman from back in the day that did a rack of state time and came back out to hook up with the team. Ace was a dude fresh out of prison who got down with the team. Shannon and his brother Knowledge were lifelong members of the team, dudes who grew up in Baisley and were down for whatever.

Tuck and Teddy were known as the money men. They were the youngsters of the team who rose through the ranks from workers to lieutenants, eventually running the spots. They were the ones bringing in the paper. They had their own crews and were making crazy money for themselves and for the team. "Tuck was a member of Prince's crew," the original member says. "He is one of Prince's men and overall a good kid." When the stash houses were raided, Prince had a crew of teenagers and small children in his employ to move the drugs before the cops showed up or afterward if they could get it out. One kid, Pee Wee, walked out of a house that was raided with a kilo of coke tucked in his waistband, right past the cops. A pair of Supreme Team workers was arrested down the street at the corner of Foch and Sutphin Boulevard, but Pee Wee escaped with the coke for Prince. Prince was making major cash profits when other hustlers were grinding for small change. As he and the team flourished, his status on the street grew to certified baller status.

"I looked up to Prince," Tuck says. "He was everything that a young kid from the ghetto aspired to be. He had money, tons of women, power and got mad respect." In the streets they called Prince the general. He was known to be one step ahead of his rivals, focused at all times, a master chess player who could be found in Baisley Projects playing multiple opponents at a time. He was a shrewd character who survived several hit attempts and dealt with enemies and friends alike with an iron fist. He allegedly once had a childhood friend beaten to near death because he fucked up some money. He showed no mercy and gave no quarter nor asked for any. "In the drug game there's no tolerance for bullshit," Tuck says. "Because the game breeds larceny, and anyone who can keep their cool in the face of all that deserves their stripes." Tuck got down with the team as a youngster, but he went onto bigger and better things quickly.

"I was in high school working at D'Agostino's; it's a famous supermarket. I was a delivery guy, seventeen-years-old and delivering groceries to fucking people," Tuck says. "I lived next to my man Black Born. We were walking to the store one day, and this God Bishme told us about Prince. He said Prince was recruiting for the team. I had never heard of the Supreme Team before that, and I lived in Jamaica all my life. I grew up right around the corner from Baisley Projects, and most of my friends grew up in the projects. I met Prince in June 1986 in front of Baisley Projects." Tuck found out that he was a born hustler and jumped into the game with both feet, never looking back.

"I went from making 100 dollars a week at the grocery store to a thousand dollars a day. I was selling hand to hand, a worker. I was seventeen and didn't have any goals. I thought I could sell drugs forever. I chose to make the streets a part of my life. Prince became somewhat of a father figure to me. Someone I could look up to. Baisley Park, that's where I hustled at, five buildings, eight floors in each building. That was where I ate. I learned how to make a thousand dollars a day for myself while making ten thousand a day for the next man," Tuck says.

Tuck started off selling hand to hand to the crack heads. "I had yellow," Tuck says, meaning Tuck worked in Prince's crew. "Our thing was hustling, getting paper and stacking it. I interacted with everyone from the bottom of the totem pole to the top. Being around guys on the team was nothing special to me. One received a whole lot of pussy though. That was the benefit of being affiliated. When you're so embedded in the life, it's hard to have friends. I don't think Prince and I ever had a friendship. I believe it was all business, but he was definitely an influence." Eventually Tuck rose up in the ranks to become a lieutenant. "I became what we called a lieutenant," Tuck says. "Once the drugs were purchased, put them in my hand, and everything is taken care of. I had no foresight to say that I'm gonna make a certain amount of money and get out of this. Selling drugs is like an addiction. The dealer is just like the fiend. The dealer is addicted to the money just like the fiend is addicted to the drugs."

Under Prince the team peaked. He was very security orientated and believed in keeping the whole area in check. There was no competition. Either dudes got down with the team, or Prince put the security force on them. The ease with which Prince dispatched rivals put him in an empire building mode. Flush with cash, Prince created a business called Future Dimension Inc. in June 1986. Future Dimensions served as a front for Prince's various real estate deals and luxury car purchases. As he consolidated his power on the streets of Queens, the money kept pouring in. By October 1986, the Supreme Team was generating 30 grand a day in drug income. To keep the profits coming, Prince had his security force deal with any problems or even any possible or potential problems. But with success shit started getting out of hand. Team members and the security force were drunk with power.

Rampant rumors of blatant crack use among the security team members ran wild as Prince tried to keep everything in control. When word reached Preme that Prince's security force was thinking of robbing other team members, Preme sent for the primaries. "Preme sent word that Righteous had better make his way up to the prison to pay Preme a visit," the original member said. "Mostly due to Righteous acting like he was ready to bring Black Just and Bimmy a move. At the time Preme had love for Righteous, but at the same time he knew dudes like Righteous and Green Eyed Born were too ambitious, and where their problems stem from is the fact that they were completely brainless. They did not have the common sense to even shoulder their ambitions."

Prince took a page from Fat Cat's book, too; he bought a ramshackle building in South Jamaica at 115-05 Sutphin Boulevard and transformed the property into the Supreme Superette. Puerto Rican Righteous worked at the store which became one part of Prince's vast network of Southside Queens drug spots that included a pair of towers at Baisley Projects as well as a building at 171st Street and Liberty Avenue in South Jamaica. The team had taken over the Southside. They were conducting business in open air drug markets while half-dead, totally zoned-out fiends roamed the streets day and night like zombies. It was the night of the living base heads for real, way before Public Enemy rapped about it, and nobody was willing to do anything about it. The regular residents were too scared to say anything. They just stayed in their apartments at night and shut out the world of terror Prince had created at Baisley Projects.

"Money was coming in so fast that muthafuckas didn't have time to count it," the team member says. "At that time period we developed coke connects of a variety of people. I had a coke connect. Tuck had a coke connect. Prince had a coke connect. Teddy had a coke connect. Muthafuckas started going on trips, like Vegas, Hawaii, Miami." When crack was king, the Supreme Team reigned as its under lords. They were the grim reapers, the horror unleashed on the community, the best in the streets at what they did.

In essence, they were the premier criminal organization of the day. Their enormous enterprise moved tens of thousands of crack vials each week.

By the fall of 1986, Prince boasted perhaps the most impressive network of any of the South Jamaica, Queens, drug crews. The Supreme Team surpassed even Fat Cat's organization in size and scope. Prince was also able to stay one step ahead of undercover cops thanks to his connections in law enforcement. He had done the ultimate and infiltrated his enemies. To say Prince was arrogant would be an understatement.

The Supreme Team was blatant and held no regard for authority. Team members would hit all the clubs, loudly making their presence known. They carried on like they were above the law. Whether posted up at a VIP table sipping Moet, sniffing lines of coke in the bathroom, or in the middle of the dance floor, or just partying while off the clock, the Supreme Team was always the flyist, boldest, and toughest in the room. They would flaunt their deep pockets and buy drinks for all of the girls in the club. With their gold chains and hip-hop gear bought from boutiques on Queens' Jamaica Avenue, they'd stunt in Gucci or Louis Vuitton leather suits. At the Copa, Bentleys, the Roxy, or Latin Quarter, Prince and his cohorts would revel in all their glory, drug barons of the underworld, rocking and bopping their heads to new rap groups like Boogie Down Productions, whose rapper KRS-One rapped about what was really going down in the ghetto streets. It was a wild time of violence, power, and crazy money for the team.

"Prince was not doing any partying at a club where they were not letting him come in with his gun; that was not happening, and his crew had to get their guns in too," the original member says. "Prince was not down with sharing nobody's gun. The only thing Prince shared were his bullets while they were being discharged. Prince was one of the strangest dressing dudes on the entire team. One time he came down on the block and walked up with a bulletproof army coat on, a bulletproof hat, and a long pair of battery operated pants; that shit was crazy. He looked like a moon man."

Even though Prince was the boss, law enforcement maintained Preme was running the show, calling the shots from prison, but they couldn't prove it. Prince wouldn't rat out his worst enemy let alone his uncle. "Preme used to call shots over the phone," the Southside player says. "Everybody knows how much Prince loved his uncle. He ran the shit, but Preme was in on it too." In the end, though, it was all about the money.

"That shit has a magnetic pull on you that is hard to escape. The more money you get, the more money you want," Tuck says. For drug dealers, the addiction was the lifestyle. The power that dudes like Preme and Prince had was tremendous. Life and death type of power, and with money, it was all possible.

"I believe now money is the root of all evil," Bing says. But at the time it was the means to an end. It was the all and the everything. To dudes in the organization like Bing and Tuck, money meant power, status, women, and material things, whatever they wanted. It was what they put in work for. It was the American Dream, capitalism unbridled.

"I came up through the ranks from the bottom doing hand to hand. I caught two cases and came out and I was a lieutenant. I never touched the drugs except to hit the workers with it. Once a guy is proven he steps up in rank," Tuck says. And the step up in rank was a step up in responsibility in the hierarchy of the team.

As Prince and the Supreme Team maintained what they'd built, the bodies started dropping. The Supreme Team's homicidal instincts knew no bounds, and they grew bolder as they strengthened their hold on the area. To Southside residents they appeared untouchable, and a team member echoed this sentiment. "We were untouchable. We were the most feared organization in Queens," he said. But not all dealers in the area bowed down. They were trying to get theirs also, Supreme Team or not. In the bustling crack trade there was a "do me" mentality which led to all out war in the streets of Queens. Dudes didn't care whose toes they stepped on as long as they got paid. That was the crack era attitude, and it evolved into the hip-hop mentality.

"There were hungry little niggas ready to hold it down and all that pussy shit was dead," the team member says. "Niggas was now on fuck Brooklyn, fuck uptown, fuck you. They was gonna eat, and if you had some weight to your ass, you was food." Prince was considered the heir apparent to the Supreme Team, but he wasn't Supreme. Preme built bridges and strategic alliances; Prince burnt and tore them down. He didn't give a fuck; it was his way or the highway. Prince was a serious, solemn dude who tended to fly off the handle in a rage and let his anger get the best of him. "In Preme's eyes and in most of the people who are really in the know, Prince is one of the main reasons why Queens got so fucked up," the Queens insider says. There was no in-between with Prince; everything to him was black and white. He was very pragmatic when it came to business and death. The warning signs in South Jamaica reared their ugly heads as the bodies started dropping, and a bloody turf war escalated.

"It's alarming," said State Senator Malcolm Smith. "We're not sure what's causing it, but there's no question about it, there's more gun violence and more murders." The killings which varied widely by motive and victim represented sixteen percent of the city's 436 slayings in a precinct that was among the smallest. The 103rd Precinct grew to number one on the homicide list among the city's 76 police precincts.

"We're all kind of a little stunned in how there has been such an increase," the president of the 103rd Precinct Community Council said. "It's been low for years, then boom, it went way up all of a sudden. We had a street crimes unit that did nothing but take guns off the street. People were scared to carry them, now there are more guns on the streets of Hollis and Jamaica, and you see more people brandishing guns."

Beefs tended to be settled quickly with extreme violence. It was the Wild, Wild West on the Southside. Dudes pulled their guns and fired, not caring who was around. It became a bloodbath which didn't stop there. "Pappy started the whole torturing thing," the Queens hustler says. "There was a fight for who could be the craziest or the baddest. They would put hot curling irons in people's rear ends or tie them up for days on end and leave them in their own shit." Supreme Team members who fell out of favor were similarly treated. Prince didn't play when it came to disloyalty. A dude on the team who ran off with some money was allegedly sodomized with a hot curling iron. Prince used every opportunity that came his way to make examples of those who crossed him. In the streets of South Jamaica, a lot of vicious and twisted shit was going down, another byproduct of the crack storm.

"There was always a lot of situations," Bing says. "Certain crews did stuff. About beef, you could tell who did it by the way the smoke was left. You always knew who did it. If niggas got beef, muthafuckas can't be freezing up. Dudes got to be ready to go on a mission. Talking about it and being about it are two different things." Supreme Team members were known for being about it and handling their business in the streets. In the violent cadences of the crack trade, most young players came and went quickly without establishing identities or organizations. The Supreme Team was different. "To a certain degree it was because of the organization we had," Bing says. "That was our real life, how we came up. In every hood shit happens. Niggas get names and get money, but with the team, we sustained our presence. People feared us." With Prince's security team, a bunch of known killers given free reign, the cops were very cautious of crews like the Supreme Team.

"We're even more fearful of the time when more large scale dealers and the mob take over the crack industry and organize it," the Queens detective said. "And that will happen eventually. There's too much money involved." In Queens it was happening before law enforcement even knew what was going down. Fat Cat's old neighborhood exploded with violence as Prince tried to extend the Supreme Team's reach. In front of a Montauk Street video game parlor, a popular crack spot, four cars cruised by, led by a white Cadillac. As the cars sped up, several young men leaned out the windows and began firing shots. Most people ran for cover, but six were wounded. One civilian was killed while trying to protect his girlfriend from the line of fire. Feeling immortal and in the grip of a strong lust for power, Prince's security team didn't care who they killed. In a crack induced haze, they became unfeeling monsters who preyed on anyone who dared to oppose them.

Within ten minutes the scene was replayed nearby. Two men arrived on foot at Farmers Boulevard and opened fire on people standing outside the Ho Ho Kitchen. Two more passersby were wounded and the assailants chased 22-year-old Larry Pearson, an alleged drug dealer, for a few yards before killing him. Deputy Chief Joseph Borelli, the commander of Queens detectives described the outburst as "something like the OK Corral." The areas involved were reportedly controlled by Prince and the Supreme Team, who were muscling in on Fat Cat's former territory. "After what's happened here, it's clear that Fat Cat no longer has control," the Deputy Chief said. "The young guys are moving in. When Fat Cat was out, no one would pull anything like this." While Prince and the Supreme Team had ties to Fat Cat, in reality he was a dinosaur to them. His time had passed, and the Round Table was no more.

A number of theories bounced around in the streets days after the shooting sprees. One held that Pappy Mason, who was in prison with Fat Cat, was trying to seize back power with his crew, the Bebos, for Cat. Another had the Corley Family from Forty Projects in a three way battle with Prince and the Supreme Team and the remnants of Fat Cat's crew. Still a third theory held that the violence was between several young, small-time crack dealers vying for space on the block. "I genuinely don't know," the Deputy Chief said. "All we know is that it was a skirmish, and there will probably be more."

With the arrests of the bigger dealers like Cat and Ronnie Bumps, the Supreme Team filled the vacuum on the streets, but with the crack epidemic in full swing, everybody and their brother was trying to get in on the action and come up. "Everyday I'm hustling," was the modus operandi, and this was long before the rapper Rick Ross. The action was thick, shit was getting hectic, and Queens was going crazy.

Right after the shootings on Farmers Boulevard the police made a show of force in the area, assigning 100 extra officers. The violence continued anyway. Three nights later, two more young men were wounded outside another video arcade in Jamaica. Two weeks later, a 29-year-old man was gunned down in South Jamaica by four men in a Cadillac. Police couldn't connect any of the incidents to the turf war that was supposedly being waged, but the shootings added to the overall sense of chaos that pervaded the streets of South Jamaica. It was a mass confusion of death, fear, gun smoke, and crack.

What really stoked the NYPD's ire was the Supreme Team's deathly impulses toward the police. Most criminals didn't go after cops as a general rule. It's bad for business, as it painted a target on the backs on the perpetrators for the police, but the Supreme Team felt they were above the law and had a license to kill. They were like Los Zetas. These guys made *The Sopranos* look like pussies. In the Supreme Team's eyes anything with a badge was a target. They had no respect for authority. "When I was young, I didn't give a fuck," Tuck says. "It was whatever." Among Supreme Team members, that was the prevailing attitude.

"The police didn't even count," Bing says. "Officers in the 113th Precinct feared Supreme Team members because of the work individuals put in. Prince was the most feared individual in Southside Jamaica, Queens." The gun became the ultimate symbol of authority as gun wielding gangsters sponsored the killings and gun deaths. Prince was a master of creating fear to suit his own ends.

Locals said that Baisley Projects was like a warzone. "We have to treat this like a war," the Queens detective said. "I'm not at the point of asking the governor to bring in the National Guard or to declare a state of emergency for the area, but what's the difference between a natural disaster or a flood and a drug disaster?" People in the neighborhood responded quietly to the drug crisis. Most spent less time on the street and installed extra security for their stores and homes. "Dealers wouldn't be in this area if they didn't have any support," the Queens detective said. "You hear a lot of anti-crack talk, but no one takes credit for tolerating crack."

With all the chaos surrounding the Supreme Team, Prince was constantly being picked up and arrested, in and out of jail on a variety of charges. In late 1986, he was arrested on drugs and weapons charges, forcing another leadership struggle within the Supreme Team. Prince trusted his man Fat Pete to run his drug spots and to stack the team's money. But when Prince came home, Fat Pete refused to return Supreme Team assets. Prince played it cool, deciding to send a message that would once and for all show who was boss of the team in his uncle Supreme's absence. Fat Pete's head was blown off in broad daylight. The killing went unsolved, but a wiretapped conversation between Prince and God B soon after Fat Pete was killed indicated that Prince knew about it. "Power, Equality, Truth, Equality," Prince said to God B, Five Percenter code for Pete.

Prince and the team proved once again that they were far beyond the typical street level drug dealers who usually only engaged in chaotic gun battles. The Supreme Team was a layered organization that worked well in the distribution of drugs, but this complex structure could also be ruthlessly effective in dispatching acts of violence, and more importantly, in masking the identity of the perpetrators of such acts. Murder suspects seemed to vanish from the streets almost daily, and with so many lieutenants within the organization, it was difficult for law enforcement to find out who actually committed the crimes. With the Five Percenter names and Baisley Project residents' unwillingness to finger any Supreme Team members, the police were at a stand still when it came to solving the shootings.

Prince flexed his muscle anyway he felt necessary and in anyone's direction. He even had Fat Cat's nephew, Tyrone Nichols, shot in the summer of 1987. "Cat's nephew was caught stealing a safe from an apartment in the Baisley Projects," Prince said. "I got a call from one of my people letting me know what was happening. My thoughts were they should put a bullet in his ass. Teach him a lesson about burglarizing people's houses in the projects. He hit two other cribs of legitimate citizens in the Baisley Projects before this one. I felt a little lead in his behind might make him seek a more legitimate occupation." The Supreme Team protected their own at Prince's behest. They held the projects down as that was where they made their money, and the legitimate citizens, as Prince called them, were under the team's protection.

"My crew must have read my thoughts," Prince said. "By the time I got to the projects, Tyrone was laid out in front of the cab stand bleeding but conscious. I told a cabdriver to take him to Mary Immaculate Hospital. Later that evening, when my man Black Just and me went to the hospital to scope out the situation, someone from Cat's family pointed us out to the police as the shooters, and we were arrested on the spot, taken to the 103rd Precinct, booked and fingerprinted. They took a custom made bulletproof vest from me that night. I was in my feelings about that shit. They charged us both for assault with intent to cause serious injury with a weapon and other lesser counts. I was placed in the The Queens House of Detention for Men." Cat's family had violated the code of the streets, but Fat Cat would rectify it.

"On October 2, 1987, I was rearrested for an unrelated murder I hadn't committed," Prince said. "They transferred me from the Queens House to the Brooklyn House of Detention which had a special floor for organized crime members, cop killers, and drug kingpins. Cat greeted me as I came through the gates of the 10th floor. He made small talk and guaranteed me that his nephew would drop the charges. In January of 1988, the charges as a result of Tyrone's shooting were dismissed." In the streets of the Southside, that was how it went down. Snitching was seriously frowned upon and not tolerated, especially among gangsters' families. The heat was on Prince and the team. Still business didn't stop in any fashion, shape, or form. The team was on a paper chase. They were going hard. But the cases started stacking up for Prince.

Prince was charged with the murder of Melvin Anderson, a 19-year-old drug dealer, who was shot once in the head at point blank range at 9 p.m. on August 21, 1987, at the corner of Foch Boulevard and 142nd Place in Jamaica. Kevin Anderson, the dude's brother, identified Prince as the killer, but before the case went to trial he retracted his statement and claimed his identification was fraudulent. He did this because one of Prince's people threatened the Anderson brother. "Shut your mouth or your whole fucking family's going to die," Prince's man threatened. The living Anderson brother knew the threat wasn't a bluff. The charges were promptly dropped. It was better to live than die, even knowing your brother's killer walked free. With Prince allegedly offering a ten grand bounty on witnesses who were willing to testify against team members, people in Queens decided to keep their mouths shut when it came to the team rather than risk death from one of the Supreme Team's hit men.

While Preme sat in jail, Prince and his crew ran wild in the streets. Their reputation for violence escalated fiercely. The drug trade induced body count in Queens grew as Prince and the Supreme Team were mentioned in newspaper headline after newspaper headline. They were the usual suspects for every murder in the borough. Their notoriety grew to startling and epic proportions, so much that the mere mention of the team elicited fear in all five boroughs. "Prince was not the monster that the government and media tried to make him out to be. The team just got so infamous that anything that happened in the hood was blamed on us. If someone got stabbed way over in Queensbridge, the team would get the blame. It just got crazy. Prince was never the monster they proclaimed. Media portrayed us as people that preyed on our own kind. We didn't hold people hostage or terrorize anyone. If a drug dealer got terrorized, that is part of the game. We weren't monsters," Teddy says. Shit in the streets was escalating though.

"I kept the peace when I was on the street," Preme said. "But with me gone, they had to show everyone they could answer the call." Protecting an outfit that was clocking 200 grand and selling 25K vials of crack per week in and around the Baisley Projects, Prince definitely answered the call. Supreme, sitting in jail, developed a reputation in the streets as the money guy, the brains behind the operation. Prince, his nephew and second in command, became known for handling the dirty work. He was the general of the Supreme Team, the street boss, the team's wildcard and stone cold killer, ready and willing to bust his guns at any provocation with a deadly security force to exercise his authority. Prince had balls of steel, too, as exhibited by his fearlessness of the police. In the summer of 1987, wearing a bulletproof hat, Prince showed up at the 113th Precinct in South Jamaica, after police asked him to help solve the kidnapping of one of his men. Prince told them he didn't know anything. But in the streets rumors flew that he was the one responsible for the disappearance. Cool and collected, Prince gave his statement and left, death and unsolved murders in his wake.

With all the killings, murder was paramount in the hood. Even Supreme Team members weren't immune to it. Several members were killed for various reasons. Even innocents were caught in the crossfire. "We did a mural for the kid on the handball court- Mo Cheeks Rest in Peace. Mo is short for Maurice, a young dude who got shot accidentally in the head. The team did a memorial, a tribute to the kid on the other side of the handball court, which was a drug spot," Tuck says. With death looming and a lucrative business to protect, Prince and the security team killed at will. They turned the Southside of Jamaica into the Old West. Prince and the team members were looked upon by residents as Billy the Kid-type, outlaw figures. They were larger than life and living in the shadow of their own immortality.

The string of murders committed by the Supreme Team during the summer of 1987, made Prince feared and respected in the streets of South Jamaica, Queens, but at the same time, attracted the attention of law enforcement. Numerous law enforcement agencies including all the alphabet boys were looking to take down the Supreme Team. At the same time Preme was fighting his case and got it overturned. "Me and Preme ended up beating the case on appeal due to a technicality," Bing says. That meant Preme, who had a nine years to life sentence, Bing who had a six to life, Born a six to life, Brett a four to life, and Eric a three to life, all got out on appeal bonds before the cases were dismissed. "Everybody beat it on appeal," Bing says. "Preme came home in 87. Born in 87. Brett in 89. I wasn't really calling people out there. I was in jail doing my time." Preme was back on the street and ready to roll. "My legal team got the case overturned in 20 months on the premise that the warrant was bad," he said. That was nothing new; the team was used to beating cases. They paid top dollar for mob counselors like Robert Simels, a popular drugs and guns lawyer.

While Preme and his co-defendants were beating their case, Queens Narcotics detectives Mike McGuinness and William Tartaglia were closely monitoring the Supreme Team's activities and recorded numerous drug buys at Supreme Team spots. Late in the summer of 1987, Queens Narcotics even penetrated the crews' inner circle, placing an informant to relay the minutes of a Supreme Team upper level management meeting directly to Tartaglia. Over the years, numerous names have been mentioned as the possible informants, including Supreme Team higher ups like Bimmy, Black Just, and Green Eyed Born, but no one knows for sure. "Dudes said that Bimmy and Black Just were rats," the Southside player says, but the informant was never exposed, and many team members defend their associates. "I've never seen anything with their name on it," Bing says. "We'll probably never know." That's because the informant never testified against the team. He was well protected and insulated by his Queens Narcotics handlers, a CI or confidential informant whose only job was to give up information, not testify in court.

Just before Preme was released from prison in August 1987, the informant told Queens Narcotics that the jailed Supreme Team leader was busily preparing the crew for his return to the streets. "He wanted to make sure all the members and various locations had their money ready," the informant told Tartaglia. Each Supreme Team member was instructed by Preme to save a chunk of their profits for the returning CEO himself. When Preme hit the streets in August 1987, he held a formal Supreme Team sit down in Baisley Projects. Tartaglia's informant was present and told Queens Narcotics cops that Preme used the occasion to take a detailed inventory of the crew. "Preme wanted to meet new members since his incarceration, and he wanted to know any fire power they had, guns, any muscle, bodyguards, connects, and what locations they had," the informant told police. Satisfied with the state of the team under Prince during his two year absence, Preme told the twenty five ranking members of the team present at the meeting to redouble their profit making efforts and to lock down all the spots they could. Preme was ready to get paid.

"In 87, Preme came home on appeal bond. He was home for two months and made like half a million," the Southside player says. Preme and the team were balling out of control, but his meticulous planning for the Supreme Team would go for naught. They already had a target on their backs. The feds were working with Queens Narcotics in their investigation of the crew, a move sparked in part by employees of New York's Specials Narcotics Prosecutor who were frustrated by the Queens District Attorney's lack of success in prosecuting Preme in 1985. In the fall of 1987, all of the major Supreme Team players were under surveillance including Puerto Rican Righteous, C-Just, Black Just, Bimmy, Babywise, Prince, and Preme. On November 6, 1987, a massive force of Queens narcotics cops and feds raided Supreme Team locations all over the Southside and Baisley Projects. When Preme found out about the raid from a police contact, he told crew members to move as much cocaine as possible and to dump the rest. The team moved eleven kilos out of Baisley before the raid commenced, but they couldn't get it all out.

FBI officers executed search warrants on a number of Supreme Team storage locations, drug outlets, and residences. With Supreme's tip off, the team was able to remove $200,000 from the targeted premises, but authorities nonetheless seized an array of weapons, narcotics trade hardware, photographs, and documents. An FBI agent reported seeing kilos of cocaine drop from the building tops. Chaos prevailed that day as cocaine rained down from Baisley. Drugs were tossed out of project windows and flushed down toilets. Triple beam scales and measuring instruments were found covered in cocaine and heroin residue. Red Supreme Team jackets were left in stash houses. In one apartment cops found books with titles such as *The Silencer Handbook*, *Methods of Disguise*, *Point Blank Body Armor*, and *Improvised Sabotage Devices*. In another apartment, police scanners, a variety of scales, and thousands of yellow top vials were found. The raids sent both Prince and Preme back to jail. Puerto Rican Righteous put himself in charge and shut the team down. He fired everyone, closed all the drug spots, collected all the money owed, and handed it over to Supreme's sister.

"If Preme and Prince both went to prison, there was no boss, niggas free styled," Tuck says, "but there were always a select few that remained loyal to them whether they were in or out." But without their leaders, the team wasn't the same. A couple of long time lieutenants held the remnants of the team together. "Bimmy and Black Just were holding the team down," Bing says. With their crews they did what they could. "When Preme and Prince were gone, Bimmy and Black Just ran the team," the Queens hustler says. But without the security force regulating the streets, a new generation of Queens drug dealers starting taking over retail spots. They wilded out, with no regard for human life. They worked from the psychotic playbook of Prince without realizing that his murderous M.O. contributed in large part to the Supreme Team's demise. Crack was fueling this homicidal new ethos, but the disappearance of the cool headed, older bosses like Supreme and Fat Cat contributed to it as well.

Ever since his acquittal on the state charges, the feds had their eyes on Preme. Through snitches and wiretaps the feds were able to make a case against Supreme. The feds tapped his phones and recorded his conversations. They tried to get his beeper numbers, bank records, or anything that could lead to a potential record of drug or money transactions. This was the feds method and routinely it entailed digging through their target's belongings. In the police sweep of the Supreme Team in 1987, the feds got what they needed. They gathered an array of evidence that tied Supreme to drug dealing.

"The feds came in and said they were tipped off," T says. Mike McGuinness of Queens Narcotics arrested Supreme on the corner of Foch Boulevard and Guy R. Brewer. Even though there was no primia facie evidence that the allegations were true, Preme was taken to jail.

Upon his arrival at MCC New York, Preme was greeted like a celebrity. "The inmates were calling out his name," remembered Detective McGuinness. "He was a very well thought of criminal, very well recognized." Preme's street star status was intact and certified.

Experienced in the ways of the judicial system that was set up to hasten his demise, Preme could see that a guilty verdict was certain. "When I came home, the feds promptly picked up the case," Supreme said. "This was a pivotal point for me because I just beat the same charges in the state. I was adamant about proceeding to trial, but upon consultation with some O.G.'s I met at MCC, I conceded to the situation. They advised me it would be prudent to relent and satisfy the government's thirst for blood than to engage in a drawn out battle with no assurances. I was sentenced to twelve years." Preme knew he was hit.

"The feds got him in 1987," Tuck says. "He copped out to twelve years. No co-defendants. The feds just wanted him." Supreme was charged with running a continual criminal enterprise, the drug kingpin statute. In court Preme played it humble, hoping for leniency. The judge ran down the charges.

"The government has that in connection with the plea to this superseding information, that I should ask you whether you involved in at least three narcotic offenses in connection with engaging in the continuing criminal enterprise that was set forth in the superseding information," the judge explained to Supreme. Preme admitted to being the "organizer, supervisor and manager" of the Supreme Team. The humbling Preme received in the courtroom was eased by the light twelve year sentence Judge Thomas C. Platt handed down. With good behavior Preme would be out in less than ten years. Supreme's CCE charge and kingpin status conferred by the feds immortalized him in the eyes of Queens urban youth. Hip-hop artists had always made mythological ghetto heroes out of crime figures, rhyming about Harlem drug lords

Alpo and Rich Porter, Chicago gang leader Larry Hoover, Colombian Cartel head Pablo Escobar, and even fictionalized characters like Nino Brown and Tony Montana. With his arrest and conviction, Supreme was added to the list. "Supreme was indicted by the feds in the fall of 1987, and entered a guilty plea in U.S. District Court on a charge of engaging in a continuing criminal enterprise. Supreme was sentenced to twelve years in the BOP, a relatively short sentence given the charges against him and the significance of the street empire he created," Ethan Brown says.

"They always gonna remember him as a top legend from the hood," Bing says. "He was one of the main generals who represented Southside Jamaica, Queens, to the fullest. He's a person the streets will always remember as a legend. He repped the hood and made Southside Jamaica shine." By acknowledging that he ran the Supreme Team, Preme insured that his rep would survive during his time away. All he had to do was a short stint in prison, and the streets would welcome him back home with open arms. In the aristocracy of the crack trade, the life that Supreme had lived up to that point was the stuff of gangsta rap legend. As Supreme did his time, paying his debt to society, his name was ringing bells in the streets as Prince was crowned.

CHAPTER 5
PRINCE IS CROWNED

"Prince from Queens and Fritz from Harlem/Street legends, the drugs kept the hood from starvin'."
— **Nas, Get Down from God's Son (2002)**

"Whenever Supreme went to prison Prince was the boss. And when the feds got Supreme, it was Prince's show."
— **Don Diva, Issue 23**

"Prince, a volatile figure two years younger than Supreme, took the organization in a brutal new direction."
— **Vibe Magazine**

Newspaper accounts said Prince inherited leadership of the Supreme Team in 1987 when his uncle Supreme went to prison. After being acquitted in state court for numerous homicides, he emerged to much fanfare in the streets. He was the undisputed street boss of the Supreme Team, and he had the makings of an army under him. Prince solidified his control of the team by increasing the security force and employing it against team members suspected of disloyalty. His philosophy was "get down or lay down" and he kept it close to home. "Baisley Projects," the Supreme Team member says. "That was headquarters." The Supreme Team held it down in the projects. It was their own personal fiefdom, to rule like feudal lords and control how they saw fit. With the crack wars in full swing, Prince and his crew terrorized the streets with a vengeance and continued to carve their niche and perpetuate their legend.

The team was run like a crime family that rivaled the old style mob crews. There were certain protocols and procedures to follow, as well as a hierarchy to uphold. Prince had two rules- do what he said and don't snitch. There wasn't much more to it than that. Dudes who stood strong and held their tongues were rewarded. Those who didn't suffered the team's retribution. In the streets Prince was a fearsome figure. His wrath was as absolute as it was legendary. And law enforcement was hot on his trail, trying to get team members to turn on their leader. "Niggas weren't snitching on Prince," the Queens hustler says. "They was scared." But that didn't stop dudes from gunning for him. Prince had enemies, lots of them, some even within the ranks of the team. Legend has it Prince engaged in gunfighter type duels and laid down the law with rapid fire submachine guns. The security team did drive-bys and peppered enemies with bullets. They practiced the art of street warfare with Sun Tzu flair. Law enforcement and federal officials considered Prince one of the most violent drug dealers in the city during the 1980s.

"Prince was the most intimidating individual in the Southside of Jamaica, Queens," Bing says. "Wasn't no one trying to cross him." New York's tabloid newspapers called Prince, Mr. Untouchable. He was like the Teflon Don, John Gotti, as nothing would stick. Cases would be brought, and Prince would end up walking. The indictments were thrown out. In and out on murder charges, he beat them all. His cunning in the streets was backed up by his legal shrewdness. His leadership outlook consisted of "doing me" and to hell with the consequences. When Prince took over the Supreme Team, he ratcheted up the violence, collateral damage be damned. Residents of the 113th and 103rd Precincts who hoped that Supreme's incarceration would lead to the demise of the team were in for a surprise. With Prince back in control, violence was as much a part of life as trips to the shops along Jamaica Avenue were. "The police were nothing to us," Bing says. "We didn't give a fuck about them." On the Southside that was the overwhelming attitude. They were like N.W.A.- *Fuck the Police.*

In his book *From Pieces to Weight*, 50 Cent wrote about Prince and his reputation, 50 called him King in the book. "King was, in a word, notorious. He had previously been an enforcer for the organization, but the feds had indicted the leaders of his crew a few months before. The old bosses still ran things from the pen, but King was left in charge of the street operations while his bosses' lawyers scoured the law encyclopedias for appeal loopholes. King's rep was built on disappearing Colombian connections, tortured workers, and public murders. People who were set to testify against him usually changed their minds, couldn't remember what exactly had happened, or claimed that the police misunderstood their statements. Word was that King even took the life of his best friend over a few thousand dollars that went missing."

With a network of connections to Colombian cocaine dealers through

Latino members Puerto Rican Righteous and Gus Rivera, Prince set out to make the team bigger and more profitable than ever, using violence as his main operating tactic. To celebrate his ascension, Prince bought himself a $65,000 BMW and sent it to the shop for $50,000 in James Bond upgrades. The car was armored, equipped with oil slicks, and electric door handles. "Prince had that 750 BMW, white on white," Bing says. On the Southside of Jamaica, Prince was a gangster prodigy. Everything he did was first class. In one of his boldest moves, he corrupted a New York state parole officer named Ina McGriff and had her accompany him to the car dealership to buy the Beamer.

"Prince had over 100 muthafucka's that was involved in certain activities within the team," Bing says. "He put me, Tuck, and Teddy as his top lieutenants. We only answered to him. We all had certain areas, locations. I served a whole area, Tuck had his, and Teddy had his. As it went along, we were back at our fullest form. We maintained all of Southside Jamaica, Queens, selling drugs, doing our regular, always everywhere, over Queensbridge too. Prince had shit out there. Prince was about his money. If someone fucked with his money, they were hit." The Supreme Team began to reclaim its hold on the area's drug trade and built its gross receipts up to $10,000 a day.

It was a time of murder and chaos in the hood. Despite many team members struggling with crack addiction, and the regular busts of stash houses and hand to hand dealers, business still flourished for the team, generating tremendous profits for Prince and the crew. But with all the drug money came a litany of problems. Prison, beefs, robberies, and murders dominated South Jamaica and came to define what the Supreme Team was about. It was a change from Supreme's era of styling, profiling, parties, and hip-hop. The so called wonder years of the team were over. With the coming of crack and Prince's coronation, a reign of terror was unleashed.

"That third floor of the Baisley Projects was like 5th Avenue at Christmas time," Assistant U.S. Attorney Leslie Caldwell said. "Peddlers started selling without having to worry about retaliation." As the team grew bolder, they attracted more wholesale dealers to sell them weight.

"You gotta have different connects," Bing says. "Some got better prices, better coke. There were a lot of different people we were buying coke from. We had like three or four connects." Like any business, the crack trade ran on raw materials which was namely, high grade cocaine in large quantities.

Gus Rivera, the cocaine distributor who pleaded with Prince to join the Supreme Team, was introducing the crew to new and bigger connections.

Rivera's friends Fernando and George, a pair of Colombian distributors who only went by their first names, were fast becoming the favorite suppliers of the Supreme Team. The duo would bring major weight to 116-80 Guy R. Brewer Boulevard at a moment's notice. "Gus would beep Fernando and George," Assistant U.S. Attorney Caldwell explained, "and they would show up with duffle bags and the deal would be done." These transactions were so effortless that the pair of Colombians had no idea who or what they were dealing with.

During the mid to late 1980s, the Southside of Jamaica had seen countless murders committed by the Supreme Team and other drug crews, but the slaying of Mildred Green, a grandmother and a Big D's Car Service employee for more than a decade, was an authentic turning point in the history of the neighborhood. The cycle of shootings, slayings, and dramatic police raids that wracked South Jamaica in 1987 barely made an imprint on the city's consciousness, but Mildred Green's murder changed all that, bringing with it an intolerance of the drug business that would doom crews like the Supreme Team.

On September 2, 1987, the 61-year-old Green was working at Big D's Car Service at 150-01 Linden Boulevard when a heated argument over a fare broke out between one of the company's drivers, Joel Johnson, and a passenger Derrick Kornegay. Kornegay was a local drug dealer of some repute but nowhere near the level of dealers like Prince and the Supreme Team. Kornegay was mad because he thought Johnson overcharged him five dollars for the fare. Only in the Southside of Jamaica, Queens, could a murder result from the trivial amount of five dollars. Like they say on *Boondocks*, Kornegay had "a nigga moment."

But it wasn't the dollar amount that was important, it was the respect factor. The fact that some chump cabdriver would try to get over on him infuriated Kornegay. He knew damn well that no cabdriver would ever try to get over on the Supreme Team, and he fancied himself in the same category. Call it delusional or whatever, but Kornegay and his friend Reynaud Chandler, feeling disrespected, angrily demanded a refund from the bosses at Big D's. When another driver entered the debate, Chandler pulled out a .357 Magnum and began firing, hitting himself, Johnson, the other driver and Kornegay, a real gangster move. All four were treated at the hospital and released. Chandler was charged with the shooting and jailed at Rikers. Mildred Green was unharmed but witnessed the shooting.

The week after the shooting at Big D's, Green testified about the incident in front of a grand jury at Queens Criminal Court. This action marked her for death in the eyes of the Queens underworld. They labeled her a snitch, and Chandler's crew started calling her and threatening her to retract her statements or change her testimony. These were routine mob tactics that were perfected by crews such as the Supreme Team. But Chandler's crew was not the Supreme Team, and Green refused to refute the charges. She saw them as bumbling gangster wannabe's. Chandler was a nobody, not of any stature or affiliated with the likes of Prince or Supreme, so any respect he earned would be at the point of a gun. Green felt she was safe, but that proved to be a deadly mistake.

Waddell Winston, Chandler's 37-year-old uncle, decided to make sure Green didn't testify against his nephew. He would serve street justice, Queens style. He and Tracy Middleton walked into Big D's on Linden Boulevard and killed Green with a single shotgun blast to the head. Her body was discovered at around 4:40 a.m. on October 4, two days after she received the phone calls threatening her life. The city was outraged with the killing. Mayor Ed Koch offered a $10,000 reward for information leading to the arrest of those responsible.

"These drug guys are absolutely nuts," Thomas Reppetto, president of the Citizens Crime Commission, told *The New York Times*. "They're way worse than any Mafia. They're so young and so violent that they don't have the restraint that the more traditional organized crime guys have." The community was astounded at the brazen, bold, and violent killing. And in reality Mildred Green wasn't a snitch. She was a civilian, unaffiliated with the drug game or any crews. By telling the police what she saw, she was just doing her civic duty as a citizen. Sometimes dudes in the street get shit twisted. A snitch is someone who betrays his comrades to get out of a jam. Green was a witness, not a snitch. The high profile murder was quickly solved. On October 9, 1987, a team of six police officers and detectives raided Waddell Winston's home at 135-55 232nd Street. Winston was arrested and charged in the Green killing. Eighteen-year-old Tracy Middleton was also arrested and charged in the killing.

In the hothouse atmosphere of the South Jamaica drug scene, the killing of a grandmother was big news. But bigger news would soon announce itself. NYPD Detective Robert Colangelo admitted to *The New York Times* that "the totality of the police response in this situation was insufficient." With their witness murdered, the NYPD would be on guard in the future. Green's killing set off a chain reaction that still reverberates to this day. The NYPD was gripped with a sense of outrage and powerlessness that crews like the Supreme Team magnified with their blatant, rude, and outlandish chip-on-the-shoulder attitude toward the police and the community at large. The drug crews didn't give a fuck, and they didn't care who knew it. The young black crack dealer became a figure of scorn in the media. The NYPD was fed up with feeling impotent when it came to drug dealers. At long last they were ready to take back the streets of South Jamaica, Queens. They put a target squarely on the chests of every young black male in the city.

Law enforcement's consciousness wasn't put to rest by the arrests of Green's killers. A culture of terror had been brought into vogue in Queens. The Southside Jamaica crews were threatening to murder witnesses for testifying even in insignificant cases. During 1987 alone, Prince and the incarcerated Supreme were suspected of ordering at least eight homicides. The Supreme Team had created and fostered a climate of death that infected the streets of South Jamaica, and now all the drug crews were trying to one up each other. One Queens resident, a Guyanese immigrant named Arjune, wasn't dissuaded by the atmosphere of intimidation created by the drug crews like the Supreme Team. He lived at 107-05 Inwood Street in South Jamaica. By the end of 1987, his block was so overrun with crack heads and dealers it resembled an open-air drug bazaar. Arjune made it a point of pride to call the 103rd Precinct to complain about the dealers, users, and lookouts and even played the informant role for police.

Due to what hustlers perceived as his snitching, dealers from the remnants of Fat Cat's crew and the Bebo's tossed three Molotov cocktails at Arjune's Inwood Street home. Later they threw three more, two of which crashed through the window. Before the fiery homemade bombs could do much damage, Arjune picked them up and threw them back out the window. Arjune quickly reported the incident to police. Stung by the criticism about their inaction that led to Mildred Green's death, law enforcement took an unusually strong action in the wake of the firebombing. They put cop cars in front of Arjune's house 24/7 to protect him. They didn't want to lose another witness like they did in the Green case. The NYPD thought a solid police presence would deter any further harassment of Arjune or a repeat of the Green murder, but they were wrong. At the time, though, no one knew how wrong they would be.

The event that forever changed the perception and image of the Supreme Team was an act that they didn't even commit. In one of the city's darkest moments, as the drug wars reached their peak, rookie Police Officer Edward Byrne was shot and killed on February 26, 1988, while sitting in a patrol car on 107th Avenue guarding the house of Arjune. Officer Byrne was parked in a marked patrol car when two suspects approached him. One of the suspects knocked on the passenger window to distract him as the second suspect ran up to him at the driver's window and opened fire, striking him in the head five times. Two additional suspects served as lookouts. The perpetrators were linked to the remnants of Fat Cat's old crew and to "that of his enforcer Pappy Mason, who ran a crew called the Bebo's," prosecutors said.

The round-the-clock police presence was a message to dealers that the Mildred Green situation wouldn't be repeated, but it turned tragic. The killing of a uniformed patrol officer was an act so brazen that the NYPD never believed it could happen. But with the crews getting crazier and crazier, it was just a matter of time. Queens had turned into the Wild, Wild West and law enforcement had lost control. The police had good intentions, but a message of a different kind was sent when five gunshots shattered the pre-dawn silence and tore through the officer's skull. The message to the police was "fuck you." And it wasn't an N.W.A. song. It was a real life 187 on a cop.

Byrne, a second-generation police officer, lay dead in his cruiser. The NYPD was astonished and infuriated. After the initial shock, they demanded retribution, and there was no stopping them. The drug dealers had crossed an impermissible line and the NYPD, with the feds' help, would hold them accountable. The cop killing changed the course of Queens history and quickly hastened the Supreme Team's demise even though they had nothing to do with the murder. They were guilty by association. Byrne's murder became a symbol of the nation's failure in the war on crime, and, instead of declaring defeat, the government stepped up their efforts tremendously.

Within days, four suspects belonging to the Bebo's were rounded up and charged with the crime. Three of the four suspects made videotaped statements implicating each other; one even claimed the order came from the imprisoned drug lord Fat Cat, who was still trying to run his crumbling empire from prison, albeit, not very successfully. "Edward Byrne was a rookie police officer that was on guard duty watching a witness that was in protective custody," Lance said. "Byrne was murdered execution style. Although Pappy Mason and four others pleaded guilty and are serving time for this crime, authorities still linked all the Queens crews to the murder." In law enforcement's view, all the crews were guilty, and they would all face the consequences.

"Edward Byrne, all that stuff could not have happened without crack," Ethan Brown said. "Crack was really the end, not the beginning." The violence, perpetrated in a crack induced haze, focused the spotlight on the South Jamaica crews. What was considered a local problem or a ghetto problem was now national news. "There's the killing of a white cop and suddenly it's on everyone's radar. There's no accident there. I think the cops were focused on the Mafia before that. They didn't take this stuff seriously. They thought black neighborhoods, who cares? It really took crack and Edward Byrne to put this stuff on everyone's radar," Ethan Brown said.

"Supreme was locked up when the cop was shot. He was basically locked up from 85 to 93 under the old law," Tuck says. But it didn't matter. The cop's death infuriated the NYPD and the feds. The national media had a field day with the story running headline after headline. The young black male became public enemy number one. Things in the Southside of Jamaica, Queens, would never be the same. The feds would wage an all out war against every crew from Queens, including the Supreme Team. Officer Byrne's slaying provoked calls for sterner tactics against drugs- in particular against the violent and sometimes chaotic world of crack sales. This event ushered in a new stage of American politics called the War on Drugs and the 100 to 1 crack to cocaine ratio.

To NYPD top brass, Byrne's killing was a throwing down of the gauntlet that had to be answered and punished severely. A line had been crossed and law enforcement was ready to bring the cop killers and everyone associated with that world down. Any and everybody involved in drugs in Queens were to blame. "This was not an order, not for the murder of a particular police officer, but of any officer, for the sole purpose of delivering a message of death to anyone who opposed crack dealers," Lieutenant Phillip Pansarella, head of the Queens Homicide Squad said. The streets were quickly strangled by the law's long arm and angry fist. Outposts sprouted up overnight like weeds, and patrol cars rolled through Southside streets. For a minute the Southside looked like what it could have looked like if no one had invented crack, but it was a show of force, nothing more. It wouldn't, couldn't last because it didn't deal with what was really going on in the community. The problems of poverty, drug abuse, and a lack of jobs were ignored. Law enforcement was just looking for revenge and people to hang cases on.

The rookie's murder was front page news all over the nation and kicked the War on Drugs into high gear. Mandatory minimum drug sentences and federal sentencing guidelines had already been established the year before, but then came the Anti-Drug Abuse Act of 1988, which called for a federal death penalty for drug kingpins and ensured that convicted drug offenders would serve at least 85 percent of their jail sentences. President Reagan signed into effect the tough new federal drug sentencing laws, as Officer Byrne's father, Matthew, attended the White House signing ceremony.

"I found out that the only coverage of this stuff starts in February/ March of 1988, when Edward Byrne was killed in the line of duty. None of this stuff was paid attention to by the media until that happened," Ethan Brown said. As long as it was black on black crime, the media didn't care, but when a white police officer was killed, the newspaper shined the spotlight on South Jamaica's drug crews and the lives they led. The Reagan government saw an opportunity for national exposure and ran with it using politics to grandstand in the media. It was political propaganda at its best with the losers being the fabled drug crews of Queens.

It was this murder more than any other that started the crackdown in the 103rd Precinct, a place many law enforcement officers came to view with distaste bordering on hate. This also led to the creation of police units like the Tactical Narcotics Team (TNT) and the Street Narcotics Enforcement Unit which gave the police an unprecedented amount of power to deal with street hustlers. The new program, called TNT for short, was described as a coordinated citywide multi-agency approach involving the Police, Fire and Building Departments, the Queens District Attorney, the offices of the City and State Criminal Justice Coordinators, the State Office of Court Administration, the City's Special Narcotics Prosecutor, the Federal Drug Enforcement Administration, the Joint Narcotics-FBI Task Force, the City's Corporation Counsel and the City's Correction Department.

The stepped up drug enforcement program included the addition of more than 100 police officers who would be unleashed on South Jamaica. Commissioner Ward said the new program would include the areas covered by the 103rd, 105th, 106th and 113th Precincts- about 22 square miles of southeastern Queens. The Police Department provided one lieutenant, fourteen sergeants, 70 investigators, 28 undercover officers and five civilian support personnel. The operation was aimed at purging the area of its flourishing drug trade. Mayor Ed Koch said the newest drive, prompted by the officer's murder, would be the first to employ the concerted resources of so many government agencies. The attack on the Queens hustlers was wholesale.

It wasn't safe for dealers to keep drugs on them anymore. It wasn't safe to even be around the drugs, or in the vicinity of them. When TNT swept in, everyone in the area got arrested, even innocent bystanders. The TNT tactics changed the dealers' logic. As police squads began to stake out street level hustlers and make arrests based on observation of sales, dealers began to run when the police jumped out. It became a game to the Southside crews, a game they found they could win, at least in the short term. The Supreme Team prospered by having their operation up and running in Baisley Projects. Their sales were harder to observe as cops couldn't even get in the building. Pappy Mason and four Bebos took the fall for the murdered police officer, but that didn't stop law enforcement from exacting retribution. They were out to arrest any and all. All minorities were fair game. And Prince and the Supreme Team were at the top of the list.

Prince was an enigmatic figure to the streets of South Jamaica. Investigators said Prince and his henchmen terrorized the area, murdered suppliers they double-crossed, killed confederates who fell out of favor and potential rivals. To law enforcement officials trying to police the relentless drug trade in New York City, Prince was one of the most savage and successful of the flashy young kingpins who dominated the lucrative crack enterprise. It was said that Prince wore a bulletproof baseball cap and that his Mercedes 500 was rigged up James Bond-style with oil slicks, smoke screens, gun ports, bulletproof glass and all. He was a hero to his hood and the greater New York area, an outlaw hero like Jesse James.

With the security team, retail spots in Baisley Projects and their numerous stash houses, the Supreme Team operated with impunity. Prince was picked up numerous times on drug charges and always walked. He also faced a series of murder charges and beat them all. With the best drugs and guns lawyer money could buy and a fearsome team of killers behind him taking care of any and all potential witnesses, Prince had the game on lock. It was just that easy, with his well deserved rep and cadre of gun thugs, he was the reigning overlord of the streets, a brutal drug kingpin whose word and whims were law, a heavy handed gangster who did as he wished. In the Southside of Queens he was like a modern day warlord come to life out of ancient Japan with an army of Samurais beside him enforcing his will.

In the interim Prince was always getting locked up, but the charges never amounted to anything. "The majority of the top people affiliated with the team, when they caught a state case, they beat it," Bing says. "Our lawyers were so good it was unbelievable the cases they got thrown out. With money anything was possible." A lot of the team's core members were in and out of jail. With the TNT task force ripping and running through the Southside, dudes were getting arrested like crazy, but most of the time they ended up beating the cases. "I came home in January 1989," Bing says. "Preme and Prince were both locked up, Supreme in the feds and Prince in Rikers fighting a murder beef. C-Just was home, Black Just was home, Bimmy was home. Other dudes were home that I knew, but I didn't really fuck with them. I started fucking with Black Just. He was in charge of the family when I came home. He had stuff jive in order. He used to go see Preme."

Even with their members scattered, fighting various charges, the Supreme Team ran like a well-oiled machine. "It's called the Supreme Team," Bimmy says. "Preme was not by hisself and he was in jail for the most part. Myself, Just, Prince took care of Preme. Preme been in jail, me and Just took care of Preme. Nigga, I'm a boss to this day. I feed the jails. I took the team to the next level." They had meetings in the prison visiting rooms. The lieutenants and security team would come to see Prince so he could pass down orders and control his empire. He was calling shots from a jail cell. If shit got hectic, Prince would restore order as well. His word was law, and he had the respect of everyone under him. In the prison visiting room meetings, Prince had to reign in his younger charges to curtail their reckless ambitions. When disputes arose, he settled them, making sure his crew didn't take advantage of the other members. A decree Prince enforced for Preme. Even among his crew he was held in awe.

After Preme's incarceration though, the team was increasingly divided into factions. With Prince's crew growing more violent by the day and taking their security force reputation to heart, the other crews wanted nothing to do with them or their brutal tactics. What Supreme held together by force of will and his own engaging charisma fell apart and divided when he wasn't on the scene to mend fences, placate egos, and practice his diplomatic skills. He tried to direct traffic from federal prison. But since he was so far from home and was being transferred around, it was hard for him to keep a firm grasp on the team which left it in Prince's hands.

Babywise, Black Just, and Bimmy did their own thing as Prince did with his sub-organization although everyone still operated under the Supreme Team banner and flew its colors. Some of the more ambitious members on Prince's team like Puerto Rican Righteous wanted to bring a move on Preme loyalists like Black Just and Bimmy, but Preme made Prince put a stop to that. Whether Prince was ultimately behind it, no one knows, but more than a few times Preme had to instruct his nephew to get his guys to back off. With the lines drawn, the Supreme Team became a very fragmented organization with crews within crews, all flying the Supreme Team banner.

"Some dudes hated practically everyone who made Preme happy, and Black Just and Bimmy did a lot to keep Preme happy in the early part of his bid," the Queens insider says. "When Preme got short, things fell apart for Black Just and Bimmy in regards to the money they were supposed to be turning into Preme as long as he was locked up. But for 75 percent of Preme's bid, Black Just and Bimmy were the team's greatest earners if not the only earners. No one can dispute that." It was a tight rope some of the other team members had to walk with Preme in prison and Prince in charge. But they played a major part in forging the team's mythology. The violence committed by Prince's security team, though, kept everyone in check.

"Prince had the streets shook," the Queens hustler says. "He was the man. He kept the team in order. He held the team down for Preme. Preme was still running shit from the pen. Black Just used to go see Preme and pass messages from him to Prince. Prince loved his uncle. Preme was in FCI Talladega at the time." Prince was feared by most and respected by all, but his uncle was still the more legendary figure. Prince had the streets in a chokehold, but Preme held the mythical quality possessed by all outlaw heroes. He was the icon, the gangster god of Queens, the modern day urban outlaw. In the streets, though, Prince was the boss. He was the villain at large. His reputation spoke of violence and wild abandon. To the black underworld, Prince simply didn't give a fuck. He would get his and nothing would stand in his way.

"Prince and I had a business relationship," Tuck says, "and a friendship, but I believe business eventually ruined our friendship, but I know Prince the way most don't. Prince is a real good dude. Very well respected and feared too. He was highly motivated, very organized, and extremely intelligent, a real master at gamesmanship." The Supreme Team, for all their murderous faults, provided order in South Jamaica and Baisley Projects when crack was king. It could have been much worse on the Southside. To an extent Prince and the team curtailed crack related crime. They took care of the civilians and frowned upon random acts of violence, unless they were committing them. They were the big dogs and kept all the other wild dogs in check. Everything was about keeping the money flowing. Prince believed in taking care of business. But with the team's leaders incarcerated, total chaos reigned. Security team gun thugs smoked crack and robbed people, even other Supreme Team members. It was a dog eat dog world in South Jamaica. "The majority of the security team was bank robbers and sneak thieves," the Queens hustler says. With their boss locked up, they did them. With friction between the factions, chaos erupted and crack left an indelible trail everywhere it went.

"Prince wound up beating the murder beef and built the team back to its usual self," Bing says. "Prince came home toward the end of the summer of 1989. He bought a new 750 BMW as a coming home present for himself. Prince was the top nigga out there again." The streets welcomed Prince back. He was a brutal but firm and fair task master. He'd cruise the streets letting everybody see him stunting and shining. In the chaos of the crack snowstorm, the community welcomed the stern hand of the man known as the general. He was going hard, as he wanted his and he wanted it quickly. Prince was on a mission. He knew time was short. He dove headfirst back into the game, and the streets of Queens would never recover.

One violent summer under Prince's reign, Supreme Team members went crazy, ripping off and killing their connects for no apparent reason. In the swirl of chaos and bloodlust, few in the Supreme Team were worried about the prospect of getting caught. They were still under the pre-Edward Byrne killing assumption that law enforcement was preoccupied with the Mafia, but to their detriment that had changed. President Reagan had started the War on Drugs, and the Queens dealers were prioritized. With the cop killing, they had a target on their back. They just didn't realize it. "They made it seem like we were ruthless, like we killed at will," Bing says. The Edward Byrne killing also changed the lenient federal drug sentences. The Queens dealers thought a federal charge meant a short prison stint, but as the War on Drugs ushered in mandatory minimum sentencing, that was all about to change.

At the end of the 1980s, Prince and the Supreme Team's reckless violence gave the residents of South Jamaica the impression that the Supreme Team ruled the streets. But the endless murders were a sign of chaos, not power. The Supreme Team had nothing to gain from the killings other than relatively small amounts of cocaine. As law enforcement boasted in *Newsday* that "the four legs of the stool" of the major Queens drug dealers had been broken (meaning Fat Cat, Supreme, Tommy Mickens and Wall Corley), the Supreme Team was left standing. Like a punch drunk fighter, they danced around the ring arrogantly.

Fueled by crack addiction and hubris they were behaving like the uninitiated and undisciplined freelancers who were beginning to dominate the streets instead of the feared and respected organization that they were. Like the Supreme Team under Prince's management, these new jacks on the streets of Queens, Brooklyn, and the Bronx were engaging in senselessly violent, open ended free-for-alls that ratcheted up New York's murder rate to previously unseen heights. The crack era made New York the murder capital of the world as the Supreme Team developed a gruesome reputation for killing, killing and more killing. It was total anarchy in the streets of Queens.

"The Colombian murders, that was the first time that shit ever happened. Prince was locked up for that shit. I didn't even know about that shit 'til I got arrested," Bing says. The butchering of four Colombians at Baisley Projects was the Supreme Team's most infamous crime. With numerous Supreme Team members being jailed at the 113th and 103rd Precincts, fighting cases at Sutphin Supreme Courthouse, the Supreme Team's coffers had been decimated. Also Prince's personal finances were a mess.

"Prince had about maybe 250 thousand dollars in his stash when he got busted," the Queens insider says. "His older brother, Wise, stole most of that and smoked it up. What could Prince do? Nothing. Wise is his older brother and Preme's other nephew. Prince's older brother's name is Darryl Miller aka Wise. This guy is Prince's real brother, same mother, same father, but he was a complete fuck up. When Prince went down on this bid he is doing, his older brother fucked up most of Prince's money. Whatever Prince had left, he fucked up. Wise had a crack problem. I mean a real problem. But because he is Prince's brother and Preme's nephew, Prince had to swallow his losses. I think he stole between 200K to 300K of Prince's money. Wise was never any kind of hustler, but he always kept a job. Him and Prince look exactly alike except he is lighter than Prince."

With more cases mounting up, the team needed money and fast. Pookie allegedly came up with a plan to ambush the team's cocaine connect that Gus Rivera had introduced them to. Supreme Team members had done many transactions with the Colombian pair Fernando and George, so they were taken completely unaware. Pookie assembled a crew of the Supreme Team's toughest members including C-Just, Puerto Rican Righteous, and Big C to help execute the plan. But before they made their move on Fernando and George, they needed permission from Prince who was in jail on state narcotic charges. Prince gave the order to take out the Colombian dealers over the prison phone. "Do it, just as if it were me," he ordered. Puerto Rican Righteous gathered the entire Supreme Team security force at Baisley Projects. He was purposefully vague. He told the security team that there would be a major transaction the next day, and the entire security force needed to show up.

The next day the whole security team was outside 116-80 Guy R. Brewer Boulevard. Only a couple of increasingly unreliable members were absent. They were out somewhere in Manhattan smoking crack, a growing trend among the security force. Everyone was surprisingly calm, given what was about to take place, except Gus Rivera who was fucked up that the distributors he'd hooked the Supreme Team up with were about to get murdered. Rivera put a brave face on when Fernando and George showed up with their duffel bag of cocaine. C-Just, Shannon, and Pookie then allegedly led the Colombians up to apartment 3K, a one bedroom that Pookie was renting. Soon after arriving in the apartment, the security team forced Fernando and George to the ground and tied their hands with rope. A dresser was pushed up against the door to block anyone from entering.

"Take the cocaine," Fernando pleaded. "Just don't kill us." Pookie smacked Fernando in the head with a gun to quiet him. The mood in the apartment was suddenly tense. C-Just allegedly instructed Puerto Rican Righteous to go downstairs and see if anyone was waiting outside for Fernando and George. Puerto Rican Righteous saw a pair of Hispanic looking men sitting in a car. He went back upstairs to get instructions from C-Just.

"Go outside and get them," C-Just allegedly said, assigning Shannon and Puerto Rican Righteous the task. Puerto Rican Righteous told the men in Spanish, "Fernando wants to see you inside." Puerto Rican Righteous drew his gun and brought the men inside the apartment and pushed them to the floor.

The Supreme Team's original plan was to murder only Fernando and George, but now four men were lying in wait to be executed. They struggled to come up with a method of murdering the entire group. "What should we do? Slit their throats?" They wondered.

Frustrated with the crews bickering, Puerto Rican Righteous left the apartment. "I'm going out in the hall," he said. "You decide." But these were the words of a man who turned rat. "This nigga did not 'go out in the hall.' He said this to take himself out of the murder equation," The Queens hustler says. "Righteous was the one running that shit. He just put everyone else in it and blamed them to save himself." As in any scenario, the snitches painted the picture, conveniently removing themselves from the scene and placing the comrades they betrayed squarely in the thick of the action.

As Puerto Rican Righteous allegedly waited outside, Supreme Team enforcer Big C arrived, "What's going on? Are they here yet?" Puerto Rican Righteous nodded his head, and Big C went inside. His presence spurred the Supreme Team to action. The Colombians were strangled with ropes and beaten in the head with hammers. As the killing took place, Prince phoned a downstairs apartment, 1K, from prison. "How much do you think you got?" Prince asked Puerto Rican Righteous. "Five," he answered. "You didn't get ten?" Prince said. "He only brought five. C-Just said it was five," Puerto Rican Righteous answered. "What are you doing with the guys upstairs?" Prince asked. "They're chilling," Puerto Rican Righteous said. "They're on ice."

The responsibility for disposing of the corpses of the Colombians fell to the security team. They had given the coke out to the Supreme Team's distributors, but now they had to make the bodies disappear. The crew hoisted the Colombians, wrapped their bodies in huge garbage bags from the New York Housing Authority, and then tied the bags with ropes in order to keep the bodies in place. Puerto Rican Righteous served as lookout while the lifeless Colombians were brought out one by one to a blue Ford Taurus. The last body to be removed from 116-80 Guy R. Brewer Boulevard was so bloodied that the gun thugs were forced to wrap it up in a thick piece of carpet pulled from apartment 3K. As Puerto Rican Righteous dragged George's body down the stairs, he slipped and fell on the blood that had been seeping from the corpse. The other Supreme Team members found Puerto Rican Righteous' predicament hysterical.

"Righteous got all soaked up in blood," Big C laughed. To him it was funny. After the bodies were loaded up in the Taurus, they were dumped at a series of locations- 145-40 155th Street, 167th Street, 120th Avenue, 174th Street and 116th Avenue- all just blocks from Baisley Projects. The Supreme Team's enforcers didn't even bother to remove the New York Housing Authority garbage bags from the corpses and left a green laundry bag of a make that was used in the Baisley Projects on one body. To say they weren't cautious would be an understatement.

Speaking in Five Percenter code that night, C-Just, according to police, informed Prince that the deed was done. "Born, Cipher, Divine, Whys," C-Just said. The code police said was an acronym for bodies. "When they got busted, Prince was still giving out orders," the Queens insider says. "He was trying to run that shit from jail, but everything was falling apart, and the whole team was about to go down. Dudes were getting cased up and needed money. He did not have any money to help any of his men's financial problems. He could not even support his own financial problems." Prince needed more money, so he set up another mission for his crew.

Prince was pleased with the Supreme Team's work, but instead of laying low after the quadruple homicide, he decided to strike again. Jaime Padro, a cocaine dealer Prince met on Rikers Island, told Prince he could hook him up with a new pair of Colombians to get work from. Their names were Fernando Suarez and Pablo Perlaza. With Fernando and George permanently out of the picture, the Supreme Team needed a new connect, so Prince took Padro up on his offer. Prince put C-Just in contact with Padro who introduced the enforcer to Suarez and Perlaza. Just as Fernando and George had done before, Suarez and Perlaza showed up at apartment 3K at 116-80 Guy R. Brewer Boulevard at Baisley Projects with a duffle bag full of cocaine.

The Supreme Team's relationship with Suarez and Perlaza was beneficial to both parties, but the team wanted more. They were disappointed at coming away with only five kilos from the Fernando and George move and wanted a bigger lick. With their war chest coffers low and Prince's trial on a variety of charges looming, they needed more money and they needed it fast. On August 22, 1989, C-Just allegedly called Suarez at his New Jersey home and requested a major shipment of cocaine. When Suarez and Perlaza arrived at 3K, they put their duffel bag on the dining room table and unzipped it to reveal just two kilos of cocaine. The Supreme Team enforcers were not dissuaded by the small quantity of drugs. As he'd done in previous meetings with the pair, C-Just walked back to the bedroom to get the cash, but this time C-Just allegedly reached down to the living room floor and grabbed a gun hidden beneath a beach towel.

Suarez and Perlaza were frozen in fear, as they faced not just an armed C-Just but several Supreme Team members including Julio, Pookie, and Big C. "Why are you doing this CJ?" Suarez pleaded to C-Just. C-Just allegedly told him that he thought they were cops or informants, a lame explanation to justify the move and the team's murderous intent. The team then tied the hands and feet of the Colombians with black electrical tape.

Julio went one step further and placed plastic bags over the heads of Suarez and Perlaza. "I could see the plastic bags like sucking into their mouths," he said later, "and them trying to gasp for air. Pookie picked up a baseball bat, banging them in the chest because they were making a lot of noise and moaning and groaning. And he hit Pablo in the head, and then blood started seeping out of the bottom of the bag; after a while, they stopped moving." While Suarez and Perlaza were suffocating, Julio said that Pookie beat their heads in with a baseball bat.

With expertise gleaned from the killings of Fernando and George, the team dispatched Suarez and Perlaza quickly, hog-tying their bodies, covering them with laundry bags, and then carrying them out to a waiting car. Once again the Supreme Team had difficulty transporting a body out of 116-80 Guy R. Brewer Boulevard. Big C struggled to slide Perlaza's body, which was hemorrhaging blood, down the stairs. Once he got downstairs, he simply stuffed Perlaza's corpse into a shopping cart the Supreme Team had stolen from a nearby supermarket and wheeled him away from the Baisley Park Houses and into a getaway car. This time the Supreme Team took a little more care in disposing of the bodies, dumping them into the thick, wooded brush in a remote area of Queens near 135th Avenue and Cranston Street. Later, knowing that her husband had gone to meet the team before disappearing, Suarez's wife telephoned them. She was told that Suarez was supposed to have met them but never arrived.

Meanwhile, Gus Rivera was stressing. He talked big when he joined up, promising this and that, but when it came down to it, he was shook. He told his girlfriend, Toni McGee, that he had killed some Colombians and taken two keys of coke. Rivera began wearing a bulletproof vest after Puerto Rican Righteous confirmed his suspicions that the Supreme Team had him targeted for death during a phone call. On August 25, Julio and C-Just staged an argument. Thinking he was safe with the crew embroiled, without even a glance at his surroundings, Rivera left the building. As Rivera pushed open the door and walked outside, Big C sprang from behind a pillar, put a .44 magnum to Rivera's head and fired. "We got to about the end of the courtyard and a shot rang out," Julio explained. "I turned and I seen Rivera falling face first hitting the ground, and Big C standing behind him with a black gun, an aura of smoke around him."

Rivera miraculously survived taking a bullet to the head and was treated at Mary Immaculate Hospital on 89th Avenue in Jamaica. The Supreme Team naturally considered the job unfinished, so when Rivera was released from the hospital on August 28, C-Just followed him back to his girlfriend Toni McGee's home at the Jade East Motel on South Conduit Avenue in South Jamaica, near JFK airport. On the way, C-Just, accompanied by Julio and Pookie, stopped at apartment 3K to pick up their weapons. Arriving at the hotel, C-Just and Pookie spotted McGee in the parking lot since she had just left the room she was sharing with Rivera. Approaching McGee, they asked for her room number. She refused to tell them. "You tell us," Pookie said. "You tell us or we'll kill you."

McGee relented. "Three hundred twenty," she said and handed over the room key. C-Just and Pookie moved quickly. They didn't want Rivera to get away. They ran up to room 320, slid the key into the lock, and burst through the door opening fire on Rivera. He was killed instantly, but in the volley of bullets one shot hit Pookie in the hand. He stumbled down the stairwell of the Jade East, droplets of his blood hitting the floor as he made his way out into the sunlight. The Supreme Team's beef with Rivera would have provided cops with potent evidence linking the crew to the killing, but Pookie's blood at the crime scene ended up making the case irrefutable.

With all the killings, law enforcement officials were busy. A number of agencies were investigating Prince and the Supreme Team and their violent string of murders. On December 31, 1989, *Newsday* marked the end of the 80s with an article- The Decade When Queens Was King. That royalty came with a price and not merely for the leaders of the

Supreme Team. Rolls Royce driving hustlers like Tommy Mickens and multimillionaire empire builders like Fat Cat were behind bars, but few were feeling safe. The avalanche of get tough legislation that passed in the wake of Edward Byrne's murder helped the United States become the world's leading incarcerator as the War on Drugs ushered in the prison age. In the 90s the federal prison population quadrupled, and the reign of the game changing iconic hustlers of South Jamaica, Queens, ended.

The higher stakes made the streets of Queens even more deadly. Hustlers were grinding to simply survive. Disagreements over turf or product that would have been settled or dismissed were now a cause for war. Major battles raged in the Queens streets. On one side was the largest police force in the nation, the NYPD. On the other were the drug dealers, armed to the teeth and with wealth untold. The feds knew something had to be done. The father of Edward Byrne was speaking loudly to America about the murder of his son. He became a one man propaganda machine. It seemed he was on every newscast or at every political rally. "I said at my son's wake our streets could end up lawless as Beirut," Matthew Byrne said. "Individually we cannot take on the drug dealers. They are an army. They are a massive army." To combat that army law enforcement formed one of their own- TNT- to take on the Supreme Team and bring them down.

A series of photographs had been tacked to a wall in TNT's office with the words Supreme Team inscribed on them. The photos were of Prince's crew with him at the top of the pyramid. With the new task force and tougher laws, law enforcement had the tools they needed to take the team down, and all the political honchos were chiming in and jumping on the bandwagon. "Drug dealers calculate the amount of money they make against the risk they are taking," U.S. Attorney Rudolph Giuliani said. "Anyone who tells you the death penalty isn't a deterrent doesn't know the drug trade." The Supreme Team, targeted by TNT, saw more than 110 of its members arrested and convicted in the late-80s and early-90s. But team members were beating as many cases as they lost. For the state of New York it was a losing battle.

"We beat a lot of cases in the state," Bing says. "Our lawyers were good. They could beat shit in the state. Get shit thrown out. We didn't have no idea about the feds coming to arrest us. We thought everything was state. We were untouchable. The feds had to come in. The state couldn't do nothing with us." That was the prevailing attitude among members, but TNT came out and shut the streets down, closing crack dens and arresting dealers, disrupting business and stopping the flow of money coming in. But that didn't stop anything in the long run. "Many in the neighborhood were afraid and said TNT was only a band aid," The Southside player says. Because with no jobs, the ghetto was still the ghetto. All the crackdown did was help to create a more resourceful, resilient breed of hustler. As the state investigated, the Supreme Team stepped up their game. But, as they say, pressure busts pipes, and Prince in all his gangsterness wasn't infallible.

A yearlong investigation of the group of alleged violent drug barons who ran a $500,000 a month crack marketplace in Queens culminated in predawn raids on March 22, 1990, that police said put an end to the last organized crack posse in that area. "That was the last of the posses," Lieutenant Michael Geraghty, the commanding officer of the Queens Narcotics major case squad said. "It is not an end to the drug problem in southeast Queens by any means. But it puts an end to the Supreme Team. Prince was known as an untouchable. I think that dispels that myth." Investigators said Prince and his henchmen regulated the area by terrorizing its inhabitants ruthlessly and ruling the streets with an iron fist. The Supreme Team brought beef to any and all, but their violent reign was over.

"Prince and them fell in March 1990 on state charges, drugs, and murder," Tuck says. His short but brutal run in the streets had come to an end. His reign consisted of capricious violence, black on black crime and the worst sustained outbreak of territorial beef in Queens' history.

"At the time of Prince's bust, Prince's main girl was Suzette. Suzette and Bimmy's wife are sisters," the Queens insider says. "Prince did not fuck with Black Just as much as he fucked with Bimmy because Blackie did not sleep in the same house as him. Bimmy and Prince lived in the same exact house." Team loyalties aside, Prince and his crew were in some serious shit. "Bing was in jail, Dahlu was in jail, Melson was in jail back and forth. Green Eyed Born was in jail and Prince was either in jail or on his way. God B was also on his way to jail or already in jail," the Queens insider says. "Preme did the last couple of years of his bid off his stash and broads."

To law enforcement authorities fighting the War on Drugs in New York City, Prince was one of the craftiest and most cunning opponents. They were out to bury him in the prison due to his criminal misdeeds. Dudes on the team saw it differently. They saw cops harassing them for nothing. "The 113th Precinct had a vendetta against us. They had it out for us. It was something real personal," Bing says. No matter the truth, the hype and propaganda machine was in effect. New York's tabloid newspapers worked overtime printing headline after headline that condemned Prince and the team as law enforcement provided tasty sounds bites for the articles.

"They are an extremely volatile group," Queens District Attorney John Santucci said. The police thought the much feared and tightly run crew had run its course, but Prince's arrest, although it took him off the street, didn't diminish his power. His incarceration only managed to increase his and the teams infamy as they battled the district attorney, taking every case to trial and costing the state a tremendous expenditure in money, resources, and manpower. With the murders coming to light, a lot of cases were stacking up, but Prince would face them all, not giving in or losing his resolve. In that way he was admirable- to the streets and police alike. As the cases grew the accusations flew.

"They made it seem like we were monsters," Bing says, "like we killed at the snap of a finger. The prosecutor said we had no regard for human life." The wave of violence unleashed under Prince was akin to a video game like *Grand Theft Auto*. Prince believed wholeheartedly in his own myth as a type of real life *Scarface*.

Lieutenant Geraghty said the Supreme Team controlled crack selling sites in and around Baisley Park Houses and along Sutphin Boulevard nearby. "We estimate that this organization has been running a $500,000 a month crack operation in Queens," he said. After the raids, Queens' detectives remembered that when they arrested Prince's uncle, Supreme, in 1987, they believed they had put the drug gang out of business. "We took the organization down from top to bottom," said an officer who worked on the case, "but Prince, the heir apparent, and a few residual members stuck around." Supreme's legacy, though muted, remained on blast in the streets of Queens, his iconic status carried on by the brutal efforts of his nephew, who forged his own legend in the process, leaving a wedge of terror and death in his wake.

The investigation into Prince's activities with the Supreme Team began in 1989 when Prince started to piece the old crews back together. He consolidated power around Baisley Projects, according to detectives who used surveillance and the cultivation of street level informants to make the case against the gang's leaders. Police said that the Supreme Team controlled six "prime crack corners," three of them on Sutphin Boulevard and three in the projects ground. "Bing had 121 and Sutphin. That shit was booming," the Queens hustler says. The other lieutenant's spots were bubbling also. It was a crack frenzy, a seller's market, as the team supplied the quota of demand, purchasing kilos and packaging them for retail sales. Police said that the Supreme Team purchased drugs from anyone willing to sell. "They bought from Colombians, Dominicans, Americans. It didn't matter, as long as the drugs were good and the price was right,"

Lieutenant Geraghty said. With Mafia-style boardroom meetings and sophisticated covert methods Prince became the ultimate symbol of inner-city success.

On March 21, 1990, 130 cops fanned out to fifteen apartments in the area for simultaneous raids. The police said that the raid netted sixteen members of the violent Queens crack ring, who ranged in age from eighteen to forty and were recruited from the neighborhood. A team of six police officers, guns drawn and in bulletproof vests, smashed the door of Prince's apartment at 223-31 110th Avenue in Laurelton shortly after 6 a.m. They found him in bed with his girlfriend. Prince, who was dressed in boxer shorts, did not reach for the shotgun that lay beside him on the bed. "We took him right out of bed," said Lieutenant Geraghty, who led the raids. "He was extremely surprised but went out of there as meek as a lamb. He did not put up any resistance and said absolutely nothing."

Prince's bail was set at $1 million after prosecutors called him a killer, but his defense attorney Richard Giampa claimed he was a community leader who sponsored bible study classes. Richard Giampa said that his client was vice president of the Justice Organization, a group that fed the homeless. State Supreme Court Justice Charles Thomas kept bail at $1 million and granted a prosecution request to examine the cash's source if the bail was met. Giampa claimed that James Quinn, Chief of the Narcotics Bureau of the Queens District Attorney's Office, was prosecuting Prince for revenge.

In September of 1989, Prince was found not guilty by a jury of a drug related murder in South Jamaica. Quinn was the trial prosecutor in that case and was promoted to Chief of the Narcotics Bureau shortly thereafter. To Prince it seemed they were obsessed with him. He faced obstacle after obstacle thrown in his path. The government wanted to put him away for life. The team's enemies were in position to orchestrate their inevitable downfall. And the enemies were turning out to be more than just law enforcement as several comrades flipped the script and turned state's evidence. Prince remained in jail, as a lot of team members did, but that didn't stop the Supreme Team. They kept operating in a less proficient, but ever more deadly way.

After beating a murder charge for the 1987 killing of a rival drug dealer in the September 1989 trial, Prince was arrested again six months later in the simultaneous morning raids. Prince was charged with running a crack ring and was also charged with his second set of murder charges in two years. He was indicted with four others in a fifteen count indictment for the savage beating deaths of the four Colombian drug dealers in Pookie's apartment in the Baisley Park housing projects. *Five Indicted in Slaughter of Drug Dealers in Queens*, The *Newsday* headline read on July 13, 1990. Queens Executive Assistant Attorney Phillip Foglia, who headed the eight month investigation, along with Police Lieutenant Phillip Pansarella said the victims were beaten to death because their assailants were afraid that gunshots would attract too much attention at the housing projects.

The Queens District Attorney's office said that Prince ordered the killings from jail because profits were down. They also contended that he operated his drug empire by telephone using code words to direct his underlings. The state was pulling out all the stops in their attempt to bury Prince and the Supreme Team. They called it "taking back the streets," but in the courts the juries would decide otherwise. "Prince was being charged with ordering a quadruple homicide from prison. He was also charged with being a kingpin. The state had wiretap evidence and everything," the Queens hustler says. It didn't look good for Prince's crew.

"The killings occurred between July 15 and July 31 of 1989," Queens District Attorney Santucci said. The exact date was unknown, but the bodies began appearing in large plastic bags in different locations throughout Queens. The first body was discovered on July 31, 1989, the second four days later, and the third was not discovered until January 20, 1990. The dead men were never identified because their bodies were too badly decomposed. Police believed that four people were killed, but only three bodies were found. They were described in court papers as South American drug dealers who walked into a trap as they brought eight kilograms of cocaine to the Supreme Team, only to be murdered and robbed. Prosecutors said Prince instructed his gun thugs to rob the Colombians of the $200,000 worth of cocaine and dispose of the bodies.

While being held in jail on those charges, some of Prince's co-defendants agreed to cooperate with Queens District Attorney Santucci's office. They provided information to the grand jury that indicted Prince and four other men who had allegedly carried out his orders to kill the Columbian drug dealers. To make matters worse, Puerto Rican Righteous was arrested and held on charges that he tried to kill three police officers in an unrelated incident. As other Supreme Team members turned against Prince, so did his main man Puerto Rican Righteous. He agreed to testify against Prince in exchange for a promise of a sentence of eight to sixteen years in jail on the attempted murder charges. Everything was closing in on Prince and the Supreme Team.

"They got arrested March of 1990 for the state," Bing says. "Teddy was on the run. Tuck had a state beef. That case started from Righteous and Pookie. I don't know which one was first. Pookie used heroin heavy. He caught a body, beat the case, came home, and got down with Prince. He caught a hand to hand, went to cop some heroin, got caught up in that shit. Warrant pops up. He started giving info up on the team. He was supposed to be a loyal soldier. Anyone that is a drug user is a liability. They can't hold their own weight. Righteous wasn't a drug user but his reason for telling was that Prince had sex with his wife while he was in jail." The original member disagrees, "Puerto Rican Righteous snitched because he felt he needed to, not because Prince fucked his wife. His wife was straight crazy. She started a beef between Dahlu and Righteous alleging the same thing. I keep it 100 percent when someone snitches. For some reason they always try to come up with an excuse for why they told, and nine times out of ten the only reason they told is because they couldn't do time." Whatever the reasons, the team was crumbling in on itself as others helped to hasten their demise.

"Cat led the federal authorities to believe that I was responsible for numerous homicides," Prince said. "These lies brought major attention from law enforcement toward the Supreme Team. He also told them that I assisted him in the killings of his enemies, when in fact he manipulated and used Puerto Rican Righteous to do his bidding behind my back. Cat, Mike Bones, and Righteous all knew that I was the next big fish the state and federal authorities wanted to hook. When all three of them flipped, they pointed their fingers at me for crimes they conspired to commit without my knowledge." The drug game breeds larceny, and with all the vipers in one basket, one was bound to get bit. The worst was still to come.

Law enforcement, acting on tips from their snitches, drained Baisley Park Pond and found ten dead bodies. They were working furiously to connect all these murders to Prince and the team. The NYPD had a full court press on the team. "You can be violent and as long as people don't speak about it, it's a good thing," Bing says. "That's how you don't get charged with certain things. The less people knew about you the better. Some people didn't care; they wanted people to fear them. They wanted people to know what they did." In the streets reputations were paramount, without one, dudes were nothing.

Assistant District Attorney Eugene Kelly called Prince the mastermind behind the Supreme Team which controlled the drug trade in the Jamaica section of the borough. Kelly said that he planned to call the bodyguard and chief of security for the Supreme Team, Puerto Rican Righteous, who would describe how the four Colombians were tricked into coming to Baisley Projects with cocaine to sell, and how they were each systematically beaten to death, their bodies put into plastic bags, and dumped. Puerto Rican Righteous would be the star witness against his former comrades, spinning the stories to lessen his culpability and maximize others. He was a grand story teller on the stand, a super snitch, and a professional rat.

The quadruple murder trial started on February 6, 1991. Prince's case was severed from his co-defendants. Judge Lawrence Finnegan denied Prince's request to throw out the murder indictment. Prince argued that the grand jurors had not been told of the cooperation agreement his alleged accomplices, Puerto Rican Righteous and Serious, had reached with the District Attorney's Office in exchange for their testimony. Mr. Santucci's office promised the two witnesses who testified before the Queens grand jury that it would make recommendations for reduced sentences on other cases pending against them. Puerto Rican Righteous was still eligible to be prosecuted for his participation in the killings if he didn't fulfill his part in the agreement, the judge determined. "In view of the strength of the people's case in the grand jury and the fact that the witness is still subject to prosecution, I hold that the people's failure to inform the grand jurors of the cooperation would not have materially influenced the grand jury investigation," the judge said.

The apartment at 116-80 Guy R. Brewer Boulevard where Pookie lived "was a real house of horrors. We found handcuffs, ropes and blood at the scene. It was virtually a slaughterhouse," Assistant District Attorney Foglia said. Police were led to the apartment by an informer's tip. "The fact is these four people were slaughtered," Queens District Attorney Santucci said. "They were handcuffed, gagged, strangled, and then they bashed their skulls." Prince was charged with ordering the murders from his jail cell. He was also charged with criminal possession of drugs. The identities of the victims were never determined. A fourth man was killed, but the body was never found, and police had only the word of Puerto Rican Righteous that the murder happened.

"Prince was back and forth fighting murder cases. They called him Mr. Untouchable in the papers because every single case he beat at trial," the Queens hustler says. "The quadruple murder joint didn't look good for the team, but they still took it to trial."

Puerto Rican Righteous, who was convicted of conspiracy to murder three police officers, testified that Prince telephoned him from Rikers Island or the Bronx House of Detention sometime between July 15 and July 31, 1989, and ordered him to set up a fake drug deal with the Colombians, murder them, and dispose of their bodies, because the dealers refused to sell more than three kilos of cocaine at a time to his organization. Puerto Rican Righteous testified that he watched as several other hit men bound and gagged the drug dealers, and then stabbed, garroted, and beat them to death with hammers. Another Supreme Team member, Serious, who was convicted of armed robbery, testified that Prince told him he ordered the murders. Serious appeared to be unruffled when he testified that Prince just smiled when one of the hit men described how the drug dealers were beaten with bats and choked to death. "The majority of that shit they say on the stand is true," the Queens hustler says. "You be gritting on those muthafuckas, mad as shit because that shit is true."

When Serious was scheduled to testify for the prosecution, his brother William received communications of threats to himself and his family if Serious testified. In anticipation of his testimony, his wife and child had been relocated. In a taped conversation with William before the trial and after the relocation, Prince noted that Serious had "sent them away," but pointed out to William, "He ain't send you away, he ain't send his moms and them, you know what I'm saying. If you notice, Robin's still staying in Baisley. If I really wanted to do anything to anybody, it would be a snap of a finger."

The security at the State Supreme Court in Kews Garden was intense as Serious and Puerto Rican Righteous testified against their former cohorts. Serious testified at the state murder trial that Prince confessed to the entire crime and showed him where the bodies were dropped. "When Prince was on trial in the state in 1991, a guy named Serious, who was a childhood friend of Prince, testified against him," Tuck says. "The day after Serious took the witness stand, two of his family members were murdered." *Two Found Dead after Relative Testifies, The New York Times* headline ran on April 19, 1991.

Police said there was a "strong possibility" that the victims were killed because of the witnesses' cooperation with the prosecution. A police spokesman, Captain Stephen Davis, said that Serious' relatives, Clifton Carrington and his daughter Robin Carrington, had both been stabbed multiple times, the father ten times and the daughter twenty, and that Robin had also been strangled. The two were found about 11:30 a.m. on Friday, April 18, 1991, in an apartment at Baisley Projects. Captain Davis said that Mr. Carrington was found in his underwear and that his daughter was naked. "They will do tests to see if she was sexually assaulted," Captain Davis said.

Law enforcement officials said they believed the stabbing deaths were an attempt by Prince or his organization to intimidate Serious. Serious' attorney, Donald Schechter, refused to say whether Serious was informed of the deaths. Asked if Serious was afraid to continue testifying, the attorney only said, "Does he look upset?" Serious continued testifying against Prince and the team. Prosecutor Eugene Kelly said that Serious was "very upset" when informed of the killings. "The Carrington's were offered protection but declined," Kelly said. Some relatives of Serious received protection from the Queens District Attorney's Office, but the Carringtons had not. The spokesman from the District Attorney's Office said, "I understand the two victims declined an offer to be in the witness protection program." Police reported that Ms. Carrington had been stabbed numerous times, her head was covered with pantyhose and a pillowcase, her hands were bound, and the first letter of Prince's nickname, P, was allegedly carved into her torso.

The murders first appeared to be part of a bungled robbery. The bodies were mutilated, and the apartment ransacked. But when police began focusing their investigation on the Queens courtroom where Prince was on trial, it all became clear. "There's a lot riding on this case," the Queens detective said. "This puts all the witnesses and their families on notice: 'Don't come forward.'" The spokeswoman for the Medical Examiner's office declined to comment on how long the victims might have been dead before their bodies were discovered. Law enforcement authorities said the Carringtons, who lived in the drug plagued Baisley Park Houses in South Jamaica, were killed on the orders of Prince as a message to others who would testify against the powerful drug kingpin. A law enforcement source told *Newsday* that the manner in which the bodies were mutilated appeared to be the signature of the accused drug kingpin.

Due to the killings, Justice Lawrence Finnegan, who was presiding at Prince's six week old trial, ordered the jury sequestered. The jurors had been allowed to go home each night, but now the judge sequestered them at a hotel. The judge did not tell the jurors why he was sequestering them. It appeared that he was concerned that if the jurors weren't sequestered, they might learn from news reports that people linked to Serious had been killed, and that this would prejudice the case against Prince. The judge didn't want Prince to have any reasons to overturn the case on appeal.

The jurors were startled in the late afternoon of April 19, 1991, when Finnegan ordered that they spend the next several days sequestered in a hotel. "I beg you to trust my judgment," Finnegan told the twelve jurors and five alternates. "I know it's horrible to be whisked away like this, but you will be surprised at how pleasant this will be." The judge refused to give the jurors a reason for the sequestering and said, "I beg you not to speculate on that." After the killings, homicide detectives received an anonymous phone call from someone claiming that the woman was a prostitute and that she'd recently had an encounter with a client and robbed him. The caller said the woman had been threatened over the robbery and that the killing was in retaliation.

Richard Giampa, Prince's lawyer, claimed that Robin Carrington was a crack user and prostitute who, along with three other women, robbed an elderly client. She left her house keys in his car, and the client went back to her apartment and killed her and her father. Giampa also claimed that the Queens District Attorney's Office was "taking unfair advantage of the situation" by implying that the slayings were related to Serious' testimony against Prince. Raymond O'Donnell, a police department spokesman, said that investigators had found markings on the bodies, but that they could not interpret what they meant. The prosecutor claimed the markings were a P for Prince. "Everything is still very much open," the Queens detective said. "If this was the reason for the killings, it would be the latest of several instances in recent years in which a witness in a criminal case had been menaced or killed in Queens." Detectives were exploring the possible connection between the murders and Serious' aid to the prosecution. But in the end it didn't matter.

Alleged Druglord Is Acquitted of Ordering 4 Killed, read the *Newsday* headline on May 8, 1991. Six days after closing arguments, Prince was acquitted of ordering the kidnapping and brutal murders of four Colombian drug dealers while he was in jail on another charge. As the jury forewoman announced the not guilty verdict on each of the fifteen counts of murder, kidnapping and robbery, Prince smiled and nodded, and his supporters and family members burst into tears. "Thank you very much. God bless you," Prince said to the jurors. As the verdict was being read, the lead prosecutor in the case, Queens District Attorney Eugene Kelly, appeared stunned, his head bowed toward his crossed arms.

"I am a little disappointed," he said. "The jury being sequestered so long hurt us." Mr. Santucci said he was "startled and dismayed" at the verdict. Three of the twelve jurors said that they felt Prince was guilty, but that the evidence was too weak to convict him. The jury of four men and eight women had been sequestered for four weeks.

"The jury speaks the truth," Prince's attorney said. Although Prince still faced drug trafficking charges and remained in jail, Giampa said he now hoped to win bail.

One juror, Bozena Dobrzynska, said she didn't find Serious' testimony credible. "The parameters of the law limited it to that, the acquittal. I don't believe there was total innocence," she said.

Juror Lucia Garcia said, "We just felt there was not enough evidence on the district attorney's side. Our gut feelings were that he was guilty, but there was no evidence. We felt our hands were tied." This was the second time in less than two years that Prince had been acquitted of murder. The mantle of Mr. Untouchable still held true.

"Prince was acquitted of the quadruple homicides, and the wiretaps were thrown out," Tuck says. "The state was defeated again. They had no choice but to let him go. Prince beat five bodies in the state. Every time Prince was charged with murder, he was acquitted. They taped his phones, and he got the tapes thrown out." To the streets and law enforcement, Prince was untouchable, a certified gangster. He talked the talk and walked the walk, backing it up with actions and deeds, not hollow words, weak pronouncements, or fake bravado. He was the real deal, all that the kids from the streets of the Southside of Jamaica, Queens, aspired to be, a true gangster who stuck to the Code of Omerta.

In the hood kids looked up to drug lords like Prince. Their heroes were the gangsters that held court on the city's blocks, the kings of the ghetto who ruled their projects through violence and gunplay, living the fast life and getting that easy dope money. To youngsters in the inner-city, that lifestyle was a ticket out of poverty. The block runners, d-boys, and four corner hustlers were on a paper chase. But the collateral damage the Supreme Team's business tactics incurred was tremendous. The Queens hustler sums up the whole era and what it was all about, "Drug dealing, killing, more drug dealing, more killing, cops getting murdered, parole officers getting murdered for violating niggas, crooked police getting paid off, police issuing beat downs, families getting murdered because other family members are testifying in court, you know, basic hood shit."

PAPPY
MASON

PRINCE

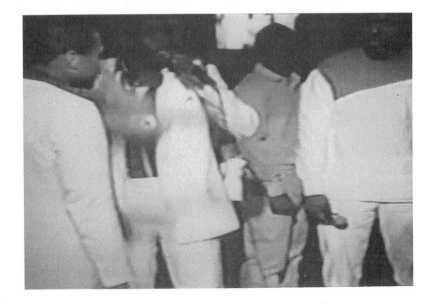

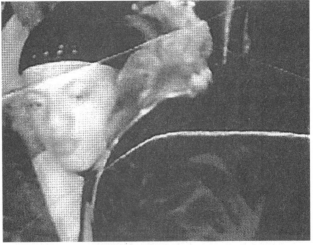

KENNETH "SUPREME" McGRIFF

GERALD MILLER

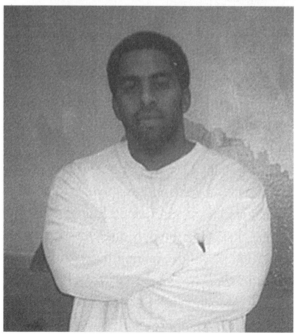

PROPERTY OF
E MONEYBAGS

PROPERTY OF
E MONEYBAGS

Kenneth
Supreme
McGriff

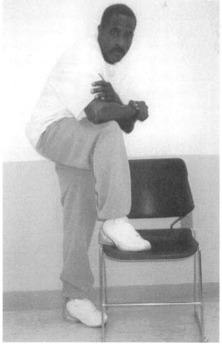

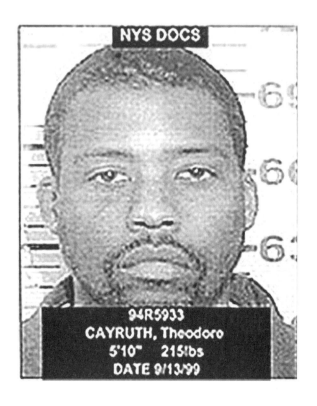

NYS DOCS

94R5933
CAYRUTH, Theodore
5'10"   215lbs
DATE 9/13/99

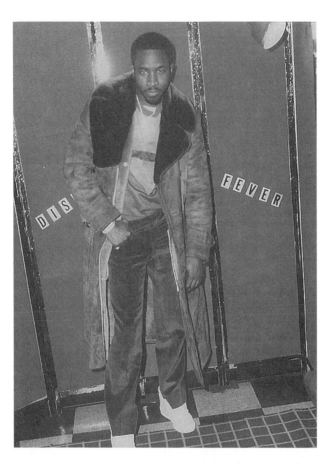

CHAPTER 6
THE FEDERAL CASE

"The first verse is just a dose of the shit that I'm on Consider this the first chapter in the ghetto's Qur'an I know a lot of niggas that get doe like Remmy and Joe And Prince and Righteous from Hillside with the mole on his nose."
— 50 Cent, Ghetto Qur'an from Guess Who's Back (2000)

"The story of Southeast Queens and of any inner-city neighborhood is that hustlers almost always end up paying for their dominance on the streets with their lives or with lifelong prison sentences."
— Ethan Brown, Queens Reigns Supreme

"One violent summer under Prince's reign, Supreme Team members butchered four Colombian cocaine distributors in a Baisley Park apartment and then stuffed them into garbage bags. Yet few in the Supreme Team were worried about the prospect of getting caught, law enforcement were preoccupied with Mafia warfare and federal drug related prison sentences were still lenient.
But that was about to change."
— Vibe Magazine

After Prince and his co-defendants were acquitted of the kidnapping and brutal murders of the Colombian drug dealers in the State Supreme Court in Queens, the feds were ready to step in and handle the deadly drug crew. "In October 1991, the feds started to investigate the team, because Prince was acquitted again in the state," Tuck says. While the U.S. Attorney's Office continued its investigation under the Federal Racketeer Influenced and Corrupt Organizations Act, state prosecutors were busy preparing yet another case against Prince and the Supreme Team on charges of conspiracy to sell cocaine. The feds weren't taking any chances though; they were ready to supersede the state charges with a federal indictment against the team.

Federal prosecutors were hoping to bring "conspiracy to run a criminal enterprise" charges against Prince and the team. Those charges in federal court carried a maximum term of life in prison without parole. Prince fully expected the case to go federal, so his lawyer started politicking. They figured why should they face two cases, the federal RICO act case and the Queens drug conspiracy case, at the same time. "The conspiracy case in Queens depends on the same witnesses that the jury did not find credible in the last case," said Richard Giampa. He knew the state didn't have a case and was ready to face the feds. So instead of fighting both cases at once, Prince's lawyer was trying to get the state case thrown out.

"The state called the feds when Serious' two family members were murdered, and the state had no choice but to let Prince go. The feds agreed to take the case from the state. There was never a federal investigation of Prince, me, or my co-defendants while we were on the street," Tuck says. "They just put all that on the team to get the feds to take the case because the state was going to have to let everyone go. Prince was acquitted of the murders, and the wiretaps were all thrown out. All the feds had were the snitches who were saying anything to save their own asses. Prince beat four or five bodies in the state. They called him Mr. Untouchable in the papers because every single case he beat at trial. That's what made the feds come and get us. It's called the Silver Platter Doctrine. The state said we can't do nothing with them. You take them. They handed us over to the feds on a silver platter."

On January 23, 1992, *The New York Times* headline read *Prince Indicted on Federal Drug Charges*. The feds indicted Prince and his crew on a fourteen count racketeering indictment that included counts for drug related murders, drug conspiracy, and drug dealing. "Fourteen counts, nine murders," Tuck says of the indictment his name was on.

Twelve people described as members of the Supreme Team were indicted in a string of violence that included at least nine murders. "Prince's fall came later but was much steeper than Supreme's," Ethan Brown says. "He was indicted by the feds in 1992 in a sprawling case that involved charges ranging from CCE to first degree murder." Investigators described the Supreme Team as one of the deadliest of the trafficking rings that plagued Queens at the height of the crack epidemic.

U.S. Attorney Andrew J. Maloney noted that the indictment resulted from a joint investigation by the FBI and the New York Police

Department. The federal authorities said that the ring sold $500,000 of crack a month and operated in the vicinity of the Baisley Park housing projects and other sites in Queens, including the yard of Intermediate School 72. "The feds can make anything look however they want," Tuck says. "It's the United States of America versus you. The whole fucking United States versus you. Their resources are unlimited. Why do you think the feds have a 99 percent conviction rate?"

By now Prince had been in state jail for three years but hadn't been convicted of anything the media or government claimed he did. They said he had victims tied up, beaten to death, and dumped in empty lots. They said he was a criminal mastermind running his drug empire from prison. The nine murders cited in the federal racketeering charge included the Colombians involved in Prince's acquittal on state charges. U.S. Attorney Maloney said federal law permitted those slayings to be included in the racketeering charges. "The feds were recharging Prince with murders he already beat," Tuck says. "That shit was unbelievable." From the early 1980s until 1987, Prince was second in command of the Supreme Team to the ring's founder, Supreme, the indictment charged. It said Prince became the principle leader in 1987 when Supreme went to prison on the CCE charge.

Besides Gerald "Prince" Miller, the other defendants were identified as Wilfredo "C-Just" Arroyo, Roy "Pookie" Hale, David "Bing" Robinson, Shannon Jimenez, Harry "Big C" Hunt, Fabio Arciniega, Julio Hernandez, Waverly "Teddy" Coleman, Ronald "Tuck" Tucker, Cynthia Brown, and Raymond "Ace" Robinson. The substantive narcotics distribution charges against the defendants focused on the period from December 1989 to March 1990 during which the state was monitoring the gang's activity with wiretaps. During that period, the Supreme Team was alleged to have conducted its business in the Baisley Park housing project. The feds said the Supreme Team terrorized and held the projects hostage. "With the federal indictment, the Supreme Team is finished," the Queens detective said. Prince's arrest and the team's would mark the end of a frightening time in the history of New York City. But detractors abounded.

Prince's attorney, mob lawyer Susan Kellman, called the case a "spite prosecution." She said, "The feds are conducting a vendetta because he was acquitted of the homicide charges in Queens. Every accusation made against Gerald has proven to be untrue." Kellman said her client had nothing to do with the murders. "I have asked for the autopsy reports ten times, and they just don't have them because it is just not true. They are trying to create a lot of sensationalism over what they believe is the last big Queens drug dealer." The feds were kicking the hype machine into overdrive while the New York City's tabloid newspapers ate it up by running Supreme Team headlines everyday and making Prince out to be the worst of the worst, a black anti-Christ. But to the hoodsters, he was a gangster god who stuck to the street code and carried his weight.

"A lot of dudes escaped that shit," Tuck says. "Their names ain't gonna come up nowhere, because dudes stood up, and their names didn't come into play. It's a lot of dudes." Most of the team members held strong. In the Southside of Jamaica, Queens, no snitching was the rule. Street rumors circulated that some of the team members that didn't get caught up in the federal indictments were hot. Team members didn't help it any by throwing out accusations.

Allegedly, it was put out that Black Just and Bimmy were snitches. "Anybody's reasoning for calling Black Just and Bimmy rats was straight up bullshit," the original member says. "Who did they tell on? Not anyone that can be named, not anyone on the team. Besides that, nobody could ever produce any proof of these allegations. Dudes make up all sorts of allegations about people. Some dudes hate anyone who is close to Preme. Black Just and Bimmy never told on anyone that I know of. Dudes never hated on original team members as much as they hated on members that did not start doing their thing until after Preme caught his case." When a big case comes about, the streets see anyone who is not caught up in it as a snitch. Sometimes that is true, but not in all cases. Some dudes don't get caught up, because people don't snitch.

"The way I grew up, and the people that I looked up to showed me morals and principles," Bing says. "They told me when you go out to hustle you hold your own; death before dishonor. You get arrested you closed your mouth and kept it shut and went to jail."

In Queens, being a stand up guy was important. It was a born and bred quality. "Stand up men are born with identifiable characteristics, meaning that true gangsters are born, not made," Prince said, and the core of the Supreme Team were stand up guys.

"That's why so many people came to support us at the state and federal trials," Bing says. "If not for the fed case, we would have retired. We would have flipped that illegal money, opened up stuff that could help our people in the neighborhood." But the feds weren't about to let that happen.

Assistant U.S. Attorney Leslie Caldwell charged in court papers that Prince and the Supreme Team had "a considerable track record of violent retribution." She said that in his previous trial, the father-in-law and sister-in-law of a key witness were killed the day after he testified, the letter P carved into their torsos. Ms. Caldwell asked the judge for an anonymous jury because of the Supreme Team's penchant for violence. As jury selection began under intense security in Brooklyn federal court, U.S. District Court Judge Raymond Dearie ordered that the jurors' names, addresses, and workplaces be kept secret to protect them from possible harm or intimidation. While Serious' relative's murders had not been solved, federal prosecutors charged that associates of Prince would not hesitate to intimidate jurors or retaliate against former accomplices testifying against him in the new trial.

In ordering the jury to be anonymous, Judge Dearie said the danger Prince and his co-defendants posed "was aptly demonstrated." The charged and uncharged counts created a circus atmosphere for the Supreme Team trial, and the government gave Prince and his co-defendants the Hannibal Lector treatment. "The court concludes that strong reasons exist to believe that the jury needs protection in this case," the judge said. "Not only are the defendants alleged to be dangerous individuals charged with large scale drug trafficking and numerous violent offenses, but the evidence also strongly suggests attempts by Gerald Miller and his associates to interfere with the judicial process." During the prelude to the trial, the judge reported that Prince, who served as his own lawyer in pretrial proceedings, was making carefully orchestrated maneuvers to delay the trial as long as possible so that witnesses could be eliminated or intimidated into not testifying against him.

"We were indicted in January 1992, but it took a while before we went to trial," Tuck says. "Prince is a legal tactician and a hell of a chess player. Jury pools were selected and then thrown out."

The federal prosecutor Leslie Caldwell had made a career of prosecuting Queens' drug dealers. She put away Fat Cat and Pappy Mason among others. She was ruthless in her pursuit to clean up the streets of Queens. "Back then there was definitely a different level of federal prosecutors at work on these things," Ethan Brown said. "Leslie Caldwell, who prosecuted the Supreme Team was a different breed." Ms. Caldwell was a nononsense, take charge prosecutor who rose to every challenge. She attributed the Supreme Team's longevity to its unhesitating use of violence and thought that the only place for members of the team that had left a four year trail of bodies and terror in South Jamaica was in the federal penitentiary. Her job was to make sure they ended up there.

A lot of controversy swirled around the snitches in the case also, as they were the same ones used in the state cases. "Serious was cooperating, Puerto Rican Righteous was cooperating; they both testified at Prince's state case," Tuck says. "Julio Hernandez was the only one of us who had access to all the floors at MCC. Seven South was notorious for rats. Julio was on Seven South. He swore to god he wasn't telling. He was coming to our co-defendant meetings. He's sitting there in the room going back and telling them, a spy in the camp. My main co-defendants Prince, C-Just, Shannon, Willie G, Ace- they were all on Rikers Island."

At first Julio held true to the code, but by April 1992, the crack head killer broke weak. In May he signed a formal cooperation agreement with the feds like Serious and Puerto Rican Righteous had before him. The government permitted Julio to remain housed with his co-defendants at MCC and to attend defense strategy sessions with the attorneys even after he begun cooperating with the government. In the wake of his decision to cooperate, his attorney and the Assistant U.S. Attorney discussed the possibility of separating him from his co-defendants, but that option was rejected because of concern it would signal the Supreme Team that Julio was cooperating and endanger his family. By July 2, 1992, his family had been relocated, and Julio was promptly removed from MCC.

Since Prince was arrested in 1990, local detectives said that homicides had dropped by more than 30 percent. They painted a gruesome picture of Prince and his crew. The feds contended the evidence against the team was abundant. Over 100 taped conversations between Supreme Team members were scheduled to be introduced at the trial. These were the same wiretaps that had been thrown out in the state case. It was a case of double jeopardy, but the feds didn't care. They played dirty and played to win at all costs. Prince and the Supreme Team were facing their toughest battle yet.

The trial on murder and drug racketeering charges was repeatedly delayed in federal District Court in Brooklyn. In part, the judge said, by Prince, who took an unusually active role in his defense, serving as his own lawyer when it suited him. "Prince knew what he was doing," Tuck says. "He stayed up in the law library." With his life on the line, Prince was as aggressive in court as he was in the street, even against the daunting odds set against him. Approximately 80 witnesses were set to testify including Puerto Rican Righteous, Serious, Julio, and Jaime Padro. They would expose the inner workings of the Supreme Team to the jury.

Prince was accused in the federal indictment of being the "principal leader and organizer" of the Supreme Team. Prince and the Supreme Team were charged with racketeering in violation of RICO 18 USC § 1962 (c) and with conspiracy to distribute and to possess with intent to distribute cocaine base in violation of 21 USC § 840, distribution of cocaine base in violation of 21 USC § 848, threatening violence in violation of 18 USC § 1969, and conducting financial transactions with proceeds of narcotics in violation of 18 USC § 1956 (a). There were a bunch of murders included in the case also. The feds claimed the Supreme Team was responsible for upwards of 30 homicides. The murders were mostly uncharged, more government rhetoric and accusations than actual evidence. Using the media as a forum for uncharged counts, the feds fired their volleys even before the trial began.

The battle was set- the United States of America versus the Supreme Team. Prince and the team fought the feds tooth and nail, but they were overwhelming underdogs. "Although I faced multiple life sentences for charges both untrue and trumped up, the gangster code is embedded in my DNA, so the thought of betraying my comrades and their families in order to lift the burden off me and mine, has never entered my mind," Prince said. "The cloth that I'm cut from is from the old and principled. Times have changed, and today they are more pranksters masked as gangsters. Soon they will be exposed for the cowards that they are and just maybe, the cloth of our elders will shelter us again."

The authorities insisted that not only was Prince a remorseless killer, but he also blended lethal wickedness with legal wiliness. The prosecutor, Leslie Caldwell, complained to the judge that with Prince showing the way, he and his six reputed associates who were tried with him, repeatedly obstructed the case. "The defendants led by Mr. Miller, inundated the court with stacks of motions, many of which were laughably frivolous," Ms. Caldwell said, asserting that Prince's goal was "to avoid trial" or buy time so that prosecution witnesses could be intimidated into silence. It was all a game within the game; it was American jurisprudence at its intolerable worst.

"I'm not trying to stall anything," Prince, who was described in newspapers as a slender, sharp featured young man responded at a court session. He insisted that he was simply seeking to assure that he had the best possible defense and that he had "no confidence" that his court appointed lawyer could provide it. Among other things, he said, his new lawyer Daniel Murphy was refusing to go along with Prince's strategy for fighting a major charge that alleged that most of the eleven murder victims in the case were killed at Prince's order. Prince said that he wanted to argue that one of his co-defendants "ordered these murders, not me."

Prince also had difficulties with his previous court appointed lawyer, Susan Kellman. Kellman withdrew from the case, on the eve of one of the several starting dates for the trial, after she told the judge that Prince had threatened her with physical harm during a dispute over trial tactics. Murphy said that because of a gag order the judge imposed, he could not comment on any matters relating to the case. Prince was entitled to a court appointed lawyer because he convinced the judge that he couldn't afford to pay for his defense. The once proud drug baron was now forced to do battle against the feds with a public pretender.

With money for their defense attorneys in short supply because Prince and his crew were broke, Prince reached out to the remnants of the team for funds. "Black Just and Bimmy looked out for Prince when he got busted but not cause they felt any obligation to him," the Queens insider says. "It was more of the fact that he is Preme's family, and they were only able to do what they were doing because of the Supreme banner that they had to fly. They had a very strong loyalty for and to Supreme, and they were also preoccupied with the "what if" factor. Like what if Prince beat the case again? Prince is somebody you want to stay on his good side. Babywise was not going to send Prince shit, especially if Prince tried to demand anything."

One result of the pretrial twists and turns was the unusual jury-salvaging session that occurred. A jury was initially selected for the trial several days before it was to open on March 15, when Susan Kellman suddenly withdrew. Judge Dearie appointed Murphy and told the jurors to return for the opening arguments. Then the judge announced a further adjournment to April 19th to give Murphy more time to prepare. The judge tried to retain the selected jurors despite the unusually disruptive jury service it would entail to avoid a third round of jury selection. An earlier jury was close to being picked in January, but the selection was postponed at the last minute.

It was still unclear who would be speaking for Prince at trial. Prince emphatically and emotionally insisted to Judge Dearie that he did not want Murphy to represent him and asked the judge to appoint yet another public pretender. "This person is not the right guy for me," declared Prince. But Judge Dearie refused to replace Murphy. "You ain't my lawyer man. Stay off my case," Prince exploded at Murphy during a court session, his obscenity laced outburst in sharp contrast to the calm, lawyer like language that was conspicuous in his previous court appearances. Prince was fucked up for the federal case because of the two state murder cases defenses he had paid for previously. He went from having popular guns and drugs lawyers to being represented by public pretenders. That was the feds tactic. Drain his money by trying him again, again and again.

Prosecutor Says Parole Officer Aided Drug Gang Leading to Dealer's Killing, The New York Times headline ran on April 22, 1993. The prosecutor asserted at the opening of Prince and the Supreme Team's trial that Prince had two moles in the State Parole Division, one of them a parole officer who provided information that led to the 1987 slaying of another dealer. "In April of 1993 our trial finally started," Tuck says. Joyce London, Prince's new lawyer called the trial a "government vendetta" against a man who was "no murderer." Assistant U.S. Attorney Mark Ressler said Prince was the leader of the Supreme Team "a vicious drug gang that turned a neighborhood in South Jamaica into a killing field."

Ressler did not identify the two women Parole Division employees who he said were moles for Prince. A spokesman for the Parole Division, David Ernst, also refused to identify the women or discuss their roles in the trial, only saying that the two employees resigned from the agency in 1990 after non-criminal disciplinary charges were brought against them. Ressler told the jury of seven men and five women in the heavily guarded courtroom that Prince obtained information from the parole employees after Lorenzo "Fat Cat" Nichols asked Prince for help in finding two dealers he wanted to kill.

"He reached out to Prince," Ressler said, and Prince found the two men. As a result, members of Fat Cat's crew killed one of the men, Isaac Bolden and wounded the other, Henry Bolden. To make matters worse, *Newsday* reported that convicted drug kingpin Lorenzo "Fat Cat" Nichols would re-emerge from hiding to testify that Prince had arranged the assassinations for him. *Turncoat Drug Kingpin to Testify; Fat Cat to Sing about Ex-Ally,* the *Newsday* headline read on October 1, 1992. Fat Cat claimed that the two men, cousins Isaac and Henry Bolden, had stolen more than $100,000 in money and drugs from him. Prince, according to Fat Cat, assisted him in the matter.

"Cat tells the feds that while we were in jail together in the Brooklyn House, I expressed my involvement in several crimes," Prince said. "He told the feds these lies to satisfy his cooperation agreement. He knew that shit he was telling them wasn't true. I was very careful about anything that came out of my mouth around him." To obtain the whereabouts of the Bolden cousins, Prince allegedly sought the help of the New York state parole officer he had on the payroll. She got the addresses of the Bolden cousins for Prince who passed them onto Fat Cat. According to government documents, handwritten notes of such addresses were recovered in a raid of a Supreme Team apartment, and Fat Cat confirmed to law enforcement that Prince arranged the assassinations for him.

Defense lawyers told the jurors that Fat Cat would testify for the prosecution in the trial, and they denounced him and the other major prosecution witnesses, who were all admitted drug traffickers and murderers, as untrustworthy. Assistant U.S. Attorney Ressler countered by saying that police wiretaps of the defendants' conversations would support the testimony. Because of this situation, Fat Cat has been forever branded a snitch, but maybe it's not so black and white. Fat Cat never testified and even Supreme spoke on Cat being a rat. "I wouldn't say that," Supreme said. "If he did tell, he held a lot back." But Prince has maintained his stance and accusations, even saying in Don Diva magazine that he was writing a book on the matter. A lot of the other snitches did testify in open court which the paperwork proves.

Puerto Rican Righteous testified that his parole officer, Ina McGriff, asked him out on a date, arranged an affair between one of her co-workers and Prince, and provided the two men with confidential information that led to two murders. Suspicious that she might be an undercover FBI agent when she asked him for a date, Puerto Rican Righteous said he sought advice from Prince before accepting her invitation to dinner. "Go with her," Prince told him. "If you have sex with her, they can't make a case." Puerto Rican Righteous said he followed the advice- including a sexual interlude- and their affair turned into a business relationship that was profitable for both the parole officer and Supreme Team.

Puerto Rican Righteous said McGriff knew who he and Prince were. On his first date with her after he was paroled in 1986, Puerto Rican Righteous said McGriff asked him if he needed a gun and told him, "I know who you are. I know who Prince is. I know you guys are getting paid and making a lot of money. I have no problem with that. One hand washes the other."

Puerto Rican Righteous reported back to Prince that he believed McGriff could be trusted. "She seems legitimate," he told Prince. "She is dirty, and we can swing with her because she is dirty." Puerto Rican Righteous testified that McGriff was in the business of selling fake drivers licenses for $100 each and had access to computers at both the Department of Motor Vehicles and the Parole Division. He testified that Ina McGriff and Ronnie Younger, a secretary in the Parole Division who became Prince's girl, often provided the Supreme Team with information from Parole Division files.

McGriff and Younger were fired in 1990 because of their corrupt relationships with Puerto Rican Righteous and Prince. The two women secretly pleaded guilty to federal racketeering charges and agreed to testify against Prince in exchange for leniency in their sentencing. Puerto Rican Righteous said that on at least five occasions in 1987, he sought McGriff's assistance in tracking down rival drug dealers targeted for death. He testified that McGriff used a Parole Division computer when finding the names and addresses of relatives of the men. As a result, two of the men were slain and a third was critically wounded. One of the victims was Jamel Page, a Supreme Team associate, who was lured to a

Brooklyn rooftop and shot to death. "Ina popped up with a sheet from parole showing he was cooperating with the Parole Division," Puerto Rican Righteous told the jury. Ina McGriff was the next to testify.

She testified that she became an informant for the Supreme Team-supplying information that resulted in two killings- in exchange for sex and thousands of dollars from gang members. McGriff, who worked for the State Division of Parole, Queens Office from 1984 to 1989, testified that she met Puerto Rican Righteous when she was assigned as his parole officer while he was in a work release program in April 1987. She said she quickly found out that Puerto Rican Righteous violated conditions of his work release program, but rather than order him returned to prison, she began socializing with him. She said he told her he was an enforcer for the Supreme Team's leader, Prince. Puerto Rican Righteous told her that Prince wanted to meet Ronnie Younger, a friend of McGriff's who worked in the Queens office. The foursome met and went to a hotel near LaGuardia Airport where she had sex with Puerto Rican Righteous, and her friend had sex with Prince.

McGriff testified that she was soon introduced to several members of the gang and regularly visited Prince and Puerto Rican Righteous at the housing project. She said Puerto Rican Righteous frequently gave her cash, totaling tens of thousands of dollars. In exchange she sold gang members illegal driver's licenses, bought them ammunition using her badge, and even cosigned a loan for Prince for a $70,000 BMW. McGriff testified about the murder of Isaac Bolden. She said Fat Cat asked her, through Prince, to obtain information about Bolden. She did and was paid $3000 for it. In November 1987 when she learned that gang member Jamel Page was being used as an informant, she told Prince fearing that Page would inform authorities about her dealings with the gang. Page was summarily executed on a Brooklyn rooftop, prosecutors said.

During the cross examination by Prince's lawyer, Joyce London, McGriff testified that she was suspended after her ties to the gang were uncovered but was later reinstated and given a settlement of more than $8,000. McGriff told London that federal authorities had offered to put her in the Federal Witness Protection program, but she refused. However, she accepted $16,000 they had given her to relocate. Ronnie Younger didn't testify at the trial. But newspaper accounts had her agreeing to plead guilty. The trial showed that Prince not only controlled the streets ruthlessly, but he corrupted the law enforcement establishment with ease. He was not above using whatever assets he had at hand. His scheming was "CIA like."

As with most true crime stories, the truth is stranger than fiction, but this case had a particular twist. Tuck explains, "At trial, one of the jurors went back and told another juror that this trial seems just like *New Jack City* and the jurors told the judge. The judge didn't know what *New Jack City* was about so he went out and watched the movie." Art imitating life and vice versa had come full circle as *New Jack City* was said to have been inspired by the Supreme Team and their takeover of Baisley Projects.

In the two month long Supreme Team trial, the government presented voluminous evidence including tapes and transcripts of wiretapped conversations among Supreme Team members, telephone records, fingerprint evidence, photographs of assembled Supreme Team members, firearms and ammunition, narcotics paraphernalia, and assorted documents. The government introduced evidence of numerous killings by the Supreme Team security force, including evidence that Pookie had killed a person named Dre, and various others had killed several people who were considered to be threats to the team's operations. When Gus Rivera was targeted to be killed, Big C shot him. When Rivera survived and was tracked down, Pookie was one of the gun thugs who killed Rivera. Serious testified that Prince wanted Tuck murdered for not "meeting a quota." The feds portrayed the team as murderous infighters. The fall was encompassed in one word- crack. The "don't get high on your own supply" edict rarely worked with crack, and what was once a structured crime machine built on the Mafia model became the province of paranoid killers, Prince included.

Among the government's approximately 80 witnesses at the trial were former accomplices including Ernesto "Puerto Rican Righteous" Pinella, the gang's chief of security, Julio Hernandez, a member of the security force, Trent "Serious" Morris, the gang's primary drug courier, Toni McGee, a gang associate, and Ina McGriff, a corrupt former New York state parole officer. Scores of federal and state law enforcement officers testified about the discovery of homicide victims killed by the Supreme Team, crime scene analysis, surveillances, and other investigative activities. The evidence was extensive.

The court found that when Prince was released from prison in the spring of 1989, he began to rebuild the Supreme Team and regained control of two of its most lucrative retail locations known as spots. The reorganized gang under Prince included C-Just as second in command, Big C as Prince's bodyguard, Puerto Rican Righteous as head of security, and Pookie, Shannon, and Julio as security workers. Tuck and Teddy managed the retail spots and supervised crews of workers. Long time gang member Bing helped supervise the drug operations and kept records. Ace assisted in arranging cocaine purchases, provided security during drug transactions, supervised the processing of cocaine into crack, and delivered crack to sales locations.

During that period, the Supreme Team conducted its business in the Baisley Park apartment of Bing's mother. Tuck, Teddy, and Bing would deliver to the apartment the moneys received at the retail spots they supervised. Prince and Serious would negotiate cocaine deals by telephone with Willie G, a supplier who had Colombian connections. Serious and Ace would then drive to Willie G's apartment with money to purchase kilogram quantities of cocaine. "Willie G was just a coke connect," Bing says. "He was like a middleman. Had Colombians he was fucking with. Went to trial for supplying drugs to Prince. He was Serious' connect. Serious used to get the drugs from him; got 30 years because of Serious." The cocaine would be brought back to Bing's apartment where it was processed as crack, packaged, and given to C-Just, Bing, Tuck, or Teddy, who in turn arranged for its sale by street level employees.

The gang also resumed its use of violence and homicide. The government presented evidence at trial, not all of which resulted in convictions, of homicides committed both prior to the Supreme Team's 1987 shutdown and after its 1989 renaissance. The court found that Gus Rivera was a Supreme Team member who introduced the gang's leaders to some of his Colombian suppliers. According to trial testimony, four of these Colombian drug traffickers were robbed of their cocaine and brutally murdered in July 1989 by Prince, C-Just, Pookie, Big C, and Shannon. But the jury refused to find that the defendants had killed the four unidentified Colombian suppliers as alleged in the indictment. Other than testimony that two of these men were known as Fernando and George, the government was unable to present evidence as to their identities, and their bodies were never identified. The jury found that these murders, alleged as RICO predicate acts, were not proven beyond a reasonable doubt. The murder of Gus Rivera was not proven in court either.

At the Supreme Team trial, the evidence included numerous conversations among its members. During the investigation of the Supreme Team by state authorities, pen registers were used on telephones at the apartments of Supreme Team members or their relatives to identify the numbers dialed from these locations. In August 1989, state agents installed a pen register on the home telephone of Polly Douglas, the mother of Shannon. The pen register indicated that the telephone was used to place many calls to telephones where Supreme Team members lived or conducted illegal business, and that several calls were received from prisons where gang members were incarcerated. A wiretap became operational in December

143

1989 on this phone which intercepted discussions of the Supreme Team narcotics trafficking between the Douglas home and Prince's home where the state obtained authorization to place another wiretap. The wiretap on Prince's phone became operational in January 1990. This wiretap intercepted the conversations of Prince, C-Just, Pookie, Bing, Ace, Teddy, and other Supreme Team members as they discussed narcotics trafficking.

State agents explained at trial that they had been investigating the Supreme Team for some years and had exhausted its battery of traditional investigative techniques with little significant success. Using normal techniques, the state had been unable to penetrate the Supreme Team or gain sufficient admissible evidence against any members other than those at the lowest echelons. The Supreme Team's leaders had insulated themselves from police contact through extensive use of bodyguards and lookouts, and when the state applied for wiretap authorization, it had yet to identify all of the upper and middle level members. In fact, they missed notable Supreme Team members like Black Just, Babywise, Dahlu, Green Eyed Born, God B, and Bimmy all together.

The state had procured the cooperation of one accomplice, but it hesitated to attempt other undercover infiltration because of the extreme violence in which the Supreme Team engaged against persons it believed were threats to its security. The state was unable to obtain physical evidence whose existence could be gleaned from conversations intercepted by wiretap, given the difficulty of infiltration by undercover officers, and the unreliability of cooperating defendants. For example, Pookie at one time agreed to cooperate, and then at various times refused to cooperate; his history of homicide and drug abuse further decreased his reliability. Plus agents never really knew if he was a double agent working on Prince's orders to act like he was cooperating to get information on what state agents knew. It was all a grand game to Prince, full of Machiavellian flair.

Supreme even attended the trial. "Preme was released from his twelve year federal bid around February 1993, so he was home when our trial began," Tuck says. "Our trial lasted exactly two months. During the testimony of one of the defense witnesses, Preme was sitting in the audience with a dude I grew up with. While the prosecutor was cross-examining the witness, she shocked the whole courtroom by turning around and pointing to Preme in the audience and saying, 'Isn't that Supreme right there, sitting with the sunglasses on? Isn't he the founder and leader of the Supreme Team?' Of course the witness denied knowing anything about him being the leader of anything."

About the trial T recalls Supreme telling him, "I wasn't sharp enough at the time to say I'm Supreme. I'm not on trial." The accusation lingered and would have serious ramifications on Supreme later. "When I was cross-examined by the prosecutor I took the stand in my own defense," Tuck says. "The prosecutor asked me did I know Supreme. My response, 'I never saw the man before in my life until the day you pointed him out in the courtroom.'"

At the Supreme Team trial, Prince was acquitted on the possession count and the count of threatening violence. He was convicted on all of the other counts on which he was tried including racketeering, narcotics, and continuing criminal enterprise. Tuck was convicted on the RICO and narcotics conspiracy counts and on one distribution count; he was acquitted on all of the other counts against him. Pookie was convicted on the RICO and narcotics and on one possession count; he was acquitted on all other counts against him. Big C and C-Just were each acquitted on one count of possession, and they were convicted on all other counts against them. Bing was convicted on all of the counts against him. The jury found Shannon not guilty on the possession count but guilty on all other counts against him. At their separate trial, Teddy and Ace were each acquitted on one distribution count. They were convicted on all of the other counts on which they were tried. It was a resounding victory for the feds. "Throughout the state and federal trials the courtrooms were packed with 103rd and 113th officers," Bing says. "They gave a hell of applause when we got found guilty. They felt that they shut down the Supreme Team organization."

CHAPTER 7

THE STORY OVER

*"Remember Prince used to push the bulletproof BM This here get you
seasick, I sat back and peeped shit The roll with Easy Rider
and they ain't get blunted Had the whole projects workin' for fifty on
five hundred"*
—50 Cent, Ghetto Qur'an, Guess Who's Back (2000)

*"Investigators described the Supreme Team as one of the busiest and
bloodiest of the trafficking rings that plagued Queens at the height of
the crack epidemic."*
— Don Diva, Issue 23

*"As Supreme sat in prison, the myth only grew, celebrated in verse, but
the world outside the penitentiary walls was changing."*
—Vibe Magazine

Prince was convicted on June 21, 1993, of supervising a narcotics
enterprise that terrorized Queens and was responsible for scores of
shootings and slayings. However, the jury found him innocent in the
murders of the four unidentified Colombian drug dealers, the second
time he had been cleared in the slayings. Still he faced a mandatory
sentence of life in prison without parole. The members of the Supreme
Team showed no emotion when found guilty of various racketeering and
narcotics trafficking charges after a nine week trial in U.S. District Court
in Brooklyn. Prince was also convicted of a murder facilitation charge.
C-Just and Pookie were found guilty of three murders. When friends and
relatives burst loudly into tears and began moaning in the courtroom,
Prince raised his right hand and said, "Don't do that." The courtroom

remained silent as the forewoman of the anonymous jury continued reading the verdicts, the climax of jury deliberations that took little more than six days.

Prosecutor Leslie Caldwell said Prince and the Supreme Team controlled drug trafficking in the Baisley Park Houses in South Jamaica throughout the 1980s. With their conviction, she had succeeded in taking down all the legendary Queens drug barons. "With today's verdicts, the government has dealt a crippling blow to a gang that preyed upon southeastern Queens for a decade," said U.S. Attorney Zachery Carter. "The Supreme Team was one of the most violent and feared gangs to ever plague the city. They were convicted of three homicides, but during the trial, evidence was presented that linked the Supreme Team to more than 30 murders."

Prince's attorney, Joyce London, predicted that an appeal of the convictions would be successful because of the government's use of wiretap conversations that had been suppressed in the state trials. "We are very happy he beat the four Colombian murder charges," she said. "He beat them in state court fair and square, and he beat them here fair and square." She contended that Prince's arguments that government attorneys used illegal wiretap evidence to win the conviction would set him free. "Prince beat all the murders and charges except one facilitation of a homicide and for the 848," Tuck says. "Big C beat seven murders, Shannon beat four, and Prince eight and half. They beat them shits."

After being convicted, the Supreme Team wasn't sentenced for almost two years. Explaining why it took so long to sentence the Supreme Team Assistant U.S. Attorney Mark Ressler said, "There were post trial motions, some of their lawyers were tied up with other cases, and some of them requested new lawyers after they were convicted."

Finally the wheels of justice moved and team members started to get sentenced. Judge Raymond Dearie told Tuck at sentencing, "You people stuck together. I'll give you that. But there's a real high price to pay for that loyalty. You're going down in flames because of your loyalty. I can understand it, but I can't condone it." Tuck and the Supreme Team's moment of truth was upon them.

"When I went for sentencing, I was prepared to do the rest of my life in prison. All of my co-defendant's PSI's came back recommending life sentences including my own," Tuck says. "Teddy was the first one sentenced. We were in MDC Brooklyn, and he came back and told me he had thirteen. I thought he was telling me thirteen life sentences." With the publicity of the case, the stakes were high. The newspapers printed daily stories of doom and gloom. The end result, though not what the government wanted, tilted heavily in their favor. Prince ended up being sentenced to seven life terms, Pookie two life terms, Big C two life terms, C-Just six life terms, Shannon thirty years, Bing nineteen years, Ace fifteen years, Tuck fourteen years, and Teddy thirteen. "When they gave me fourteen years instead of a life sentence, I thought I was blessed," Tuck says. But Prince and the security team weren't so lucky. They would be going down for life.

"Prince and eight other Supreme Team members were sentenced to long terms in the BOP," Ethan Brown said. "Including life without parole." The evidence was kind of flimsy too. Tuck explains, "I was never intercepted on any wiretaps. The feds had no pics of me. Never knew where I lived. No phone number of mine; nothing." But when the feds build a case, they don't need much. They were on some secret squirrel shit. All they needed was some snitches who were willing to put cases on people. With the feds giving out football numbers, most people were eager to cooperate and get that time cut. All that death before dishonor shit was out the window. Prince's crew, whatever their faults, stayed loyal to the end and paid the ultimate price.

"Prince's downfall had very little to do with business," the Queens insider says. "Most of the crazy shit that Prince pulled when he was out was based around revenge. He let his pride get in his way." Still Prince is a solid, respected G; a legend that will forever be remembered in the hood.

The prosecutor for the Supreme Team case was Leslie Caldwell. At the time she'd been an Assistant U.S. Attorney for only a couple of years. She made up for her lack of experience with her toughness. She wasn't afraid of anyone. To her, a criminal was a criminal, regardless of what they looked like or how much money they had. As a relatively new federal prosecutor, she had been thrust into a major role in the prosecution of New York City's most notorious drug trafficking rings. "I didn't know what I was doing," she said. But she learned as she went, going into it full steam. The state had gathered a lot of evidence against the team. Thousands of wiretapped conversations had to be digested and responses made to a flood of pretrial motions submitted by defense lawyers. Ms. Caldwell was overwhelmed. So apparent was her difficulty in coping with the ocean of evidence and defense challenges that the judge bluntly told her she was too inexperienced to handle a case of such magnitude. That only made her work that much harder.

"The cases are satisfying because you know that the people you're prosecuting deserve to be removed from society," she said. "When Prince was put in jail and Pappy Mason and Fat Cat were, detectives in Queens said the homicide rate in South Jamaica plummeted. It's satisfying to know that you contributed something tangible."

Ms. Caldwell was very adept at convincing defendants that they would never see the outside of a prison again unless they provided information or testified against co-defendants. "She knows what the score is with these people," an FBI agent said. "She doesn't pussyfoot around." For her part, Ms. Caldwell spoke simply of giving people an "incentive to cooperate." She also spoke of the lessons she learned like the "shades of grey" she found even among the coldest of killers.

"The motives for committing crimes are not simple," she said. "You can understand how on one day a person might kill someone and the next day hold his child. You see some people as irredeemable, but others as people who did something horrible and should pay for it, but who still have a future." In the Supreme Team, who was retrofitted to 80s excess and increasingly violent, Ms. Caldwell had to prosecute them accordingly. With their victories over state authorities, Prince and the team would not cop out. Despite this, Ms. Caldwell succeeded in shutting down the Supreme Team and getting convictions for most of the heavies. "We were very aggressive with them, arresting everyone who was intimately involved in their drug operations," she said. There was one key exception to the Supreme Team convictions, the gang's founder and mastermind, Supreme, an exception that would have reverberations in hip-hop as the gangsta rap era dawned.

CHAPTER 8
IMPACT ON HIP-HOP

"I been in this game for years, it made me an animal It's rules to this shit, I wrote me a manual A step by step booklet for you to get Your game on track, not your wig pushed back."
— Notorious Big, Ten Crack Commandments

"They had the money, the luxury cars, the jewelry, the girls, the respect of the streets, all of the accoutrements that would come to define hip-hop's 'bling' lifestyle in the late-90s."
— Ethan Brown, Queens Reigns Supreme

"That drug changed hip-hop. Crack made hip-hop corporate. The stories that Biggie told, that Jigga told, that Easy-E told, all of them guys that came out of the crack culture."
— Barry Michael Cooper, New Jack City screenwriter

Rap and crack were both born 30 years ago, and more than a few rappers bragged on their records about starting their labels with drug money. At nearly the same moment as Run DMC was growing to international fame in the mid-80s, crack cocaine began dominating the inner-city drug trade. Suddenly a subset of people who shared similar backgrounds was making a lot of money, either by selling crack rocks or rhyming into a microphone. "New York City rappers are so into the street legends because there are so many legends from the 1970s and 1980s, and more importantly, because in New York City we have a keen sense of our history," Ethan Brown said.

The Supreme Team and the street culture that developed in Queens in the early-80s had a tremendous effect on hip-hop. Many of Queens' early rappers ran with people in the drug world. Often drug dealers and rappers were from the same neighborhood. Others grew up on the ensuing folklore. Fifty Cent's role models were drug kingpins like Prince and Supreme. As the 1990s rolled around, the Supreme Team's influence was seen everywhere in the East Coast rap scene. The backdrop of violence and thug bravado long associated with hip-hop and fallen heroes like Tupac, Biggie, and Easy-E was bringing gangbanging, the Crip walk, and beefs to the forefront of the national consciousness. Pop culture was immersing itself in gangsterism. The line between creative expression and real life violence and illegal drug sales and thuggish posturing blurred in rap culture, where rhymes namedropped weaponry by style number and drug dealers by name.

"It all started in Queens, from *The Godfather* hats to the big rope chains," Curtis Scoon, a producer for BET's *American Gangster* series said. "Rappers like LL and Run would copy that style, and people would emulate them everywhere. The whole bling thing is a progression from the big rope chains. The genesis is right there in Queens. People talk about the Bronx being the birthplace of hip-hop, and they're correct; it's no lie. But when you look at old tapes of Africa Bambatta and Grand Master Flash, they look like Parliament or the Village People. What you see in hip-hop has Queens all over it. When you see the Lost Boyz and dreadlocks and all that, it's from Pappy Mason. There are so many little things the rappers picked up on from these guys and presented to the world."

In the 1980s the rappers were attracted to the drug dealers and the money they made, but by the 1990s there was a role reversal. The crossover happened quickly. Drug dealers, murderers, and robbers all saw the money rappers were making and wanted a piece of it. Rap became the new crack game. "During the mid-1990s, when the murder rate in NYC was beginning a precipitous decline, and highly organized crews like the Supreme Team no longer ruled the streets, rappers looking to be seen as street credible were forced to look to the past for inspiration," Ethan Brown says. "Rappers could be nostalgic for the streets of the past because for the most part, they had not been affected by the fallout- crack addiction, federal indictments, murdered friends and relatives- from that era. Only 50 Cent could legitimately claim a connection, albeit a minor connection, to the days of Supreme and Fat Cat; 50's mom had once hustled on the same block in southeast Queens where Fat Cat plied his trade."

Known drug dealers and felons started attaching themselves to hip-hop artists as security guards, label backers, or whatever. Many hustlers were able to enter the lucrative hip-hop industry as managers, promoters, producers, or muscle. Drug money started to fund studio time for up and coming artists with strings attached, of course. The genre's late 1980s golden years were underwritten by the gains (financial) and losses (psychic) of the crack trade. The drug pushed rap toward a faster, harsher quality. With the War on Drugs, the real hustlers needed a new hustle.

The rise of gangsta rap in the early-90s, complete with its glamorization of violent street life, offered a viable alternative. In this era of hip-hop domination, inner-city proliferation, and everything bling-bling, gangsta rap, like the Mafia before it, took siege of the mainstream, making the transition from the underground to the suburbs and from the prisons to Wall Street. The world of rap went Hollywood, and everything chic, trendy, and hip became straight gutter. In popular culture and the music world, being a thug was considered a benefit on someone's resume. The criminal element was alive and well in the industry.

"Hip-hip's dalliance and fixation with the streets can be traced back to the borough of Queens," Curtis Spoon says. "While Bronx artists such as Grandmaster Flash and the Furious Five or Afrika Bambaata and the Zulu Nation performed in costume, the artists from Queens opted to emulate the local ghetto superstars who were, in all actuality, the neighborhood drug dealers. During the 80s and the genesis of commercial rap, the black gangsters of Queens like Supreme, Prince, Fat Cat, and others were in a class by themselves, especially in the style department. The designer jogging suits and excessive jewelry that became synonymous with rap even to this day, started with artists like Run DMC and LL Cool J attempting to be identified with the success, flair and swagger of the drug crews in Queens like the Supreme Team."

Sometimes the drug dealers and gangbangers wanted to get on the mic themselves. They couldn't decide if they were criminals or entertainers. Drug dealers didn't leave their previous lifestyle behind when they joined the hip-hop party, they brought it with them. They didn't see the music business as their chance to go legit, but as an opportunity to expand operations, an opportunity to hide behind legitimacy while still carrying it gangster. The results in hip-hop were an extended cycle of violence, murder and corruption that mirrored the exploits of the Supreme Team. Violence is ingrained in rap; it's a celebration of bitches, guns and cash. Rap's lyrical lore holds all kinds of murder and mayhem, police and thieves, bloody money and crack dens.

"These people had so much of an impact on the whole game. Whether it's streets or entertainment," Curtis Scoon says. From LL Cool J to 50 Cent, making paper has been their legacy. "Without crack cocaine, half the narratives of hip-hop would've been erased; the street cred, the danger," Curtis Scoon says. Legendary figures of the crack wars had been the province of myth and hearsay, a tendency aided by the "had to be there" king making of 1990s hip-hop. Hip-hop artists have often made mythological ghetto heroes out of crime figures like the Supreme Team, bringing the legends from their hood to the masses. As hip-hop colonized the world, hustling went mainstream with reality television, in a tragic "rags to riches" storyline in which the 1980s gangland figures were at the core.

"At its core gangsta rap is crack era nostalgia taken to the extreme," Curtis Scoon says. "The Queens hustlers were known for lavish parties, mansions, yachts, and even bulletproof luxury automobiles." Prince and the other Supreme Team members became models for gangsta rappers, who celebrated the drug dealers by name. On *Get Down*, Nas spit, *Prince was from Queens and Fritz from Harlem/street legends, the drugs kept the hood from starving.* Supreme, Prince and other street stars were lauded in song, their lifestyles celebrated in verse. Hip-hop became infatuated with all things street.

Today's rappers brandish their crack dealing credentials as a badge of authenticity. Biggie even wrote the definitive rap to selling rock, *The Ten Crack Commandments- Rule numero uno, never let no one know how much dough you hold, cause you know the cheddar breed jealousy especially if that man fucked up, get you ass stuck up.* Crack has been a subject of rap songs since day one. As early as 1983, songs like Grandmaster Flash and Melle Mel's anti-cocaine anthem White Lines noted the sale of rocks, *Hey man, you wanna cop some blow, sure what you got, dust, flakes or rock?* As did the Beastie Boys 1986 hit, *Hold It Now, Hit it* which boasted- *I'm never dusting out cause I torch that crack.*

The crack cocaine epidemic spawned gangsta rap and a lot of today's biggest stars- Russell Simmons, Irv Gotti, 50 Cent, LL Cool J, Run DMC- started in Queens where the crack game was nothing if not serious. But a lot of the rappers have come off as studio gangsters. "Gangsta rap today is about as reflective of reality as a reality show," Curtis Scoon said. "Gangsters have pedigree. Most rappers don't." Still storied street guys were making their presence felt in the industry. The ascendance of ex-street guys like Suge Knight with Death Row records, James Prince with the Geto Boys, and Tupac's partnering with Jimmy Henchmen led to a lionization of street characters like the Supreme Team. But it also led to attention from the feds.

With hip-hop blowing up like it did, label owners who boasted of ties to crime figures were being profiled because they were black men with a lot of money and growing power. Law enforcement had always tried to find drug money and big time gangsters in the rap game. There was a long history of suspected and real life ties between organized crime and the music business, just look at Frank Sinatra and the Italian mob. In the mid-90s federal authorities in L.A. investigated claims that Suge Knight was backed by jailed L.A. drug dealer Michael "Harry O" Harris. In Houston DEA and local police tried to tie James Prince and Rap-A-Lot Records to narcotics trafficking in the city's gritty fifth ward. To the feds the rap game was the new drug game.

"Rappers are in the business of selling records. Lots of times they rap about what they think their consumers want to hear. They do what they do," Tuck says. "The rapper Capone is not Al Capone. Real gangsters don't talk shit on MTV *Rap City* or BET's *106th and Park*. Real gangsters do shit. There's nothing wrong with being a rapper, and if you've lived the hard knock life and want to rap about it, then by all means, let the world know your story. But don't act like you've never smiled, and all you did your whole life was pop your gat and sell drugs. Most of the so called gangsta rappers are faking." But this was the post crack era, post Supreme Team world where the lines between entertainment and reality blurred.

"They were looking at rappers like they used to look at the Mafia," Ethan Brown said. "They were trying to find crime in entertainment." Surveillance of rap events to track allegiances, hierarchies, and feuds was commonplace. Informants were scattered throughout the music world, giving up info to all the alphabet boys, the hip-hop police, and other government agencies. In the gangster's paradise snitches ruled. This was the atmosphere Supreme stepped into when he was released from prison. Ex-con, street icon, ghetto star- his rise in the world of hip-hop continued the Supreme Team's legacy.

CHAPTER 9
SUPREME'S RISE

"Funds unlimited/backed by Preme Team crime representatives."
— **Ja Rule, Survival of the Illest**

"The feds can't stand it when a gangsta goes legit. It's okay for the Kennedys but when a black man goes legit it's a federal crime."
— **Don Diva, Issue 23**

"He's a progenitor of that movement- of Puff, Of Dame, of Jay-Z, even Cam'ron. He had confidence, with intelligence, style and danger. These guys have this because the record business is dangerous. That's like the drug game. And the drugs is the music."
— **Barry Michael Cooper, Stop Smiling Magazine**

A lot happened while Supreme was away in the feds. The world and landscape of Queens had changed. In Preme's era the rappers hung out with the drug dealers, but now it was the other way around. With dark glasses and a baseball cap pulled low, Preme attempted to stay inconspicuous, but he was too big of an icon for that. Everybody knew who he was, and the feds were keeping tabs on his every move. "He was under scrutiny from day one," T says. "Every time he goes to the street, the police are in his backyard. This man was targeted from the word go." The feds wanted Preme back in jail; they were on him like Bin Laden. But in the streets his fame had the opposite effect, he was idolized and worshipped. His folklore resonated the most with the young hustlers and rap impresario's of Queens. With hip-hop becoming more main stream by the day, hood stars like Supreme were in big demand. Supreme was a towering street legend mythologized for his crack era crime exploits by hip-hop artists, including rap superstars like Biggie, Nas, The Game, and 50 Cent.

"When the old heads like Supreme and them came home, I was in place already," 50 Cent said. "I had the 400 SE Benz, and I was nineteen years old. I'm talking way before the record deals. I really couldn't comprehend the respect level these niggas had. Whatever they said about the old heads putting in work was black history to me. I had conversations and relationships with the old heads, those niggas know me in the streets, all of them know me. It's hard for some of the old heads to respect you if they could have birthed you. They look and see us as a bunch of babies." According to 50 Cent, he was getting his in the streets, Supreme Team style. He modeled himself after and looked up to the old heads like Supreme.

"These niggas is gangstas. I came up under these niggas. I was raised under the Supreme Team," 50 said. "They came at a time- early-80s into the 90s. Everybody that was from that area fall under that umbrella at some point. If it wasn't under Preme, it was under Cat and Corley or somebody down there. You looked up to all of them niggas that ring them kind of bells, course they doing what they doing, and they count so much more to the streets at the time based on their reputation, what they accomplished. I came up under all these niggas. Initially I didn't know Preme like that. I knew Preme through Black Just. Blackie was cool with me. He was calling me Curt when everybody was calling me Boo Boo or 50. He financed the boxing program; he was that nigga to me. When I wasn't killing time in school, I was sparring in the gym or selling crack on the strip."

Unlike Preme, Prince and the rest of the team, Black Just avoided serving any substantial amount of jail time. He slid through the cracks, so to speak, and was holding Preme and the team down through thick and thin. "Anytime one of us came home we went to mostly Black Just for funds," the original member says. "You might have got some sneakers or an outfit from Bimmy; he was not about taking care of any grown ass men. When Bing came home and got rolling, a team member could count on him to look out without question. When Preme came home the first time, he was really upset with practically everyone that was down with the team. Nobody had anything for him. Everything was fucked up and basically gone." The team was still fiercely loyal to Preme even if their finances were fucked up.

"Black Just bled Supreme Team," says the Queens hustler. "He held them niggas down and kept it going." Black Just was in the streets, so he knew what the score was when Preme came home. A few other prominent team members like Bimmy, God B, and Babywise had avoided the federal RICO cases also.

"Everybody on the team has done a bid- God B, Black Just, Bimmy, Green Eyed Born. Babywise has caught a number of cases in his life, but he only did one bid back in the early-90s. He did two and a half years, came home, and never went back to prison. He caught another case, but he beat it. It was a North Carolina case. When Preme came home the first time, it was Dahlu, B.J., and sometimes Shabu before they all got violated from parole," the Queens insider says. "The dude Shabu was Black Just's right hand man bar none. He was a third tier team member, but he was official. B.J. was Bimmy's right hand man, but when Preme came home, he took him from Bimmy. He was what Shabu was to Black Just, only to Bimmy. Everybody had a right hand man except Dahlu and God B. Their right hand men were drugs. But they were both closest to Preme." The young 50 Cent was up under Black Just and Bimmy when Preme came home.

"Preme came home from jail, and these niggas was in the club with me," 50 said. "I'm nineteen, and I'm kinda hot. Bitches is looking at me. I was already 50 before my record came up." In reality Preme probably hardly noticed 50. He wasn't worried about the youngster even if 50 was seriously sweating Preme.

"Before Preme came home and before 50 Cent was anybody, Black Just and Bimmy were very tight with a young Curtis Jackson. I don't know much about 50 Cent's drug game ventures, but I do know that he never reached a level above street corner. He was basically a sidewalk kid from the beginning," the original member says, but 50 idolized Preme. Preme didn't have the time to fraternize with fans, though, as he was trying to get his life together.

"I was dead broke," Preme said. "And everybody from the original Supreme Team was home waiting like, 'Supreme, whatever you say.' And I'm like, 'Good luck on y'all venture.' I wanted to be able to walk in the street or go to a club by myself and not have security. I just wanted to be a regular person." That was Supreme's story, but, for real, he wanted more. With his notoriety in Queens, Supreme could never be a regular person. He was a living, breathing, walking legend, a myth out of hip-hop lore come to life, back home to the streets that spawned him. He was the favored one, the ladies man, the superstar, the chosen son. Supreme was, right or wrong, a legend, and as he would find out, that status granted him a tremendous influence over the New York rap scene.

Everybody else of his stature was either dead or in the feds doing big numbers. All of his peers- Prince, Fat Cat, Wall Corley, Pappy Mason-were all in prison, but Preme was home in Queens. "He was like a magnet," T says. For women, for wannabe's, for dudes in the street trying to get a rep, Preme was far from a regular person. He was a ghetto celebrity.

"He's a stand up dude," Choke, a friend of Preme's said. "Straight forward. He values nothing but friendship, loyalty, and respect. He got a platinum heart. Everybody like him."

Living in his father's house in South Jamaica, he tried to subsist by selling pornographic pictures to inmates. "When Preme first went home, he started up Picture Perfect," Tuck says. Being the ladies man he was, it was easy for him to get girls to take their clothes off while he snapped the pictures. It was rumored he even got some of his old cohorts' seeds to strip for him. Every young lady in Queens knew who Supreme was, and to the young impressionable ghetto girls, he was movie star like. "His first venture Picture Perfect was selling photos of women in bathing suits," T says. "In the 80s when he seen so many thousands of young guys that grew up similar to him that were never getting out, he decided to do legitimate stuff." Living at home with his father and three siblings, Preme worked his hand with the mail order service offering revealing photos of women to prisoners.

He also started a hair salon for his sister. "A lot of people were coming there on the strength of his name," she said. Preme had used his time in prison wisely, as he had a plan to start different ventures in the hood and capitalize off of his notoriety.

But the lures of the drug game were always there. Preme was well schooled in crack cocaine and the drug game. Preme would only go back to hustling as a last resort. In truth Preme hoped it never came to that. "Black Just and Bimmy were around, but Preme was not really fucking with them when he first came home," the Queens insider says. "Neither of them had anything to offer Preme upon his release, not saying anyone else did. But he didn't expect anyone to have anything but them. Black Just had a drug problem, and he was broke. Bimmy did not have much of anything, and what little he had was going to his numerous families. Babywise was the only member in pocket." Preme wasn't trying to get back in the game anyway.

"Kenny saw the light after spending time in jail," said Robert Simels, Preme's long time popular guns and drugs lawyer. Preme was smart enough to know that he could capitalize off of his infamy and reputation. His way of life and legend was celebrated in hip-hop circles. When he first got out, Nas shouted the team out in verse on 1994's *Memory Lane*, *Some fiends scream about Supreme Team/a Jamaica Queens thing*. This wouldn't be the first or last time the team was glorified in rap. With men like J. Prince, Suge Knight, and Jimmy Henchman building companies and finding a second chance in the hip-hop industry, it was plausible that Supreme's street credibility could do the same for him.

"After a run in with the law and several years of incarceration, Preme rectified the elements of criminal thinking that led him to prison," Prince said. "Upon his release, Preme implemented his own ideas of entrepreneurship. Preme's rehabilitation wasn't due to prison programming but to his own will and determination to succeed. With this in mind, we must then realize that when your leadership isn't certified or sanctioned by the government, then you pose a threat to their plans to keep many urban Americans in poverty. Preme never obtained degrees from universities, so it is difficult to gauge and measure the extent and effect of the brainwashing techniques used through the educational system and prison rehabilitation programs." Preme was finding it wasn't easy to get ahead. Sure, he was celebrated, and everyone wanted to know him, but his notoriety would only take him so far. This was a big plus, and Preme knew it, but it wasn't putting money in his pocket. The respect he got left him in high regard to the denizens of the block. But that wasn't paying his bills. Still, he used his stature and reputation to make inroads into the hip-hop community.

Preme was making his rounds and hitting the clubs like The Tunnel-hip-hop's ground zero was considered thug paradise. "Music industry executives go to The Tunnel to play catch up with the streets," the Queens hustler says. "The Tunnel's street cred stamp is invaluable. This is the Apollo, but on a hip-hop level." At The Tunnel Supreme could rub shoulders with hip-hop's elite and up and coming stars. New York's hardest of the hardcore hip-hop parties was staged there, where alpha males and b-boys sported typical hip-hop wear like Mecca hats, Avirex jackets, and Fubu jeans, where shoes were inspected for drugs and weapons, where ballpoint pens were considered contraband, and fights decided hit records. To Preme and the Supreme Team, though, the wannabe gangsters and thugs of hip-hop were nothing.

"The rappers were straight jokes to us," the original member says. "One time we were at The Tunnel, and Preme was kicking it with this cutie pie. While Preme was talking to her, this kid out of Puff Daddy's click got in Preme's conversation with the broad. We are standing around Preme, and I step to the kid and tell him to raise up out of my man's conversation. The kid said, 'Yo, I'm trying to get at her too.' It was obvious he did not recognize our type. So I said to the kid, 'Don't play yourself; we ain't no rappers or no shit like that.' But the kid would not give up. In fact he started to get reckless out the mouth with Preme. Man, he got the shit beat out of hisself. I'm talking about a royal ass whipping, and while he is getting fucked up, club security is just standing there looking, not doing nothing until after he finished getting fucked up totally. After it was over and the kid was twisted, club security came over and started to fuck dude up some more for messing with us. It was incredible.

"When we leave the club and get outside, in front we see Puff Daddy. In Preme's mind nobody is above him, so he did not speak to Puffy. Puffy recognized or knew not to approach Preme, so he and I started having a conversation about his boy's show of disrespect. Puff Daddy was scared as a muthafucka. He started talking like, 'Yo, brother dude was wrong, he deserve what he got.' It was crazy what he was saying. He was rambling on so much and scared. I thought he was some type of counselor dude who tries to get dudes not to be violent. He was like, 'Brother, we black, we shouldn't be fighting, killing each other.' He was getting his Martin Luther King, Jr. on. He was trying to make sure we were not getting ready to whip his ass. He was shook. I could smell the fear running out of him. We did not even whip his ass, and he had me feeling sorry for him. He had me thinking that we had violated one of the rules of black power. Malcolm X could have been Puff Daddy that night. He invited us to one of his parties in Mount Vernon or Yonkers. We went, but when we got there, they was on some Versace dressing type shit. We was some Timberland boot wearing dudes, all dressed in black, murder wear, so we did not even bother to go in, just hollered at a couple of broads outside the joint and left.

"The next time I saw Puff Daddy I was going through the midtown tunnel dropping my bitch off at work, and as we are approaching the toll, Puffy and one of his flunkies spot me; they are in a blue drop top BMW. Me and my bitch are in the same car except it's black. Puff Daddy's flunky literally jumps out the car and runs over to me and hands me about 200 invites to some party Puff Daddy is giving. I just took them, looked over at Puff Daddy, and nodded my head to him. I knew he was going to be a giant of a dude. He just happened to be a giant pussy of a dude." The rappers and hip-hop dudes clamored for Preme and the team's attention. They were intrigued and in awe of them, but for Preme it was different.

"Preme never looked in awe of no man especially not no non-street dude," the Queens insider says. "I remember one time we were at Rucker Park in Harlem, and I saw Biggie Smalls, and I had lost my cool and got excited, and Preme blew a gasket on me. He said, 'Muthafucka, don't ever play yourself like that about one of these rapper ass muthafucka's. Nigga, we are exactly what they rapping about and trying to portray.' What had me a little puzzled was we were riding around that whole week, and the only tape we listened to was Biggie Small's. Preme would keep rewinding that whole tape. That whole tape was stuck in our heads. Preme said there had never been nothing like it. We were feeling that shit." But song or no song, Preme did not let anything or anyone be bigger than he was.

"One dude that was really cool with the team from the music industry is Biz Markie. He was our man, but one day I was ready to bust his head open, but Preme wouldn't let me do it. He really liked Biz Markie, and he really did not intentionally violate me. I just felt that he was too foul smelling. We went to the Jacob Javits Center for the Black Expo event, and as soon as we get inside, we run into Biz, and he starts hugging me, but the problem is Biz is all sweaty, smelling like old gorilla shit. I'm like, 'If this fool don't get off me, I'll shoot the shit out of him right here in the Jacob Javits Center,' but Preme sensed my anger and interceded and told me to fall back and just leave it alone." Preme even had an encounter with Tupac.

In 1994, when Tupac Shakur got shot at Quad Recording studios, Preme was the one who tried to dead the situation for the rapper. "He got with several of the dudes that had the conflict with Tupac when he got shot and ironed out the situation," T says. "This led to an organization where Supreme was involved with Tupac in organizing a clean up program to clean up the community." Supreme's ties to Tupac were real and could have led to something fortunate.

"Preme had a good rapport with Tupac," the original member says. "Their relationship derives from Preme's strength throughout NYC. After Tupac got shot, he was very leery of the NY scene, but he was still very much in love with NYC. So their friendship developed out of Tupac's need and want to move through NYC without further incident from the underworld on a pass sanctioned by the universally respected Supreme and his respected crew. Preme's street cred is so strong that 20 years from now he could still pass out ghetto passes, and they would be fully honored, and Tupac got wind of that back then.

"One time we ran down on the singer Miss Jones. She's a radio personality now, but Preme told me to get her name. When I asked her, she said her name was Miss Jones. I said 'Bitch, what's your name?' Preme started laughing, and then told me to leave her alone. She was with some dude that was her man. He was straight pussy. He did not say one word in defense of his girl."

The hip-hop community embraced Supreme for the legend he was. His way of life was a motif for their songs. He personified the fine line that separated art and reality in a gangsta rapper's lyrics. He was Tony Montana, Frank White, and Nino Brown. His presence gave entertainers credibility in the streets. At the same time, his past was never far behind. He was the usual suspect, high on the fed's list for recidivism. "He did 12 for the CCE," Tuck says, "and came home. His whole crew was dead or doing big numbers, and the feds wanted him off the street." To the feds Preme was public enemy number one. They would use any excuse to put him back in jail.

"He was going back and forth on violations," Tuck says, "out in 93, back in 95. At MDC in 95 he came to my floor. I laid him out, gave him whatever." Some think that Preme going back to prison indirectly led to Tupac being killed and the east coast/west coast beef between Death Row and Bad Boy.

"When he went back to jail, Tupac got killed," T says. "Preme would of been able to mediate the situation with Tupac just out of the respect he got." Preme's respect level with Suge Knight and Puff Daddy was high.

"Preme and Suge was tight. They came to the video shoot," the Southside player says. Preme was making inroads into the hip-hop community, but he was still a gangster, and the loss of Tupac was a setback. "He'd be out and about, but then one time when Preme was with Dahlu in Harlem, he got caught with a gun. Dahlu took the charge for Preme and got four to twelve for the state. Preme got violated," the Southside player says. Without Preme to mediate, Tupac was killed. Preme's calm demeanor, and the respect that he held could have averted the deaths of two of hip-hop legends and the most famous hip-hop beef of all time. But it wasn't to be.

During his time in prison on the federal parole violation, Preme contemplated more on his grand plan. "He did time at FCI McKean, FCI Talledega, Allenwood low, and one of those joints in Florida," Tuck says. He passed his time reading books of his favorite author, Donald Goines, a hustler from Detroit who cranked out 16 books on urban street life before he was murdered in 1974. With titles like *Black Gangster, Crime Partners,* and *Daddy Cool,* Goines novels were very popular in the federal system. With the 100 to 1 crack to cocaine ratio, where five grams of crack carried the same ten year mandatory minimum sentence as 500 grams of cocaine, the war on drugs was incarcerating young black males at an alarming rate.

With NWA, Snoop Dog, and Death Row dominating the hip-hop scene, Preme believed that Goines' novels could be turned into big screen gangster epics like *The Godfather,* especially if he could use his hookups in hip-hop to get some big time rappers to act in the movies and contribute to the soundtrack. "When I was incarcerated, I asked myself, 'Why hasn't anyone brought any of Donald Goines novels to life in a movie?'"

Preme said. "I told myself, 'When I get out, that's what I'm going to do.'" Wayne Davis from Harlem was one of the dudes Preme shared his idea with while locked up.

"I met Supreme while we were incarcerated," Wayne said. "Once you get incarcerated, and you find out what you gotta do and how much time you gotta do, you start remembering the mistakes you made, and you start introspecting and retrospecting on what you can do and what you not gonna do again. We were talking about what we were gonna do when we get home, and he told me he wanted to bring Donald Goines to the movie screen. At that time I looked at him like he was crazy." But Preme wasn't crazy. He was a visionary. Just as Preme set trends for the rappers with the Supreme Team in the 1980s, he was clearly a man before his time. Long before Denzil Washington's *American Gangster*, Supreme had the vision to bring the urban landscape and inner-city hood stories to the screen.

"I was always good with reading, but Donald Goines reintroduced me to reading," Preme said. "I started out by reading his novels, and from there I started reading Sidney Sheldon, Robert Ludlum, and so on. Each of Donald's books captivated me; it was like I could see the blood dripping. That's when I said, 'Man, this right here would make a good movie,' and I wondered why it never got done. That's when I decided that if I ever got a chance, I would do it; I would make the movie. I read all of Donald's books including *Donald Writes No More*, and there's no comparison."

Preme was hooked, and he had his vision, his way to go legit. But it wouldn't be easy. Preme was a product of the streets, and his past would always come back to haunt him. It was something he could never out run. "I got a basic hood background, you know. I came out of Baisley Projects in Queens," Preme said. "I was in the streets for a little while before I got locked up. I did about two years in the state, and then I went to federal prison to finish my time. That's where I met Wayne. I served eight more years there, and during that time me and Wayne established our bond." Back on the parole violation, Preme served another two and half years.

As Preme finished up his parole violations, the team he founded was non-existent. With defections, dudes turning snitch, and Prince's RICO act trial, the team was no more, only a footnote in hip-hop history. "He was terribly disappointed at the rate of informants," T says. "He was disappointed that people that came up with him and after were telling." A couple of the team's members were still on the street doing their thing, but more likely than not most of the ex-hustlers were trying to get involved in the hip-hop industry by trading off on their notoriety as members of the infamous crew.

Preme decided to do the same. Armed with more creative ambition than professional experience, Preme set out to make a name for himself in the hip-hop business. He knew he needed to use his street fame to bring his Donald Goines vision to life. In hip-hop circles and in the street, his credibility was paramount. Preme knew he had a good chance to make it. As Preme contemplated his future, the incarcerated members of the team were going hard in prison, trying to solidify their reputations by any means necessary.

Prince was battling furiously, trying to hold the New York car down in whatever prison he was at- USP Allenwood, USP Leavenworth, and USP Beaumont. He was checking in snitches and making sure New York dudes stuck together. When the rat Clarence "Preacher" Heatley hit the compound at USP Beaumont, which the C/O's and convicts alike called "Bloody Beaumont," Prince tried to check in the Harlem gangster, who had snitched on his own kids, and they had a knife duel in front of the chow hall. "Prince was always in the mix, creating chaos." The Queens hustler says. "He was either playing chess or on a mission. I know Prince; we were in Allenwood together. We always been alright. My assessment: he's a solid dude, just a little crazy like the rest of us." As their legends and exploits grew to epic proportions in hip-hop rhymes, gangster magazines, and hood DVDs, Prince and the other team members sat on the sidelines in prison.

"In spite of my sentence, life goes on," Prince said. "The sun that shines on that side of the wall also shines on this side of the wall, so the experiencing of life itself is the same. I make every effort to surround myself with those who enrich the quality of my life. I have become consumed by my own project and my federal appeal, which has been pending before the trial judge. I try to stay productive in spite of it all." In the streets things were still moving fast and furious, all legends aside, but the police discovered something that cast doubt on Prince and the Supreme Team's RICO act trial.

On July 18, 1997, a convicted robber on probation for life was arrested by the Police Department's Cold Case Squad and charged with murdering his ex-girlfriend and her father in Queens six years before. The ex-convict, Rodney Morris, of 67-50 G 195th Street in Queens was charged with killing his girlfriend, Robin Carrington, and her father, Clifford Carrington, in April of 1991. "The motive was robbery," Officer Olga Mercado, a police department spokeswoman said. At the time of the double homicide, investigators had thought they were connected to the trial of Prince and the Supreme Team. The Prosecutor Leslie Caldwell had even claimed that Robin Carrington had a P carved into her chest, and that this was a tell tale sign that Prince had ordered the murders.

The Carringtons were described by police at the onset of the murders as the sister-in-law and father-in-law of Trent "Serious" Morris, who was in protective custody and testifying that Prince ordered the Supreme Team to rob and kill four South American drug dealers. The papers had a field day with the double homicide, blaming it all on Prince and the team, but it was all hype. In response to the killings, Justice Lawrence Finnegan sequestered the jury in the Supreme Team case. A police department official finally admitted six years after the fact that the killings weren't related to the drug case. But the damage was already done. Prince and several team members were doing life, making their bones in the pens, due in part to an accusation that wasn't true. As Prince battled his case and enemies furiously in the federal penitentiary, Supreme was back in Queens trying to turn his dreams into reality. He was employing all his charm and grace to get himself in position in the hip-hop industry.

"Supreme's very personable," T says. "You can automatically see that he's very charismatic. He's definitely the type of individual who deserves the type of respect he got from his peers. He deals extremely well with his notoriety. He was never anyone else than Supreme. He was familiar with people coming up to him, but he had very few intimate friends." Preme set out to connect with those who mythologized him as a true hustler, the wannabe G's of hip-hop. Thanks to the myths of the crack era and the tabloid headlines about the Supreme Team, young rappers and hip-hop executives were in awe of Preme. They were raised on the Supreme Team, as 50 Cent said, hearing the street tales and legends since they were shorties.

Preme knew there were hustles to be had that were legitimate. No matter how much the streets called, he needed to resist the lure. Even with his old Supreme Team cohorts like Black Just, Bimmy, and Babywise still knee deep in the game urging him to jump back in and open up shop, Preme had to resist the temptation. "In the 90s when Preme had gotten out, we weren't promoting ourselves as the team," the original member says. "We were hardened convicted criminals trying to survive by simply making money. We still went out and partied hard. We were doing our thing and making out pretty good, but nowhere near the level of our 80s heyday and, for the most part, not in New York. Preme was fucking with Black Just when he came back from parole violation. He was not fucking with Bimmy on any business type shit, but he would let Bimmy hang with us. Bimmy had long been suspected of being a CI, but trust me, if

Preme thought there was any truth to what dudes tried to put out there about them, he would not have been dealing with them. Preme was only fucking with Babywise, B.J., Shabu, Black Just, and Dahlu who had just come home also."

While many of the infamous figures heralded in hip-hip lyrics were either dead or in prison, Supreme paid his debt and reentered society. His reentry was accompanied by a reentry into rap's lyrical lore. He was an exciting, charismatic gangster who really captured the imagination of the public. But Preme didn't want to be a hip-hop legend; he wanted to make money and live the high life. He wanted Supreme Team type money, so he could live in the style he was accustomed to, and he saw movies as his ticket.

"Kenny primarily was involved in trying to write scripts," Robert Simels said. "He was smart enough to understand the real money in today's world is in the entertainment business, not any other kind of activity." Another street legend, Chaz Williams, was already in place making moves in hip-hop with Black Hand Entertainment. Chaz and Preme knew each other from the 80s, so Preme decided to take his idea for the Goines movie to Chaz. "Supreme brought the idea to me; he was trying to get me involved in the movie aspect. I had other film aspirations," Chaz said. "After a year of him trying to convince me about the project, I kind of took a look. He knew that I knew about the Donald Goines series. What always impressed me about Donald Goines was he wrote his stories and kept it simple. They were very popular in the prison system.

"I saw guys that couldn't read learn to read Donald Goines books and go on to get a GED and a college degree. I felt Donald Goines helped a lot of brothers become literate and educate themselves. I still wanted to control the film part of it. So I was trying to raise the capital. I came up with doing the CD. I wanted to introduce Donald Goines to the youth because he was a black writer from the 70s. So I wanted to show a relationship with what was happening right then with DMX, Jay-Z, and Ja Rule. I thought that would make the younger consumer realize who Donald Goines was plus raise some capital. Supreme didn't have the capital at that time either. He couldn't raise it, so he went his way, and I went mine. The idea for the soundtrack was mine. Supreme brought me the idea for the film project, but I was already involved in my own script."

Preme agreed to the idea, thinking *Black Gangster* would impress hip-hop people, and with Chaz at the helm, the newly released Preme could get his feet wet in the entertainment business. At Black Hand headquarters on 139th Street in South Jamaica, Chaz and Preme held studio sessions. "I was spending my money on the *Black Gangster* soundtrack," Chaz said, "which had Jay-Z, DMX, 50 Cent, and Ja Rule. That was my first musical project. I was co-managing 50 Cent at that time. Fifty and Ja didn't really see each other back then. Their beef started soon after. This was before either of them had made it." Preme also got to know the rappers including the soon to be superstar 50 Cent.

"We used to talk all the time. As a matter of fact, I told him, 'I want you to be in this movie I'm getting ready to do,'" Preme said. "And this is when he wasn't nobody." Fifty was up under Preme just like the other rappers and wannabe gangsta's who idolized him. Fifty used to run errands for Preme and just hangout, trying to be down. Preme was more concerned with finding financing or a backer for his film idea than cultivating a friendship with the young rapper. Preme was an opportunist and was looking for a situation that he could work to his advantage. He wanted the film project to get off the ground, and he wasn't about to give up. Enter Irv Gotti.

Irving Lorenzo was born in Hollis, Queens, in 1971, the youngest of eight siblings, who pooled their money to buy Irv his first DJ rig. DJ Irv became a minor star in the Queens hip-hop constellation. One day a rapper called him Gotti in homage to the former Mafia boss, and the name stuck. Irv was big on imagery, and he knew the lineage of Queens drugs lords well. He even said that his rise in Queens was not all spinning turntables at house parties. He openly discussed his relationship with drug dealers in his youth. He made them mixed tapes and was eventually lured into the business. "I don't recommend it," Irv said.

As Preme neared the end of the *Black Gangster* soundtrack with Chaz, Gotti had finally gained a foothold at Def Jam with DMX. With DMX's success Gotti secured deals for Ja Rule and Ashanti, who would become stars and media darlings. After years of grinding at TVT and then at Def Jam, Gotti was rewarded with a label of his own which he christened Murder Inc. His idea was to go all the way gangsta. Gotti craved street authenticity. He hired all types of ex-felons for different jobs. "Most of the guys, even those with priors, wanted to put the bullshit behind them, clean up their acts and succeed in the music business. People like Irv were the only ones that would take them in, give them jobs, and keep them off the streets," T Says.

A chance meeting on Guy R. Brewer Boulevard, when Gotti was filming a video for Cash Money Clicks' single *Get the Fortune*, proved pivotal for Supreme. Irv agreed to meet the South Jamaica hustling icon. "I met him after he got out of prison around 1995," Irv said. "I was shooting a video in front of a cleaners across from a Kentucky Fried Chicken where Preme used to hang out. Like everybody in Queens I knew who he was but had never met him. Preme says, 'Yo, so you know how to shoot videos? Do you think you could shoot a movie?'" With the introduction to Irv through B.J., Bimmy's former right hand man, Preme felt he had the connection to make his film aspirations come true.

"He seen me shooting the video, and he said, 'Hey I got this movie idea,'" Irv remembered. "He had a dream about doing movies. He felt that Goines's movies was gonna be big with the urban world." Gotti's position offered Supreme the chance to apply his hustling skills into a legitimate business. In Preme, Irv and the soon to be superstar Ja Rule had a true street legend to be associated with, improving their street credibility tremendously. In the rap world, the criminal element proved influential for reputations, muscle, or whatever. Their fast friendship was a win for both men. To Irv it was the chance to earn authenticity in the hood, and to Preme it was an opportunity to pitch his dream project to a person that could possibly make it happen. Gotti was proud of his street connections and bragged to everyone of the criminal associations that worked for him at Murder Inc.

"You got C.C., who's a Crip. One Stop is a drug dealer. Preme is a gangster. Wayne is a gangster. And when I say gangster, I'm talking gangster. B.J.- thug," Irv boasted. He loved the notoriety of his new friends, even if he didn't know the extent of their background.

"B.J. is Bimmy's little man. He was in the music business. He introduced Preme to Gotti," the Southside player says. John "B.J." Bryant and Eric "Shabu" Stuckey were second generation Supreme Teamers who were tight with Preme when he got out in the 90s and got down with the hip-hop industry like Preme. They became the wolves behind the rappers, their protection so to speak. Irv made no secret of his associations; indeed, he hid them in plain sight. This piqued the interest of overzealous investigators when they looked at the label whose catchphrase was "Murder." Gotti had always envisioned running a rap empire, and due to his success, eight platinum albums released through Def Jam and numerous Top 20 hits in the late 1990s, Gotti godfathered a new subgenre- gangsta pop. And real gangsters like Supreme came along for the ride.

"I took a liking to him instantly," Preme said of Gotti. "We'd be out, and he'd be like, 'Yo, I got to go and pick up my mother.' That struck me as responsible. To be out with your dudes and stop what you're doing and go pick up your mother." As Murder Inc.'s star rose, Preme rode shotgun.

"Anybody that succumbs to hip-hop or thug life would actually like or want to be associated with somebody like Supreme because he was a real gangster who did time," T says. It was a match made in heaven or maybe hell if they knew what the future held. But for the moment it was a party, and nobody partied like Murder Inc.

"We were wilding," Irv said, "living the life of rock stars." Preme, fresh out of prison, enjoyed the lifestyle. He was a real life Tony Soprano who played the part of Murder Inc.'s gangster henchman.

"Every Monday night they played ball at Chelsea Pier in Manhattan next to The Crack house," the Southside player says. "They would all go to Bar 89, a very sexy club right in the village. I seen Preme in there." Preme was no stranger to the party scene, and he was used to being the center of attention.

"Dudes stop him, shake his hand; they just want to be seen talking to him," Choke says. Preme, the storied ex-hustler and charismatic ladies man, often outshone the platinum selling artists. Everybody in the industry wanted to meet Preme and hang out with the drug baron from Baisley Projects. With Murder Inc. hosting the gala and footing the bill, Preme held court.

"Money was raining from the sky," Irv said. "I did like 120 million two years straight. Big wigs loved me cause I was an earner." And Preme loved Gotti for letting him relive his glory days. But Ja Rule and Gotti took the gangster stuff too seriously.

They tried to live off Supreme's rep, often making problems and then depending on Preme to solve them. They were entertainers, not gangsters. They weren't even thugs. They played a role and promoted the image of Murder Inc. as a record label not to fuck with. The "most dangerous record company in show business" was how they styled it. They imagined themselves the cast of a real life gangster flick; a modern day *Scarface* movie. And Preme, the real life gangster, was trying to get out of the life. He knew the consequences of the criminal lifestyle, his nephew Prince was never getting out of prison, and Preme had served hard time. Gotti and Ja Rule were living the studio gangster life depicted in their videos, threatening to shoot up the club, and give out beat downs. They were out gallivanting flamboyantly, the stars of their own film. It was a fantasy gangster epic to them. A movie in which they were the A-list stars. Funds unlimited, backed by my Preme Team crime representatives, Ja Rule free styled on a Def Jam compilation. To them Preme was *The Godfather*-type figure. Murder Inc. boasted of their connection to Preme at every opportunity to solidify the link. Ja Rule also name checked former Supreme Team member Hobie "Robo Justice" Townsend and even Black Hand's Chaz "Slim" Williams in rhyme. As Preme tried to get away from the thug life, Gotti and Ja Rule went all Tupac and gravitated toward it. "I go to this club and bump into Irv," Mic Geronimo, from the Cash Money Click/DJ Irv days before Murder Inc. said. "He was a little inebriated. I'm like 'What's up?' He's got a bottle in his hand, running around with 20, 30 dudes, and is like, 'Yeah, what's up?' Very nonchalantly. It was then I realized this is not the same DJ Irv. This is some sort of concoction called Irv Gotti."

With all the number one hits, magazine cover profiles, and videos in rotation, Irv was in hip-hop heaven. Highly publicized, hyped, written about and sensationalized, the headline grabbing Gotti celebrated the often violent history of the Southside of Jamaica Queens, especially with Preme at his side. But Preme was trying to get his movie made. That's what the connection was to him. Sure, he enjoyed the life, but it was all something he had experienced before. He figured with all the money floating around Gotti and Murder Inc., they could provide him finances to do him. "He brought me some Donald Goines books and told me to read them," Irv said. "You know how big Stephen King's books are in the horror flick world? That's how big he thought Goines was going to be in hip-hop." Preme had a goal and stuck to it, never giving up or compromising his vision.

"Preme always told me that the game was over," T says. "Everybody in that life should know there are two endings to it: you're dead or you go to jail. There are no exceptions to the rule." Preme was adamant in finding another way, and his ambition was strong. He had the will and with Murder Inc., he had the way to turn his vision into a reality. Since Chaz used the Goines novel *Black Gangster* for his concept album, Preme decided to use another novel from the Goines collection for his movie. *Crime Partners* would be the basis for his first film.

Partying nightly at New York clubs with Irv and even attending family functions Preme felt comfortable approaching Irv about investing in *Crime Partners*. Irv Gotti decided to invest $50,000 of his own money in the film and got Def Jam to sign a $1 million distribution deal for the Crime Partners soundtrack which Gotti would produce and get Jay-Z and his other acts to contribute too. "Suge was gonna help him do the soundtrack too. I seen Preme in L.A. a couple of times," the Southside player says. With Preme getting $500,000 up front he went into production. Gotti found him a resourceful director for the low budget film in J. Jesse Smith.

"Preme made this movie by stretching out every single dollar he had," Smith said. "He believed in this project and so did I. Preme was on the set every day. He was very hands on." Due to his affiliation with Murder Inc., Preme got some of the labels talent, including Ja Rule, Charli Baltimore, and Cadillac Tah for small roles. He also got Snoop Dog and

Ice T to play small parts in the film, an impressive lineup for an upstart first-time producer.

"He was passionate about making the film," Bentley Morris, the L.A. publisher from Holloway House, who sold Preme the rights to *Crime Partners* for 135 G's said. Gotti proved to be a tremendous boon for Preme, a godsend in fact. With Gotti's backing, Preme made legitimate strides in the film industry. He was an aspiring scriptwriter and film producer.

"Preme knew for the most part it ain't a black or white thing, it's a rich or poor thing." T says. Supreme's dream of producing Crime Partners was about to come true, thanks to Irv Gotti. "A lot of dudes getting legitimate money wanna touch gangsterism, but when it comes time to help somebody realize their dreams, they back off," T says. "Irv Gotti didn't; he tried to help someone who was through with the life."

Preme's film company, Picture Perfect Films, spent about $1 million to make the movie. They released it straight to DVD and kept ownership of the whole project. "It's the hottest thing out there right now," the owner of a movie outlet in Brooklyn said. "We're ordering as many as we can get our hands on. This movie is extremely brutal and realistic. Everyone wants it." The DVD was to be the start of Supreme's success as a legitimate hip-hop player. Gotti put up $140,000 more to buy the rights to four more Donald Goines titles. Preme already had plans for future film projects. Preme envisioned a series of hood flicks based on Goines novels- *Black Girl Lost, Death List, Kenyatta's Revenge*, and *Kenyatta's Last Hit*. He hoped to make his name and fortune with *Crime Partners*, but he was also busy learning the ins and outs of the music label from Gotti.

While immersing himself in the business, Preme encountered more and more ex-Supreme Team members in the hip-hop industry. A lot of drug dealers from the crack era were in the industry. They saluted Preme and Murder Inc., wishing him luck with his DVD venture and success in the genre. The *Black Gangster* album sold 150,000 copies, and Preme saw *Crime Partners* with the soundtrack and contributions from his hip-hop buddies doing bigger numbers. It seemed a dream come true for Preme. From the moment he got out of jail, all he wanted to do was to buy the rights to a bunch of Donald Goines books and make the films. Finally he succeeded. "Shit was good. I was glad for that," Bing says. "He was going legit. He was with a legitimate organization that was making millions, that was like hitting the lotto, especially how they looked up to him like they did." It was an ideal situation for Preme, one that his cohorts in prison took note of.

"I silently applauded him," Tuck says. "They interviewed him and

Wayne Davis on BET news. Everybody saw that." The street legend was on his way, and he was being celebrated and recognized all around. It wasn't very often that a criminal made the transition to entertainment, but Preme was like Frank Sinatra, doing it "my way."

"Everyone in Queens knew of Supreme," Chris Gotti said. "I'm pretty sure it echoed out further than Queens. Everyone knew Supreme and who he was. This dude had a dream to make a movie which he did. And you could probably count on one hand how many dudes in the hood had a dream and made it come true." The DVD, released in 2001, was a testament to Preme's evolution from crack kingpin to rap industry insider.

"I heard Irv say, 'I always believe in helping the men around me. I can't be the only guy with all the money,'" J. Jesse Smith, the *Crime Partners*' director said. But amidst the success and legitimate front, things behind the scenes were a little sketchy. Preme was leading a double life.

"First and foremost Preme was a street nigga," T says. "He did what he had to do to make ends meet." Tasting the trappings of success while riding with Murder Inc., the money couldn't come fast enough for Preme. He wanted to eat, he was sick of being broke, and asking for handouts. He was an experienced drug dealer and knew the trade firsthand. The hustles of the past were never far behind Preme. The feds said he continued to be involved in illegal activity following his release from prison, including homicide and extensive narcotics trafficking. His Picture Perfect partner Jon "Love" Ragin was running credit card scams out of a business front called Tuxedo Rentals. Love defrauded American Express card holders and customers for hundreds of thousands of dollars, transferring money electronically to his Tuxedo rentals account at Chase Manhattan. He was also running an ecstasy ring. Whether Preme was in the know or not, he was guilty by association, and the feds were on to Love as the *Crime Partners* production was in full swing.

"Success would of been insured without interference from the feds," T says. "Everything that he did when he came home was legal. But the feds said it was drug money." Preme was in the eye of the storm. Events happened around him right and left that made him seen like the nexus and put him in the spotlight. He was the only kingpin and street legend from the crack era that emerged from the 80s unscathed. All his contemporaries were doing time, long stretches of it. Prince, C-Just, Big C, Pookie, Fat Cat, Pappy Mason, Tommy Mickens, and Wall Corley were all in jail while Preme was on the street.

"Too many comrades done lost their life and have a lot of time in prison," Bimmy says. "I have respect for every man walking. C-Just is my brother." The drug game had left tremendous casualties on the Supreme Team, but Preme was unscathed. Dudes looked up to him, but he wasn't calling shots anymore. Everybody got their fifteen minutes, and Supreme hoped his wasn't up. He knew the limitations of his celebrity. He also knew the limitless reach he had in the underworld. Supreme made real efforts to go legit, but he was a criminal at heart, a true gangster who took what he wanted.

"I run with real dudes and these guys are my friends," Irv Gotti said, and the whole Murder Inc. crew played off Preme's notoriety. They were make believe gangsters living in a fantasy world that they created through music videos and interviews. Their studio gangsta personas were so good that it pulled the feds in and with Supreme riding with them, the feds decided there was something tangible to investigate. Murder Inc. wanted the reputation that Preme had. They craved the criminal reality, the authenticity. But gangsters don't do interviews. They don't advertise on TV.

It's like T says, "Gangsters choose to keep silent on their enemies." To Murder Inc. it was all about the spectacle. They were like reality TV. They were in the clubs partying with Preme holding them down. There was a general atmosphere of violence in the rap world, an implication of danger that Preme was used to. He had reigned king in the environment of crack cocaine that fueled cold blooded violence, so to him hip-hop beef was nothing.

"Preme was always aware of his surroundings and that of his crew," the original member says. "Preme would slide up on you and be like 'get on point, these dudes is getting ready to try and bring us a move.' While we were supposed to be watching his back, he was watching ours better than we watched his, and he was the boss. With us we were cool so long as they let Preme come in with his gun, cause Preme could hold us all down with his gun. As long as Preme had his gun, we were cool cause Preme always kept his eyes on all of his crew."

That is why Murder Inc. pulled Preme in, for his authenticity and credibility in the streets. But with a South Jamaican gangster like Supreme among them, the reality of it could be murder and not the "Murder" Ja Rule screamed in music videos. In Preme's world death was real and final; it was also an occupational hazard. Preme thought he was out of the life, but, like Michael Corleone in *The Godfather*, they kept pulling him back in. He couldn't out run or distance himself from the past. It was like an evil smile cruelly glaring over his shoulder. Supreme the man was constantly being called upon to live up to the Supreme of legend by Murder Inc. Preme and the Supreme Team were so steeped in street lore and hip-hop hype that it weighed heavily on Preme's shoulders, but he always attempted to live up to the stature that the streets placed on him. Heavy was the head that wore the crown.

When Preme's main man and Supreme Team stalwart Black Just was killed on December 11, 1999, it might have put Preme over the edge. A bullet struck an artery in Black Just's leg and fatally wounded him. Security cameras at a Queens' hospital showed Preme pushing a wheelchair carrying a bleeding man into the emergency room. Preme had been maintaining a delicate balance between entertainment and reality to this point, but the death of his man awoke his gangster instincts. His dream had come true, but still his finances were not up to par. It seemed Preme was living the high life depicted in Murder Inc. videos, but according to Chris Gotti, Irv's brother, that wasn't the case. "Some people think Preme had money stashed from back in the day but this guy was broke. That's the Preme I know," he said. Given the circumstances, Preme turned to what he did best.

"The boy Preme was bringing them things down to B-More, giving them to my little cousin Shabo," P says. "He went down there talking about he was taking cars and shit. He put his gorilla down. He was sending them things down. He got them niggas rich. He helped people eat down there. He got a lot of niggas started in the game; they was pushing a lot of dope for this nigga." It wasn't the Supreme Team, but Supreme was doing him. He switched it up and went from a retail market to a wholesale one, pushing those birds interstate.

"When Preme was in B-More, he was hitting off Billy Guy," the Southside player says. "That was his dude." Preme was on a mission to get money. With his Robin Hood persona he easily filled the vacuum in Baltimore and was seen as a large scale drug dealer like Avon Barksdale in *The Wire*.

Fuck the bullshit. The rappers wanted to play a game, call themselves gangsters, but Preme was the genuine article. Born and bred in the streets of South Jamaica, Queens, he wasn't faking it. Preme was the legend, the icon and myth, alive and breathing. Preme was hip-hop; he was the all of it, the whole culture rolled into one. He was the swagger, the style, the hustler, the ladies man, the smooth criminal, and the gangster. Everything hip-hop portrayed itself to be, Preme was. He decided to show them. The world wanted the street legend; Preme would give it to them. The death of Black Just jolted him. Other Supreme Team members were around. Bimmy was doing his A and R thing in the rap industry, Babywise was on the block, but Black Just had held Preme down through it all. Black Just lived for the Supreme Team, so his death was one Preme could not abide. "I think the Black Just thing, him getting killed, left a bad taste in Preme's mouth," the Southside player says.

Black Just was shot by Mobb Deep affiliate Eric "E-Money Bags" Smith, a small time hustler and wannabe rapper who lived in the Supreme Team's shadow his entire life and clearly resented that fact. His raps focused on the gun talk he prided himself on. E-Money Bags supposedly approached Preme and Black Just on the street in South Jamaica. Apparently Black Just and E-Money Bags had a long standing beef over a debt owed. Angry words were exchanged, and E-Money Bags shot Black Just in the leg. Supreme drew his gun to fire, but it jammed. "I pulled a gun; it jammed. I ditched it at the scene, and then drove Blackie to the hospital," Preme allegedly said.

"Preme was real fucked up about the whole Black Just scenario," the Southside player says. "He felt he let his friend down."

It seemed to be a non-fatal wound, but Black Just slowly bled to death and by the time Preme realized how serious it was and drove Black Just to the hospital, he was dead. The shooting was the proverbial straw that broke the camel's back for Preme, making him revert to form and regress back to his old ways after struggling to go legit. "That shit hurt Preme," the Southside player says. "Black Just was his man." Plus with E-Money Bags bragging in the streets about pulling the trigger in Black Just's murder, Preme was enraged. "Preme wanted to get that nigga E-Money Bags," the Southside player says. "He owed him big time and with Preme all bets were off. The debt would be paid." But with the coming 50 Cent beef, Black Just's death would pale in comparison. The brewing cauldron that was about to blow would shake up the hip-hop world and became news fodder for the world. And 50 Cent, Supreme, and Murder Inc. would be at the center of it.

CHAPTER 10
50 CENT BEEF

"Fifty, who shot ya? You think it was Preme, Freeze or Ta-Ta?"
— 50 Cent, Fuck you, Guess Who's Back

"You wouldn't deceive top dog Supreme Team/How and why would you try to fuck us? On the real."
— Ja Rule, Survival of the Illest 2

"According to Supreme, he was trying to squash the beef between 50 Cent and Murder Inc. It was agreed that the beef would be squashed...But 50 Cent didn't stay true to his word."
— Don Diva Magazine, Issue 30

The murder of a prominent Supreme Team member and Love's credit card schemes cast a dark cloud over the *Crime Partners* production, but Preme kept forging ahead, as he was a man on a mission and keeping it gangster was his M.O. The Murder Inc. crew tried to keep it gangsta also, but whereas Preme's gangster meant bodies dropping, Murder Inc.'s meant hip-hop and industry beef in which they engaged in faux posturing, albeit in an increasingly violent style, to settle their rivalries. For Murder Inc. and Preme a little known rapper cum thug who called himself 50 Cent became their target. Curtis Jackson, who lived with his grandparents in Queens, adopted the moniker 50 Cent from a Billy the Kid-type crook out of Fort Green projects in Brooklyn whose government was Kelvin Martin. He was known for robbing rappers and died at the age of 22, gunned down in the projects. "I took the name 50 Cent because it says everything I want it to say," 50 said. "I'm the same kind of nigga 50 Cent was. I provide for myself by any means."

Portraying himself as a "reckless street nigga," 50 Cent was quickly becoming known in Queens as a rapper who wasn't afraid of controversy. Among his supporters in the industry were Jam Master Jay of Run DMC and Chaz Williams from Black Hand Entertainment. Fifty had tasted a little success and notoriety from the *Black Gangster* soundtrack and wanted more. He put himself on the map with 1999s *How to Rob* or as it was better known in the streets, How to Rob an Industry Nigga. In his debut single 50 created the ultimate beef record by taking on literally every notable rap artist of the day, describing how he would violently stick up all the big names in hip-hop. *How to Rob* instantly made 50 Cent notorious in hip-hop circles. It also made him a target. But 50 used beef to further his career, and Murder Inc. was the first to fall for the bait.

"I think it started with a video shoot that I did on Jamaica Avenue," Ja Rule said. "We're all from the same neighborhood. I think when he seen how much love we was receiving from all the people, he didn't like the fact that I was getting so much love."

Irv Gotti backs this assessment up, "The hate from 50 came from pure jealousy. We were on Jamaica Avenue shooting the *Murder for Life* video, and I had the real O.G.'s out there- Supreme, Slim- and they all giving us love. Fifty came up to Rule to give him a pound. I don't know if Rule gave him a pound or not. Nigga we weren't thinking about you. Who the fuck are you? You're just a meaningless face. Now that face turned into the biggest rapper in the world, that's just our luck. This is honest to God shit. That's why when me and Rule think about the beef, we are like, 'Maybe we should have just given him a hug.'"

According to Supreme's partner Chaz "Slim" Williams, 50's vendetta originated when Ja Rule brushed him off. At that point, 50 took offense and deemed Murder Inc. his mortal enemy. Whether it was true animosity or opportunism- a beef with the label could help him make a name for himself- 50 wasn't shy about making his feelings known. To 50 though, it was deeper than that. "He was filming a video on Jamaica Avenue and the whole hood was out. Ja started running his mouth about me and telling people I couldn't rap. He was sabotaging my fan base," 50 said.

Fifty also dates the beef to when a friend robbed Ja Rule of some jewelry. "This nigga from Baisley Projects, Lil' Troy, robbed Ja. He saw me with this nigga in Club Amazura in Queens and after he saw me say what's up to this nigga, he started acting different," 50 said. "Like I'm not going to say what's up to a nigga cuz he robbed you. Niggas was grinding and hungry, so he robbed Ja's punk ass. He knows I didn't have anything to do with this nigga too. So I go backstage and say what's up to this nigga Ja, and he is hesitant to say what's up back. After that situation, I was like, 'Fuck him.'" With the snubbing of 50 by Murder Inc. and the chain snatching, it was on. After the robbery, Ja Rule told Gotti who in turn contacted Supreme. Supreme went to Lil' Troy and got the chain back for Ja.

"It didn't take intimidation. It didn't take threats for me to say, 'You got to give it back,'" Supreme said. "I always see these articles where 50 is saying that his man robbed Ja. But that's my man. I raised him."

Fifty couldn't let it rest though. "Lil' Troy, the nigga that robbed Ja, is in my era. We did shit in the street together. While Preme's always talking about the nigga that took the jewelry from Ja was raised under the Supreme Team, under him, that's true. But I used to be cool with him," 50 said. The incident became a flash point for tensions between Murder Inc. and 50. It was also later cited to support the FBI's theory that Supreme served as protection for the label in exchange for funding for his movie.

"After that I had a conversation with Preme. He was like, 'Yo, leave this little nigga alone. You know they pussy. But this is my food.' I was like, 'Okay.' Ja had the *Holla, Holla* record out. He felt that he was invincible. Right after that, I dropped *How to Rob* and after that the first thing I did was get in his ass," 50 said. The song sparked more beef for 50 with Murder Inc. "We were supposed to do a show in the Atrium," 50 said. "I get to ATL, there's eight niggas standing in front of my hotel. I get out of the car. I'm laughing at this nigga. He got a little bat. We walk in the hotel. I tap this nigga Ja, like, 'Yo, let me holla at you.' At first everything is fine. I'm explaining to this nigga why I made the record. So he starts talking, 'You should have talked to me like a man,' waving his fucking hands, talking loud, looking toward his niggas, so they can see him screaming on me. So I had to punch this nigga in the face. Then they jumped on me."

Out of respect for Supreme, 50 tried to dead the situation but he still had to defend himself. In the fight that ensued 50 walked away with another piece of Ja's jewelry which was another slight to Murder Inc.'s street cred. "I had popped his chain off while we were fighting and told him to come get it," 50 said. "But by that time the police were coming and everybody dashed off." When 50 got back to New York, Supreme approached him about what had happened. "I explained the situation to him," 50 said. "And he understood why it went down the way it did. He said he couldn't blame me and gave me a gold watch in order to get the chain back." The bad blood was split. Murder Inc. was enraged. They were out to bury 50 Cent. They were trying to blackball him from the industry.

Supreme was trying to mediate the situation because to him it was all just some little rapper bullshit. "I was intervening to squash the issue," Preme said. "I thought it was meatball. I think he said Ja Rule didn't say hi or something." He tried to assert his influence on 50.

"Preme's telling me, 'Chill.' And then the nigga goes and says something new," 50 said. "He came down there several times and said, 'Yo, leave these niggas alone.' I went to see this nigga Ja on the Coliseum block. They was shooting a video back there. Nigga called me from the barbershop; told me them niggas was up there shooting the shit. So I went; got the pistol. I went there on the motorcycle cause I wanted to see what its about. The nigga see me. Supreme see me from across the street, walking down toward the shoot and says, 'Hey. Come here; don't even do it. I see you.' Pulls me to the side, and I'm like, 'Yo what's up with this nigga?' And he's like, 'Nah, nah. I told you; leave them alone, man. You know they ain't gonna do nothing.'" Out of respect for Supreme, 50 left it alone again. But Murder Inc. had a different take on it.

"As soon as I heard a peep out of him, I should have went right into the studio and wrote a song about how I punched him in the face. If you know a nigga like 50, he is not your man," Ja said. "I'm like, 'This nigga is a nobody; let it ride.' The only bad thing to happen is he got with Eminem and Dre. Now he became a somebody, and niggas wanted to hear what he had to say. I started the beef. Y'all niggas think this fuck nigga started it. I brewed it, and he turned it into a rap beef. The thing was on the streets way before it got into the music. Fifty hid in the booth and rhymed about it. I am the only nigga that stepped to his business."

While Ja Rule and 50 were wilding, cooler heads, who knew the finality of death, were trying to squash the beef. "The Ja Rule/50 Cent beef was partly because Supreme spoke up for Ja Rule and 50 Cent took this as a rejection of him," T says. Chaz Williams and Supreme interceded trying to iron everything out.

"They tried to arrange a meeting for me to go meet with him and Chaz at Black Hand. At the time, Chaz, we was cool with each other. All Murder Inc. is there with Preme, and I'm supposed to go in there with Chaz and squash the beef," 50 said. "Listen, they was supposed to fuck with me, the old heads in my hood. Why? Because they know I'm authentic. Period. Any move I decided to make they were supposed to roll with me because I'm actually from the same fucking cloth. I'm an offspring of them. I'm not a relative. I'm not a brother or sister to these niggas. I'm a distant cousin. I'm from down the road. Everything that's fucked up about me comes from these muthafuckas. Most of the niggas out there who talk gangsta and thug shit in raps don't really want to be a part of the stuff they're putting on their records. Ja was never on the street, he didn't hustle, he didn't bust his gun, he didn't do any of the stuff he talks about on his records."

Fifty Cent was in his feelings due to Preme's rejection of him, but Preme was riding what he thought was the winning horse. How was he to know that 50 Cent would blow up like he did? At that time Murder Inc. was on top of the rap world and Murder Inc. wanted to crush 50 Cent, despite the sit downs. The real gangsters, Preme and Chaz, engineered the sit downs. Murder Inc. was just playing its role, the role that had been perfected in the videos. Fifty was from the hood, but many of the old heads felt that he got a pass around the neighborhood because of who his mother was. In the hood they knew the truth. "Fifty ain't half the man Brina was," the Queens hustler says.

"Now, what the fuck would I be doing walking into a room when everybody in the room is cool but me?" 50 said. "I had a Mac-32 shot clip. I came to the building and didn't go in, cause my brain tells me, don't walk into that situation. It's a bad situation. Niggas will say the wrong thing out they mouth cause they got that comfort zone; they got you in a room all by yourself. You kill somebody in the building; then you're done. So I don't go to the fucking meeting. Chaz, the same nigga who's supposed to be cool with me, was setting up the meeting so we can squash it. He's calling this nigga his friend now, so you know the nigga was on the gate the whole time." After 50 didn't show for the meeting, Chaz called him and told him he was on his own. He washed his hands of 50.

Retribution related to the beef continued just before 1 a.m. on March 24, 2000, when 50 Cent was attacked by the Murder Inc. posse at the Hit Factory, a midtown Manhattan recording studio on West 54th Street. "The story was 50 was in the studio, Murder Inc. go up there, lights go off, someone stabs the shit out of 50, then he runs into someone else's session, locks the door and calls the police," Superhead said. Fifty was treated for a laceration to the chest and a partially collapsed lung at St. Luke's Roosevelt Hospital and later received an order of protection against Murder Inc. The Source magazine published its content in an issue, and the website getsmedia.com posted the order with the message, "Real street niggas don't snitch. Fifty Cent does not rep the street. He is a coward and a liar; you cannot deny court documents."

Fifty Cent addressed the order of protection in Don Diva magazine, "I never went to no precinct to file an order of protection against nobody. I know everybody involved in my situation. I figured we'd handle it in the streets."

The rapper Scarface checked out the supposed court documents and defended 50 Cent. "This is bullshit, man," he said. "That kid is real; this is fuck shit here. You can't even really read this shit; it's a copy of a copy."

Fifty wrote in his autobiography *From Pieces to Weight*, "If there's one thing that it's not cool to be in the streets, it's a snitch. You sentence a nigga to death when you call him that." Murder Inc. stood by the paperwork.

"We had actual papers showing that Curtis Jackson and Marvin Bernard (Tony Yayo) had an order of protection and that they were suing us," Ja Rule said. "Fifty dropped his shit because he got his deal, and he knew it would ruin him. But Yayo got paid. I bought Yayo his first chain, and I bought him his first car. I might have paid him about 50 G's, and he sued Sony and the Hit Factory. He went in on everybody. Fucking faggot ass nigga." The Murder Inc. camp and Preme were not happy with 50. They were trying to crush him in anyway possible and on all fronts.

Ja Rule took the beef lyrical with his intro on *Survival of the Illest 2- you wouldn't deceive top dog Supreme Team/how and why would you try to fuck us? On the real.* "I should have squashed him," Ja Rule said. "I should have put out more records to let the public know how I feel about this guy, and who this guy really is. He's saying 'Fuck Ja Rule, Fuck Murder Inc.'" But at the time, Murder Inc. was Goliath to 50 Cent's David, so they really didn't see the need. "He is making all types of fuck records about me but at the same time he is telling the police that he is scared for his life because of us," Ja said. "Now I don't know what to do because I don't want my lyrics in court. Sometimes in beef and battles, that's what it's all about, it's for the fans, it's like a big show and for me it wasn't that, it was very real. But 50 made it into a show." Fifty Cent was talking that street shit, so Murder Inc. took him at his word.

"We were on top of the world and 50 hated us," Irv Gotti said. "He turns on the radio, hears us, and hates us. You didn't snatch the chain. I knew the guy who snatched the chain. I never told anyone not to sign him. But when people called me I was like, 'I don't like the dude, and I'm not fucking with the dude.' If that's blackballing, then that's blackballing."

Murder Inc. wanted to bury 50 Cent for even daring to come at them or fuck with them. "They were trying to blackball 50," the Southside player said, but 50 persevered.

"Irv Gotti does not have enough power to shut anything down," 50 said. "But he threw dirt in the game." As the flavor of the moment, Murder Inc. had pull, and they had Supreme riding with them. With that influence on multiple levels, they thought they could crush 50. But as they craved more street authenticity, they fell under Preme's sway. Preme had big juice in the streets and at Murder Inc. headquarters. He was like Don Corleone.

"I knew Irv was the boss on paper," Superhead said. "But when Preme walked through the house and said something, everyone listened. Maybe Irv was the boss in the Universal building, but when Preme walked in the building and if he said something, that's how it went." Preme even had keys to the Universal building and came and went as he chose. He had the run of Murder Inc. headquarters as did a lot of his criminal associates. Exactly what Supreme was doing at Murder Inc. was the question a lot of law enforcement officials were asking themselves. Early in the investigation they followed him to the slickly appointed Manhattan headquarters of the Universal Music Group on Eighth Avenue and 50th Street where he passed through security and disappeared up the escalator to the elevator bank. A security guard identified him to agents as "Mr. Supreme" and added that he worked upstairs at Murder Inc. But the agents weren't buying that Preme was an executive at Def Jam, Murder Inc.'s parent label. They suspected something far more nefarious.

Preme was playing the game though. He was playing his position and warned all comers, "Never fuck with Murder Inc." He knew they were his meal ticket, so he was protecting his interests. Preme was into a lot of different things at the time, entertainment and street. He was leading a dual life. To him the 50 Cent thing wasn't about nothing, but 50 wouldn't shut up. "He's temperamental and says what he feels. I'm pragmatic and stick to the facts that don't change every time I speak," Preme said. The facts were that Murder Inc. and Preme dominated the hood and music industry. On a desolated "drug trade dominated" block in the 103rd Precinct, the facts were in plain view. "Its Murdah," Murder Inc.'s slogan was emblazoned on the graffiti strewn walls making sure everyone knew who ran the block. Life had come full circle for Preme. It was the same wall where "Supreme Team" had been written in the 80s.

"Me and Preme had a relationship," 50 said. "At one point we would speak to each other, and we would kick it. But we have so much in common we can't get along. He's just not gonna like me, and I'm not gonna like him. His outlook on things is he should do what he wants, and I feel the same." Fifty knew the Murder Inc. crew was trying to blackball him too. "I took a meeting with DJ Clue and Rich Skane, Clue's manager, to do a deal," 50 said. "The first thing he says to me is, 'Yo, I spoke to the wolves. Niggas told me it's all right to sit with you, do business.' Cause Preme thought I tried to kill him at the gas station. Somebody shot at him and tried to kill him at the gas station. So Skane's saying, 'I spoke to Preme, and he was like, yo, it's okay to fuck with you.

He thought you tried to kill him, but he found out it was something else.'"

Since Preme was back in the streets, his life was tried a couple of times. "You have a younger generation out there who believes Preme's time/era has come and went. They don't respect anyone," Tuck says.

At the gas station they almost got him. "Tried to hit his ass up," the Southside player says. "But Preme was a good driver and got away."

Even though Murder Inc. was hell bent on blackballing 50, Preme still decided to give the kid a chance. Preme was a real gangster, so the rap shit was nothing to him. "I think Preme feels if a situation can get to the point of physical violence, and he knows both parties, he would feel obligated to put himself in the middle of that to find a peaceful solution," T says. "He's a very diplomatic individual who feels that violence is an option that can't be afforded. But him showing love to Murder Inc. ostracized him from their counterparts." Namely 50 Cent, and even a gangster trying to go legit can be pushed to his limits. "After the sit-down where 50 didn't show up, Preme washed his hands of the kid," T says.

Supreme abandoned peacemaking efforts when he realized 50 was an agent provocateur, a billing 50 would live up to with the song *Ghetto Qur'an (Forgive Me Part 1)*, which was leaked to the streets in 2000. Chaz warned 50 that many of the hustlers named in *Ghetto Qur'an* would be unhappy with the song but 50 persisted. It would be on his newly inked Colombia debut, *Power of the Dollar*, which Jam Master Jay had helped to produce. Chaz had bid 50 good riddance after helping him to ink the deal with Colombia. With 50 going to the studio and needing controversy to mark his debut, he started doing what he did best, talking shit. "Preme loves to be out in the eye," 50 said. "He wants to be a fucking celebrity. This is why when he first heard the record, he told me he liked the record. He liked *Ghetto Qur'an*." The song provided a family tree of Queens drug dealers, and the lyrics paid tribute to the legendary figures of 50's childhood- including Preme and Prince.

"The Vietnam War veterans got the wall and all the niggas from Queens got, the ones that was doing something back then, is that song," 50 said. The song was a tribute to the street figures he looked up to. He wasn't trying to snitch on them, but somewhere from the vocal booth to the streets the song became synonymous with disrespect toward Queens legends.

"I can't stand the interpretation that Preme thought 50 was snitching on him through *Ghetto Qur'an*. It wasn't anything said in the song that annoyed Preme. It was the fact that it was put out there at a real vulnerable time for him. Preme made it very well known that he was unhappy about

Ghetto Qur'an and all those mix tapes. He didn't like being described as the businessman, and Prince being described as the killer," Ethan Brown said. While some pointed to the song as the start of a bloody rivalry between Preme and 50, others dismissed the notion. "I think there was some interaction there, but, other than that, I don't think there's been any interaction. Absolutely zero overlap," Ethan Brown said.

"I didn't really think nothing of it," Bing says. "It was all cool and good. But at the time that I heard it was nothing as important to me as my family, so I didn't feel a certain way about it. I felt different about it later. But it was good that they paid homage to us for who we were and what we did. It is what it is."

Tuck says about the song he first heard in prison, "I don't know 50 Cent but as a rapper. I like 50 Cent. I like his music. He's from my town. He represents where I'm from, and he's made it." The song sparked controversy in the streets. But 50 was talking about ancient history. He wasn't out there in the 80s and neither was Murder Inc. Ethan Brown stressed, "They weren't on the streets when Supreme was on the streets." In the Y2K era, though, Supreme was back on the streets with a vengeance.

"People looked up to them," 50 said. "They had the neighborhood, they had the influence. Pappy Mason was more dangerous in my eyes. Prince was a killer. Supreme, finances made him serious." By airing out Supreme's legacy on *Ghetto Qur'an*, 50 knew he could lure Ja into battle. "Supreme doesn't have a voice, so Ja said something back," 50 said. "Before that Ja felt that he was too big to address me." With Gotti and Murder Inc. blurring the lines between hip-hop and hustling by aligning themselves with Preme, they created a surreal world where entertainment and crime clashed. By vividly chronicling the South Jamaica crack trade from the 1980s, 50 pulled the past into the present, a tactical move that suited his purposes.

Supreme allegedly sent a message to 50, "Stop rapping about me." But in truth, why would he put himself in that position? Fifty had yet to make it, so in reality he was a nuisance, a pest, a nobody to Murder Inc. and Supreme. But what must have galled them was his audacity. They must have been thinking, "Can you believe the nerve of this little muthafucka?" Fifty's audacity made him a serious threat. Or maybe Murder Inc. was just so power mad that they thought they could get away with "Murder" like they screamed in their videos. Without Chaz's backing, 50 was seemingly fair game in the streets of South Jamaica, and with his constant jabbering and provoking of Preme and Murder Inc., he had definitely made himself a target. In their eyes, it was open season on 50 Cent.

"If you're in the life, it's always been a thing where you handle your own," T says. "At no time do you verbalize a situation that you can handle physically. Speaking out is the first sign of being a rat. Men don't do that. That's kid shit. Supreme has never been accused of being a stupid person. He's not an abrasive dude. He thinks 50 Cent is an angry young man that's been venting, and his venting could be construed as ungangster because real men don't put stuff out to the public that could bring about an investigation. Preme looks at dude like he's confused. Men that have been in the life, you just don't put your business on wax. The chump 50 Cent wouldn't even be a factor in the rap game today if his lyrics weren't snitch oriented. He owes his success to the media and his beef with Murder Inc." As *Ghetto Qur'an* put Preme's business under the spotlight, he continued to live his life. Fifty was left defending his song and fending off allegations of being a dry snitch.

"The Qur'an didn't make reference to anybody who was actively doing something at the time. It was all past shit. I'm just saluting niggas," 50 said. "The cops come asking me questions. I said, 'I ain't got no answers for you.' They talking like, 'C'mon 50. You always don't give a fuck. You always say whatever you want.' I'm like, 'Man, listen. Listen to my music, like everyone else listens to my music.' I'm telling them, 'Listen to my lyrics like everyone else does, and what did I say that they don't say?' The worst thing you could be where I'm from is a snitch. They don't like that shit. So that's what they try to make me out to be based on. If I'm a snitch, who's in jail?" But real or imagined, the song rubbed people the wrong way. It added fuel to the fire.

"It was factual," Supreme said of the song. "He said, 'Supreme was the businessman and Prince was the killer.'" But Preme still felt 50 shouldn't have aired out the dirty laundry. "When we was coming up, there was a code of conduct." Supreme said. "You didn't speak about dudes who may still be in the streets." Tuck sees it differently though, "How could Preme be upset about a song that says he's a businessman. Even Prince couldn't be upset. He's lived with that moniker for almost his entire adult life." Even as 50 beefed with Murder Inc. and called them studio gangsters, he tried to get Supreme in his corner with the *Ghetto Qur'an* song. To 50 it was a tribute to his idols. He fancied himself a protégé of the team, and the continued rejection by Preme was like the ultimate putdown for 50. His love quickly turned to hate. "Now he doesn't like that I'm airing dirty laundry?" 50 said. "He done put the laundry out on the line. Look, O.G. stands for Old Goat to me. I don't like none of them old niggas. They whole style is obsolete." But obviously it wasn't. The Supreme Team and the Southside of Jamaica, Queens, was stamped all over hip-hop.

Fifty wanted to be down, but everyone abandoned him. He fronted like he was a street guy, but they called him a snitch due to his song that was supposed to be a tribute. He couldn't win, but in the end he did. Fifty turned failure and controversy into success. He wouldn't go away and kept rearing his ugly head. Every time Preme and Murder Inc. turned around, 50 was there taunting, questioning their manhood. In one song he rapped *Scream murder. I don't believe you.* Even a gangster trying to go legit could only take so much. Preme and Murder Inc. eventually decided to get rid of 50. "Fifty ain't never been in the life," T says. "He's a perpetrator to the death of the game. Fifty ain't ever been nowhere but boot camp, a place where guys like Supreme wouldn't ever go, with dudes yelling in your face telling you to do 100 pushups." Fifty was dismissed from Preme and Murder Inc.'s mind. They attempted to make him obsolete. "Kid you've never been through nothing," Preme said. "I was around wolves, man. I walked among giants." But even the best laid plans can backfire.

On May 24, 2000, as 50 and a friend sat in a car outside his grandmother's house on 161st Street in South Jamaica, a gun thug rolled up in a vehicle on 50's left side and pumped nine shots into his body, hitting him in the hand, hip, calf, chest and face. Rather than die as his assailants intended, 50 survived. "When I got shot nine times, it was 12 o'clock in the afternoon, so it wasn't safe for me at anytime." 50 said. "In the daytime it was on wherever you are, you could be coming out of the supermarket with your moms, and it was still on. I'm not saying I am the hardest, but you have no choice when you're dealing with real niggas. It happens so fast that you don't even get a chance to shoot back. I was scared the whole time. I was looking in the rearview mirror like, 'Oh shit, somebody shot me in the face. It burns, burns, burns.'" Lieutenant Richard Bellucci of Queens Homicide Squad was the reporting officer. According to Bellucci, 50 was in a car when two other cars blocked him in, at which point some guys jumped out and shot him numerous times.

Fifty wouldn't cooperate with police, cursing everybody out on the way to the hospital. Lieutenant Bellucci wasn't wasting a lot of time trying to convince 50 to talk, especially if he didn't want to cooperate. As a result, no one figured out who shot 50. In his book, *Queens Reigns Supreme*, Ethan Brown reported that Darryl "Hommo" Baum shot the rapper. Fifty even supported this accusation. In an interview on Hot 97, 50 identified Hommo as the shooter and in verse he rapped, *Hommo shot me/three weeks later he got shot down*, implying that he had something to do with the deed, but Ethan Brown sets the record straight. "What happened to the guy who shot 50 has a lot less to do with hip-hop and 50 than what

50 would like people to believe. The guy who shot 50 was from the old stick up era," he said. It was all just a smoke screen though as 50's more recent comments and trial testimony gave the real story.

Supreme's *Crime Partners* cohort Love claimed that Supreme, alleged triggerman Robert "Son" Lyons, who was Ja Rule's bodyguard, and original Supreme Team member Chauncey "God B" Milliner met in a Brooklyn garage immediately after the May 2000 attack. Love said Preme and the two others ambushed 50 outside his grandmother's house and was shot for name checking Preme in the song *Ghetto Qur'an*. Believing 50 had been murdered, the trio met up with Love, washed their hands with rubbing alcohol, and came up with an alibi that they had been shopping downtown Brooklyn. "Supreme said, 'I got him,'" Love related. "I didn't know who it was he got, and Supreme explained that he got 50 Cent. He thought 50 Cent was dead. He got shot so many times at close range and there was so much blood. He explained to me that they caught him coming out of his grandmother's house, and he got into a car, and that's when he got shot." Love claimed that Preme hired Son to carry out the hit on 50, and he claimed that Son wiped gun powder residue off his hands with rubbing alcohol after the shooting.

In Supreme's and Murder Inc.'s eyes, 50 got what he deserved, hood justice. That was how Preme dealt with problems; he eliminated them. He was a gangster. With Murder Inc. blurring the lines between entertainment and reality, the results seemed justified to them. When Chaz cut 50 loose, he was condemned to death. With no O.G. to protect him, he was fair game. The wolves controlled and influenced the artists in the hip-hop industry and any viable artist needed an O.G.'s protection. Fifty didn't have anyone backing him. He became a target to anyone in the streets, marked for death.

"After I got shot up, I call my grandmothers house," 50 said. "I say, 'Anybody call me there?' She said, 'No.' I said, 'Ma you sure nobody called there for me? The old man didn't call there for me?' Mind you, these niggas is 50 and 47 years old. I'm like, 'An old man didn't call there for me?' She goes, 'No.' So in my head, if Chaz didn't know exactly what the fuck happened before it happened, then he knew already. That's why he didn't call. And they wonder why I don't fuck with him." In 50's eyes Chaz betrayed him, hence the song *Many Men* in 2003 off *Get Rich or Die Tryin'* in which 50 raps, *Slim switched sides on me/let niggas ride on me/I thought we was cool/why you want me to die homie*. But immediately 50 had more pressing concerns. "I had to move my son to the Pocono's to get them out of harms way, so when I healed up, I could come back." Fifty made up the scenario about Hommo being gunned down three weeks later to prove to Supreme he wasn't a snitch. Fifty set out to prove his gangsta to Preme also.

"I slept in front of Baisley Projects, in front of Supreme's grandmother's house in a 1993 Dodge Caravan with three hubcaps waiting to kill him," 50 said. "So niggas have never been in that frame of mind before. When I had a beef with Supreme, I was not comfortable unless I had a bulletproof vest and a pistol, and someone else that was with me had on a bulletproof vest and a pistol. These niggas is real niggas. So what do you think my thought process is. I tell him, 'Fuck you. I see you; I blow your head off 12 o'clock in the afternoon.' Now this is really getting interesting to niggas in the hood, cause they go, 'Yo, this nigga got hit nine times. This nigga don't give a fuck.'

"This ain't when Preme went to jail 50 started talking crazy; when he was on the streets. He made it the way it is. If I said he had something to do with me getting shot, it means nothing, cause eveybody in my hood knows that's what time it is. But that's not the problem. It's cause he didn't see that I don't just listen. Nigga just don't tell me what to do and it's okay. Either way, he's a wrap now, because the change they don't see is the financial transition. Same way the nigga that shot me wasn't an 'inhouse' for them- he was just a shooter. I have access to that now. I have the finances. The shooters shoot as the bag is dropped. So now, either they give Preme life, or they let him go, and I give him life. They don't understand the difference. The first album I was trying to explain it, *Power of the Dollar*, they had money when I didn't have money. So I had to take bullets," 50 related.

After the attempt on his life in 2000, Colombia records dropped 50 Cent. "They got scared," he said. "To me, getting shot wasn't as bad as getting dropped. After thirteen days in the hospital, you think things are good, and you can move forward. But they said, 'Forget about him.'"Supreme and the Murder Inc. crew were ecstatic. Reportedly, a message from one of Murder Inc.'s pagers that was sent shortly after 50 was shot said, "Fuck half a dollar, me and my niggas kill for fun." Irv Gotti also sent a flurry of messages allegedly within 30 minutes of the shooting asking how many times 50 was shot and if he was killed. Even though 50 wasn't dead, which they must have found hard to believe considering the lead that was pumped into him, Murder Inc. figured he was finished in the rap world after Colombia dropped him due to the shooting. Mission accomplished. Although there was still payback in consideration for any who helped 50. And Preme definitely had revenge on his mind for Black Just's murder. The reckoning was at hand. It was time to tie up all the loose ends. Preme was taking an accounting and cashing one check at a time. Fifty didn't lie down, though; he went on the offensive. Never one to be cowed, he took the fight to Supreme and Murder Inc.

"The first song I put out was *Fuck You*, telling the niggas who shot me, fuck you," 50 said. "My situation was a public situation; people knew that I had gotten banged up. Out the gate, I was like, 'Fuck you,' to the niggas who shot me. I'm telling them to suck my dick. So what do you think my thought process is when I'm telling them when I see them I'm down for that daytime action? We can do it whatever time it is in the day when I run into you. I'm saying this on the records to these niggas before my album even come out. Before these niggas go to jail, while they still on the street with me." It was on before between 50 and the Murder Inc. crew, but after the botched hit, it was really on.

Fifty rachetted up the intensity, and Murder Inc. and Supreme got caught in the media blitz. It became more than just rap beef. When Preme and Murder Inc. raised the stakes by trying to take 50's life, he went for broke. He was literally going to get rich or die trying. Fifty took some serious street shit and turned it into a show for fans. He didn't deal with it in the streets. He addressed it in his music. "Now that it became music, I knew that we had to deal with this nigga on a different level. If it was just on the streets, hands down, we won. But it turned into music," Ja Rule said. What was hood shit became entertainment shit, and in this forum 50 found he could manipulate events like he never could in the streets. Preme was the master in the streets, but 50 quickly proved he was the student turned teacher in the entertainment world.

"You dealing with real niggas, you better come to the plate," 50 said. "You better come with your A game or get wrapped up. That's it. Niggas gave you an example. Took nine bullets, nigga. You come back saying, you know what? I don't care. I'll kill 'em. I go to jail, they going to remember me the rest of my life. Cause if I'd have seen him in the gas station or the store, I'd have wrapped his ass up. Then there would be 'Preme was a real nigga, but that little nigga 50, remember the nigga who shot him?' So even if it didn't work out for me where I could become a nigga that was able to do things in business that's respectable, they would've respected me, or remembered me for blowing his head off. You feel what I'm saying?"

Fuck You from 50 Cent's independently released *Guess Who's Back* speculated frankly about just which Queens' gangster pulled the trigger on him. *50, who shot ya?* 50 rapped. *You think it was Preme, Freeze or Ta-ta?* Ja Rule responded immediately with *Guess Who Shot Ya*, where he rapped, *Your heart ain't cut for the code of the streets/you're wondering 'Is it murder who shot me?'* Fifty responded with *Heat*, where he spit, *The drama really means nothin' to me/I'll ride by and blow ya brains out/The D.A. can play this muthafuckin' tape in court/I'll kill you- I ain't playin.'* It was a rap war. Fifty was walking the line between being a gangster and entertainer, albeit it was 90 percent entertainment, as was Murder Inc. which was directly opposite from Preme, who was walking the same line, clearly entrenched on the gangster side. Preme had a fearsome rep in the hip-hop world. Supreme was clearly and definitely who 50 wanted to be. His comments and raps stressed how gangster he thought he was, but his actions didn't match his talk. "Supreme knew that barking dogs don't bite, and that's all 50 Cent was to him, a barking dog," T says. But in hip-hop, as opposed to reality, words spoke loudly. In the entertainment world the show must go on.

Everyone in the street knew that actions spoke louder than words, and 50's actions were naught. But he talked a good game. He talked Supreme and Murder Inc. right out of business and into a federal investigation. Preme and Murder Inc. tried to murder 50. In retaliation 50 murdered their careers and put cases on them. With the dry snitching in his songs and his interviews, he was a one man retribution squad. He was on a crusade against the people that tried to end his life. "I never called him a snitch," Preme said. "I said his behavior could be construed as dry snitching. I was referring to his contact with federal agents and him telling them to listen to my lyrics." Because in reality 50 was telling the feds what they wanted to hear.

"Gangsta is something that happened to me," 50 said. "That's the way the hood made me. Irv tried to be something he never had the heart to be in his neighborhood. That's where Gotti came from. When I first came back, my intentions were to straight up kill niggas on the mic. I'm going to show these fake ass niggas you all done came through wrong. Niggas know what happens when you miss. I came out with *Fuck You*. I didn't even write that. I went into the studio and just said what's on my mind." The response from the streets sparked interest in 50 again.

His buzz was stronger than when *How to Rob* hit, especially since he got hit nine times and came back gunning, lyrically at least. He was playing up the Tupac image and killing Murder Inc. and Preme in public. Ja Rule tried to hit back with *The Wrap*, where he rhymed, *This nigga runnin' around talkin' about/I got shot nine times, I got shot/Want everybody to be muthafuckin' sympathic/A yo, 50, pull your skirt down B/A yo, niggaz get shot everyday B, you tough? Ha, ha, ha.* But 50 played the Tupac role to perfection which his fans loved. When 50 performed, the crowd would chant, "Fuck Murder Inc., fuck Murder Inc. Fuck Ja Rule, fuck Ja Rule." The backlash against Murder Inc. was tremendous. Everybody was flocking to the 50 Cent banner. He was the street smart underdog taking on the corporate hitmaker. The attempt on his life came up repeatedly in interviews, and 50 was happy to provide embellishments. *50 Cent Beats Bullets*, the newspaper headlines read.

"I still do what the fuck I wanna do," 50 said. "It's one thing if you out there popping off, and you talking about this nigga from up the block who got a verse that sound like you. It's another thing when you talking about real street niggas. Whatever same type of shit Preme has running through him, is running through me. And he can't see it enough to give me room to coexist with him. He wanted me to submit, and that's just not in me. A nigga would have to kill me to stop me doing what I want to do. That's what they tried. Its not gonna happen with a halfway mark. You really have to kill me to stop me doing what I want to do. Cause all I believe is what I think. All I believe in is me.

"My thoughts and the way I see things are my truths. It had to make sense to me and then I'm with you. I didn't feel like I feel about these niggas now. Younger, you look up to these niggas. Those are the niggas that you know made the money. And then you see what they turn into. These are lessons to kids to say no to drugs. These are perfect lessons, because you look up to them, and then you look at this nigga Preme, he did nothing."

After Preme's rejection of him, 50 tried to justify his feelings but the truth of the matter was that 50 was deeply hurt by Preme's rejection of him and his siding with Murder Inc. Fifty was even more hurt that Preme went after him with Murder Inc.'s blessing. But 50 turned the tables and exploited every situation to his advantage, pulling the strings like a puppet master.

"If I was a rapper who was pretending to be tough, that would be exploiting," 50 said. "But if your lifestyle is like that, it's just a fact. I'm not into the police. I've never known them to de-escalate a situation. They make it worse. Once a person is afraid, you might as well lay down and give up. I'm not anticipating a beautiful life. Things are going to happen. That's been my life to this point. So I expect anything." Fifty was nothing if not realistic. Murder Inc. and Supreme were less realistic, but they must have been taken by surprise. Like, "Who the fuck is this dude? Where did this nigga come from? Why didn't he just die?"

Murder Inc. upped the ante when they started their anti-50 Cent campaign, but, unfortunately, it was too late. As Ja Rule boasted of Murder Inc.'s Supreme Team connections, labled 50 a snitch, and got The Source magazine to cosign it, 50 struck back viciously. In a mix tape track called *Order of Protection* 50 rapped about Irv Gotti, *Don't nobody respect you nigga/you Preme's son nigga/muthafucka been getting extorted since day one.* "They're cowards," 50 said. "A gangsta will always side up with a weak party who needs them for strength. They take advantage of people who have talent through fear. The fear factor allows a weak artist to hang with gangstas. But that doesn't mean you're down with gangstas. That just means you're getting extorted by gangstas."

Fifty was on his way to stardom when *Wanksta*, a thinly veiled attack calling Ja Rule a fake gangsta wannabe perpetrating a tough guy image dropped. As his star rose, Murder Inc.'s crashed. "I might sign Ja Rule when he's done at Murder Inc.," 50 said. "After I destroy him, I'll rebuild him. Because he never was strong enough to individually go against me. He needs the support of everyone else to try that. And they should have been smart enough to tell him not to directly go against me." When 50 signed with Eminen and Dr. Dre, his ascension was set, and it became evident with *Get Rich or Die Tryin'* that it wasn't just an album title, it was 50's mission. He left Murder Inc. and Supreme scrambling and facing a serious federal investigation. It wasn't looking good for Preme and Murder Inc.

"Outsiders were probably like, 'Damn look at Ja, 50 is crushing him.' Nah, nigga, I'm good. I got a big ass house in Miami, and I got a whole bunch of cars," Ja Rule said. "I'm like, 'Don't feel sorry for Ja Rule because when you see me or meet me, I don't give off that energy.' I'm walking around like, 'Fuck that nigga.' Y'all don't know that nigga like I do. Fifty is a hoe. The hoe will show in a minute." But to 50, Murder Inc. was the hoe, or at least that was how 50 portrayed it in magazine interviews, always talking, talking, talking.

"When niggas tried to kill Supreme in the gas station, he thought it was me because he knew about the niggas I had around me," 50 said. "All I have to say about Supreme is if him and his niggas were who they said they were, then why didn't we have to dance? Yet, it's like the music stopped when Supreme left. It's like you see 30 niggas dressed in all black with their faces screwed up like they are hard, but the shooter ain't none of them 30 niggas looking hard; that tells me that they ain't about nothing."

But what is 50 about? His man from way back in the day, Bang'em Smurf, who 50 dropped after becoming successful said about 50, "Yeah, 50 sold drugs, but 'I'ma kill you' and all that shit, he don't do that. He ain't never shot nobody, cut or stabbed nobody, nothing like that." Smurf claimed that 50's super thug persona was just an image and a marketing tool that he concocted. Playing off the ghetto legends from his hood, the Southside of Jamaica, Queens, 50 rocketed to stardom. By repping them he attempted to become them. But in no way can you compare 50 to

Queens storied hustlers like Pappy Mason, Prince, Fat Cat, and Supreme. G-Unit was never going to be the Supreme Team no matter how much marketing and illusion 50 used. Despite all the talk about being shot nine times, in truth, according to the official police report, 50 was only hit by three bullets. To the world 50 is the gangsta rapper, the epitome of thug life. But to those who know him in earnest, he is a fraud. Fifty is a great actor though. He is very believable. He's like the Al Pacino of hip-hop, but Al Pacino wasn't Tony Montana; he just played him. But the beef has lived on in infamy.

"I don't think it's gonna define my career or legacy," Ja Rule said. "It's such a minimal thing to me. I think people are fascinated with the whole wave of what happened, the biting of my style, the fact that he shitted on me. Everybody turned on me, and he come back and did the same style I'm doing, the whole aura of it. From the fight, the whole gamut of the beef, people are intrigued by it. It's definitely one of hip-hop's biggest beefs. He's not important in my life; he's not relevant." But Ja Rule was fronting. At the time Supreme and Murder Inc. were obsessed with 50.

"That cracker is pimping him," Preme said. "He ain't nothing but a muthafucking house nigger who set everything, set us back 150 years. Next thing he gonna start doing is macaroni and cheese commercials." When 50 gets older, that might be true. He will definitely go where the money's at. He has already got all his tattoos removed as he's gotten more into acting than rapping. "People must realize that gangsters don't rap, and rappers are not gangsters," T says. "Rappers do just that, portray an image. Like Al Pacino was not *Scarface*, Curtis Jackson is not 50 Cent. It seems to me that the kid has some sort of identity crisis. Here's a guy who named himself after a notorious Brooklyn gangster who he never knew. He makes all this money and what does he do, he buys Mike Tyson's old house, a house that will forever be known as 'Mike Tyson's house.' Then he goes on MTV giving interviews titled All Eyes on 50 Cent. Doesn't that sound like Tupac? The kid needs guidance. He must be true to himself."

CHAPTER 11
BACK IN JAIL

"Don't nobody respect you nigga/you Preme's son nigga. Muthafucka been getting extorted since day one."
— **50 Cent, Order of Protection**

"Supreme is a towering street legend. He carried out Mafia style murders while moving kilos of coke."
— **Vibe Magazine**

"On December 28, 2002, the feds arrested Supreme. They didn't want him on the street. In effect, they were putting him on ice as they investigated all the murders they were tying to link to him."
— **Don Diva Magazine, Issue 30**

With all the bullshit swirling around the streets, Preme wouldn't long be a free man. The 50 Cent beef, the *Crime Partners* movie, Murder Inc.'s high profile lifestyle- it all created a no win situation for Supreme- the ex-convict, former drug baron who was trying to go legit. But in reality Preme didn't help himself. He was deep in the game, trying to live up to his reputation in the gangster fantasy climate Murder Inc. created. When entertainment became reality, it wasn't pretty. In the summer of 2001, when Preme was getting ready for the release of *Crime Partners*, everything started falling apart. His actions, combined with 50 Cent's rise and the buzz in the streets, hastened Murder Inc.'s demise. Queens' detectives were all over Preme in connection with several murders. During the nineteen months following Black Just's murder, Preme told associates that he was attempting to locate E-Money Bags to kill him and avenge Black Just's death. Preme knew E-Money Bags had gone into hiding because he was looking for him.

Three murders during the latter part of 2001 were linked to Supreme and intensified the growing federal investigation around him that eventually engulfed him and Murder Inc. as 50 watched from the sidelines, seemingly providing the feds info and cheering them on. It seemed Preme's underground life closely imitated his art. On July 16, 2001, E-Money Bags was killed in his Lincoln Navigator which was parked near Witthoff Street and lllth Road in Queens. It was a highly premeditated execution. A group rolled in on him, just like the gang in the movie *Dead Presidents*. E-Money's girl, Tomika told detectives that everybody believed Preme was behind the murder.

"No one can figure out why Preme didn't get nobody from Queens for the hit," the Southside player says. "They must of all been afraid of E-Money Bags." In the streets it was rumored that the whole hit team was from Harlem. Police deduced quickly that it was a murder for hire hit and gangland-style execution. After the murder, Preme allegedly told friends that Black Just could now rest in peace. Fifty Cent even added his two cents to the matter releasing a song titled *50 Bars of Pleasure, 50 Bars of Pain*, where he rapped, *Yo, Black is flashy like Alpo/gun happy like Pappy/ but he an O.G./remind me of Chaz and Bump/real low key* glorifying Black Just's gangster status and raising his game point average after his death. In the minds of street hustlers, Preme had exacted retribution- an eye for an eye, but he wasn't finished. Preme's life had been tried four times since his 1997 release from prison, and he had debts to pay. These debts would be paid in blood. For Preme it was time to call in all bets, and for dudes that crossed him, it would cost them their lives.

Karon Clarrett, a small time drug dealer and cohort of Preme's associate Victor Wright, was the next to be snuffed out. Clarrett supposedly helped run Preme's Baltimore operations with Wright and Vash-Ti Paylor. After a bust in North Carolina on April 5, 2001, for transporting two kilo's of cocaine, Preme's crew suspected Clarrett of cooperating with police after he fired the New York guns and drugs lawyer, Preme had hired for him. Fearing the consequences of having a snitch in their midst, they quickly arranged for him to be dealt with. Investigators learned that Supreme farmed the Clarrett killing to a Baltimore drug dealer who owed Preme a debt for narcotics. Clarrett and Dwayne Thomas were killed on August 20, 2001, at Red Run Apartments, 4319 Flint Hill Drive in Owings Mill, Maryland. The killers fucked up because the murders were committed in the parking lot across from where Preme maintained his B-More stash pad. Preme was not happy.

A confidential informant told homicide detectives that Baltimore drug lord Billy Guy owed Preme for drugs on consignment. Preme allegedly told Bily Guy he would forgive the debt if Guy took care of Clarrett. Upon searching the homicide scene, Baltimore detectives recovered various items from Clarrett's body including a piece of paper containing the number for Preme's two way, text messaging pager. From Clarrett's cell phone they found the name and number of Vash-Ti Paylor, which they traced to 4314 Flint Hill Drive. Following the homicide, Preme was angry because the murders exposed his stash house where detectives found 731 grams of cocaine, 34 grams of heroin, a Ruger 9mm, and approximately 30 grand in cash. The detectives also found some interesting videotapes. One had Supreme stuffing large quantities of cash down his pants, one of E-Money Bags the night before his murder, and various behind the scene videos of the *Crime Partners* production. The search at Red Run Apartments turned up a gold mine of evidence including the 2001 firearms training course certificate that would put Preme back in jail.

Troy "Big Nose" Singleton, another Queens hustler, was the third murder victim. He was killed on October 28, 2001- execution style- outside a sports bar called the Club Van Wyck on Liberty Avenue in South Jamaica. Big Nose was hit eight times, his body riddled with bullets. Singleton was allegedly whacked for killing two dudes during a basketball game at the Baisley Park Houses, Preme's home turf, in July 1995. He allegedly murdered Pierre Mitchell and Jamal Adams. "Troy Singleton went to prison for murder, and a prominent dude from the Supreme Team's handle was on the paperwork. Troy sent the paperwork home from prison, and the prosecution gave him a plea deal to avoid the prominent Supreme Teamer from having to testify," the Queens hustler says. "Before Troy was killed, he waited on some of Preme's dudes outside the offices of Universal and bitch slapped them around Broadway. Troy was pressing everybody who had any connection to Preme." He allegedly cornered Ron "Gutta" Robinson, Ja Rule's manager and smacked him around.

Anyone who had slighted Preme or the Supreme Team in any way was being erased. That was how it looked to the streets. With the bodies dropping, Preme was asserting his authority and flexing his muscles to show that he was indeed the premier gangster on the scene, entertainment or otherwise. But what Preme didn't account for was the tremendous media scrutiny focused on him due to 50 Cent's rise to megastardom. As 50 rose into the national scope of popular consciousness, a searchlight was illuminated over the Southside of Jamaica, Queens. Preme hadn't calculated for this happening, but how could he? This miscalculation would prove fatal as it led to Preme's inevitable downfall.

"Money laundering is one thing, murder is something else," the Queens detective said. "When you're doing an investigation and someone very close to it gets killed, it certainly increases law enforcement interest." Preme was using tried and tested Supreme Team policies perfected by his nephew Prince, and like Prince, Preme's downfall would be because of snitches. Even though snitches were killed when discovered in the ongoing Preme/Murder Inc. affair, the rats started coming out of the woodwork as the feds began their investigation into Murder Inc. in 2002.

Hip-hop insiders said that the investigation into Murder Inc. would involve separating fact from fiction in an industry of blurs, where the songs often read like police blotters. With 50 Cent telling the feds to "read my lyrics," they used his lyrics as testimony. Murder Inc. made it very speculative for the feds by releasing a CD called *Irv Gotti Presents The Murderers*, which listed Supreme in the credits under Murder Management, not a very smart move when the bodies were dropping. Nothing in rap happened in a vacuum. Everything that happened ended up in rhyming verse. With Preme trying to get away with murder, it wasn't an ideal situation. The feds had a lot of ready material to gather their evidence from. "A lot of these guys, they're really confused," Antoine Clark said. "They bring in the criminals from their neighborhood. They think they know the guy and bring the guy into the organization, and they forget what happens in the street, and there's an effect from all that."

Preme and Murder Inc. became the subject of an intense FBI investigation. Their beef with 50 Cent was just the tip of the iceberg. In 2001 the DEA intercepted a package containing five grand in cash wrapped in scented baby wipes mailed to Supreme's associate Love who was under investigation by the IRS for the credit card fraud ring. When the agents seized his two way pager, they saw a number of texts to and from Supreme using the tag line "Murder Inc." While Murder Inc. was pulling in millions of legal dollars, the feds insisted that the labels ties to Supreme were grounds to suggest that the label was operating with illegal money. An IRS agent alleged that Supreme was the "True owner of the company and was a Mafia like muscle man for the label." In light of the federal investigation, the 50 Cent beef was nothing.

"Who cares about beefs and all that shit when niggas is talking about sending niggas to jail," Ja Rule said. "They want you to pick out your friends. When you get into this business, they be like, 'Leave them niggas alone and come with us.' I'm like, 'What about them? My niggas wanna live good lives too. Preme's my nigga, that's my dog.'" But the feds were trying to separate Preme from Murder Inc. while at the same time indicting them together. Their attitude was, snitch out the ex-con, give us Preme, and we'll leave Murder Inc. alone. But Ja Rule and the Gotti's weren't going out like that.

"Preme is my man, just that my man," Irv Gotti said. "My lawyers were like, 'If you just say you're not going to be friends with him, this might all go away.' But I run with real dudes, and these guys are my friends. No one is going to tell me who is going to be my man. So if they want to lock me up, I'm going away."

The feds knew Murder Inc. was a legitimate company. They were just exploiting them, holding them up as an example for all of hip-hop. "Leave the hood shit in the hood, don't take it public on MTV," they said. The feds wanted to separate the street from entertainment once and for all. They pressured higher ups at Universal Music Groups to rein Murder Inc. in, but Irv Gotti and them weren't having it. They were standing up for their man Preme.

"People tried to persuade them to distance themselves from me," Preme said. "But if you know someone and you know what they were trying to accomplish, you don't abandon them just because the government says he is a bad guy. Should I have not taken a legal opportunity out of concerns of the feds? What aggravated the feds was that I actually made a film based on a Donald Goines book with an all star cast. You see, the feds are vindictive in nature; they believe that once a bad guy always a bad guy, and that you don't deserve to be prosperous. They sit around all day saying he's got to be doing something wrong and once they believe something, no amount of evidence to the contrary will alter their position. Long before I came along, the feds viewed hip-hop as a criminal entity. There is a tremendous gulf between us and them. Because they can't understand our vernacular or our culture, so they attack it."

Since Murder Inc. wasn't capitulating to the feds' wishes, they were against them, and the feds were hard at work trying to establish that Murder Inc. was funded by Preme's drug money. "The feds are talking crazy," Choke says. "They're saying Preme put up the seed money for Murder Inc., that he got 50 Cent shot and owned Murder Inc., that he was the power behind the scenes." These were absurd, but at the same time believable accusations, seeing as how the Gottis and Ja Rule pushed the connection. With gangsta rap center stage, law enforcement was actively looking for crime figures in hip-hop.

The federal investigation of crime in the rap music business was centered on Supreme. "They got his muscle, his backing. It's a violent industry and you need to have someone with street cred behind you to survive," the Queens detective said. Supreme was the central figure in the probe, and his name was quickly attached to any rap related crime.

"I didn't think nothing of it. Because they were always putting his name out there because of who he was. They linked him to everything because of his name," Bing says. Supreme's controversial past earned him mentions in every sensational hip-hop news story.

"Every rap related crime they bring my name up," Preme said.

Even his long time lawyer Robert Simels agreed. "His name comes up with every unsolved crime," Simels said. "He's a victim of wild innuendo." In 2002 the investigation was just heating up, but it would quickly become an inferno, especially as investigators kept approaching 50 Cent and his rote response was "read my lyrics." To Murder Inc. 50 Cent seemed like the puppet master pulling the feds string. They kept blasting him as a snitch. On *Loose Change* Ja Rule spit, *So on ya grave it's gon read/ here lies Fifty who snitched on many.* The IRS affidavit connected Preme to the 50 Cent shooting also, "The investigation has uncovered a conspiracy involving McGriff and others to murder a rap artist who has released songs containing lyrics regarding McGriff's criminal activities. The rap artist was shot in 2000, survived, and thereafter refused to cooperate with law enforcement regarding the shooting. Messages transmitted over the Murder Inc. pager indicated that McGriff is involved in an ongoing plot to kill this rap artist and that he communicates with Murder Inc. employees concerning the target."

Preme didn't help matters when again he was at the center of controversy. With murders happening all around him, Preme and a friend were arrested in July 2001 when cops stopped their BMW in Harlem and found each man carrying a loaded .40 caliber Glock pistol. "These aren't meant for you," Preme said. "It's a tough neighborhood." More than twelve grand in cash was recovered from the men, and Preme told the cops, "We were shopping. You caught me on a bad day. Usually I'm carrying more than that." Preme and his companion were indicted by a Manhattan grand jury on three counts of criminal possession of a weapon. Preme was also indicted for resisting arrest and carrying a phoney New Jersey driver's license.

Preme's lawyer, Richard Giampa, argued that the two men were shopping near West 145th Street and Broadway when several unmarked police cars converged on their BMW. Supreme was "violently approached by numerous armed, unidentified strangers," his lawyer said. "There was no use of this gun. The police were in unmarked cars; they came after them at gunpoint." Preme pleaded guilty to the top count of gun possession and remained free on fifteen grand bail. The ATF traced the gun to a relative of Chris Gotti. It was bought by Rory Lorenzo in Las

Vegas in 2000.

"Why wouldn't Preme carry a gun? Niggas was gunning for him. A young wolf could earn a lot of points for bodying Supreme," the Southside player says. Preme did what he needed to do for survival, but the police and feds were vindictive in their pursuit of Preme.

"Supreme is a guy they really want to put away," the Queens detective said. "He is viewed in New York law enforcement circles as one of the big fish who got away. He is associated with the 1988 cop killing, and a lot of law enforcement people feel he never got his just due. In their eyes he shouldn't be on the streets ever." It didn't look good for Preme despite his successes and appearances of legitimacy.

His lawyer claimed the government was unfairly targeting his client. "Despite his past notoriety," Giampa said. "Kenny McGriff is a man who is now trying to make an honest living." To the feds it didn't matter, as Preme was the usual suspect. With a long rap sheet, the deck was stacked against him.

With a sentencing date for the gun charge, Preme went to see Prince at USP Beaumont in Texas in January 2002. "Whatever you want to say about Prince, he could be the most notorious dude ever, but to Preme, that's his little nephew," Irv said. The original member backed up this assessment. "Nothing Prince could ever do would change Preme's opinion of him nor would Preme ever stop totally loving his nephew Prince." Preme tried to visit his nephew and old comrades when he could, under a false name of course, and help them out in any way he could. "At the time Preme knew he had to go to jail for the gun charge," Irv said. "Every time he goes in he always feels like it could be his last." Those words were prophetic because when Preme went in, he would never see the streets again. Irv Gotti paid for the trip and provided a limo for Preme to ride in to the jail. Prison officials noted "A sharp increase in the presence of heroin in the prison facility" right after Preme's visit.

A beef resulted at Beaumont later that year also involving Prince and Big C, who got into it with some Detroit dudes. Prince and Big C got locked up under investigation due to the altercation, but Big C hit the compound again without Prince who was still in lockup, and without his homie to watch his back, Big C was killed around Christmas 2002. This was an unfortunate situation that ended the life of Prince's bodyguard and comrade. On prison life Prince said, "My current circumstances make it necessary that I remain street smart. I'm not one who plays mind games with myself. I'm surrounded by cold brick and steel all day, everyday. It is what it is. The jungle is full of traps, weapons, predators, and prey. Therefore, it is essential that my awareness is continually heightened on every level, just like in the streets. But I like it that way. It keeps me on my feet."

While Preme visited his nephew in Texas, U.S. Attorney Roslynn Mauskopf prepared an indictment of Jon "Love" Ragin on credit card fraud. A raid of Ragin's office yielded over 1,000 blank credit cards and equipment for manufacturing more. The feds also planned a raid on Murder Inc.'s offices. With everything closing in around him, Preme stayed busy, trying to lay low and make moves, but every rap related crime was attributed to him either directly or indirectly. It was a crazy time for Preme as there were newspaper headlines trumpeting his name day after day. The press was having a field day examining and analyzing the Preme, Murder Inc., and 50 Cent connections. While awaiting sentencing for the New York City gun charge, another climatic event occurred that would prove disasterous for Supreme.

On October 30, 2002, Jam Master Jay from Run DMC was killed gangland style in his Queens recording studio. Immediately, the streets, media, and law enforcement floated Preme's name in connection with the murder. *Feds link 50 Cent, Dealer to Jay Slaying, The Daily News* headline read. The theory that emerged early on was that Jam Master Jay was killed because he helped 50 produce and put out 2000s *Guess Who's Back* mixtape that featured *Ghetto Qur'an* and *Fuck You*, songs that namedropped Supreme and heightened the investigation around him.

"Preme didn't have nothing to do with the Jam Master Jay situation," the Queens hustler says. "But the papers were trying to sell papers, right? So they make up stories." It came out that Jam Master Jay left enormous debts behind. "Even the Mafia treats its members better than the music business," the Southside player says. It was hard to believe that Jam Master Jay, who was supposedly set for life, was broke, but he was.

"Agents are still trying to determine whether Jam Master Jay's homicide has any connection to the ongoing dispute between 50 Cent and Supreme," a DEA agent said. "We are investigating the possibility that Jam Master Jay was murdered for defying the blacklist of 50 Cent." There were reluctant witnesses and witnesses who changed their stories in the Jam Master Jay case and there was a rush to judgment. People wanted to say Supreme did it because of Jay's affiliation with 50 Cent. It made for a good news story. The day after Jam Master Jay was shot dead, police offered 50 Cent 24 hour protection, but he rebuffed them. A number of guns and bulletproof vests were found on 50 Cent's entourage though. "It's about that thing in Queens," was the reason they gave cops for arming themselves. With all the gun drama, 50 must have thought he was next in line.

Another development that further clouded matters for Supreme was his indictment in Baltimore on federal gun charges for a series of visits he made to a Glen Burnie, Maryland, shooting range where he took target practice with machine guns under an alias in 2000. With the federal charges, Preme was officially on the run. The Jam Master Jay murder was a definite killing blow for Preme's hip-hop dreams even if he had nothing to do with it. The media storm that covered the hip-hop icon's death snowballed uncontrollably with story after story linking Supreme to the murder. The innuendos that 50 Cent started in the streets and the hip-hop world with his lyrics were now full blown accusations being examined by every news and entertainment media outlet in the world. The results of the criminal investigation were now a foregone conclusion. "They say he tried to kill 50 and now Jam Master Jay is dead, and they're saying Preme did it. It's a wrap. He was done," the Southside player says. The feds had all the information they needed. They were making their case through snitches and song lyrics.

"All I can say is that people fear what they don't know," Prince said. "And it's no different for the legal system. The government fears Preme because they don't know him. They didn't produce him nor have they been able to buy him or flip him. So out of their fears they made every attempt to eliminate him. As with most of our natural born leaders, they're eliminated by a system that refused to accept them. I am very proud of my uncle. He remains my commander in chief; I salute him."

Inside the fences Supreme received the ultimate respect from convicts like his nephew, but still the rumors flew. If anything, prisoners will gossip. "I just heard that he's the one who had 50 get shot," one prisoner says. "I read about him in The Source magazine. I heard his name several times. They said he killed Jam Master Jay and some other rappers. He supposedly killed his people and had a contract on 50's head."

On December 23, 2002, *The New York Daily News* headline read *Zeroing in on Raps Seedy Side, Gangsta Dough a Magnet for Queens Thugs, Feds Say.* This article put Preme on front street and connected his present to his turbulent past. The article showed how everyone he associated with in the 80s was doing life and compared Jam Master Jay's death to that of slain officer Edward Byrne, who Pappy Mason was convicted of ordering to have killed. This article drew a gruesome picture and all but assured the public that Preme was guilty of something if not everything it outlined. "One should never allow fear to curtail their potential or anything for that matter," Preme said. "What needs to take place is that we need to remove all this dichotomy and petty disputes and find some common connections that can strengthen our union, because they want to end hip-hop. I don't regret my decision to change in a new direction." But the feds weren't having it. They were moving in for the kill.

Preme moved carefully after the Jam Master Jay killing, traveling under aliases and paying for hotel and car bills in cash. By the time *The New York Daily News* piece came out, he was on the lam. "All wiretap activity stopped, and he disappeared," the Queens detective said. On December 28, 2002, the feds got Supreme. He was at the Loews Hotel in Miami Beach with a female companion where he had checked in under the name Rick Coleman. The feds extradited him to Baltimore to face the federal gun charge. "With the weapons charges pending the feds essentially kept Preme on ice," the Queens detective said. "With big issues hanging in the air, especially the killing of a prominent figure like Jam Master Jay, it's nice to know where he is if you have to go look for him."

They arrested Preme on the weapons charge as a pretext. The ties between the rap music industry and drug trafficking were the real investigation. The feds were unconvinced Supreme had gone straight. They just knew he was funneling drug money to Murder Inc. They had targeted him along with his associates in hip-hop. "He was on the Baltimore news everyday," DJ, a friend of Preme's says. "He was in the supermax in Baltimore where they hold the federal inmates. We was in the block together when he was facing the gun charge in Maryland for shooting at a gun range. He's a real cool dude, not what the media makes him out to be. He's real down to earth. All these cats was trying to leech onto him and shit. He really didn't trust no dudes. He knew the feds was trying to build a case against him and they could be planting rats. Preme always told me the game was over."

The rap industry was in flux, with Suge Knight and Supreme locked up, the power brokers behind the scenes were gone. "There is a power vacuum now," said the Queens detective. "The Murder Inc. people are scared, 50 Cent is coming up, and everybody is running around nervous. There are two aspects in the industry, the money and record sales and also the muscle side. The rappers can't exist without the muscle behind them." The investigation escalated dramatically on January 3, 2003, when federal agents armed with search warrants raided Murder Inc.'s offices and seized computers, financial records, and files. They rifled through desks and drilled open company safes looking for a link between the self proclaimed "Most Dangerous Record Label" and Supreme.

With Preme locked up, the feds moved on the other targets of the probe. On the same day they raided Murder Inc.'s 29th floor offices at 825 8th Avenue, the feds also raided Preme's *Crime Partners* co-producer Love's home in Queens, label accountant Cynthia Brent's home, and Irv and Chris Gotti's homes. "It wasn't just the office," Irv said. "It was my brother's house, the accountant's house. It was like four different locations hit simultaneously. They was acting like I was John Gotti. It's not the NYPD; it's the feds. They came at me all crazy like I'm some crime boss. You never see it cause you're on cloud nine. You don't think it's ever going to stop. You ain't seeing the feds. I don't care if I was with Supreme. I'm not doing nothing wrong." The feds were dead set on proving that Murder Inc. and Preme were crime partners. They believed 50 Cent's lyrics verbatim, and the raids were an attempt to gather evidence to prove the accusation that Preme was the "true owner of Murder Inc." who "provided the label with muscle, threats, violence and intimidation."

Though the federal investigation into Preme and Murder Inc. had been ongoing, Irv Gotti and his brother Chris were blindsided. "There was no lead up to it to think that was gonna happen," Chris said. Gotti and Murder Inc. suspected that 50 Cent was somehow behind the raid on their homes and offices. They believed he was telling the feds more than "read my lyrics." To them 50 was a snitch of the highest order, sabotaging his competition and enemies, and putting federal cases on them while he came up at their expense.

It was no surprise to Murder, Inc. that they were raided right after 50 was arrested on weapons charges outside the Copacabana, a Manhattan nightclub on New Year's Eve 2002. It was also eerily similar to them how the feds' claims mirrored 50 Cent's lyrics. Court documents even pointed to 50 dry snitching. "When agents specifically asked 50 Cent who shot him," IRS Agent Francis Mace wrote in an affidavit filed in the federal investigation into Murder, Inc., "he replied sum and substance that he would not answer that question directly and that agents should read his music lyrics." The USA Today's headline read *Probe of Rap Industry Results in Raids, Arrests*, on January 9, 2003. The media blitz was on.

On January 16, two weeks after the raid at Murder Inc., someone rode the elevator to the 11th floor of another hip-hop office, Violator Records Management, which represented 50 Cent, and fired at least six shots at the plate glass windows in the reception area. This wasn't a rap video. It was real bullets from a real gun. Luckily, no one was hit but no one was caught either. Were Murder Inc. and Supreme making a statement? Who knows? But the Queens detective warned that, "If you know somebody that's in a pattern of criminal behavior and you're with them all the time, you can very easily get caught up in that." Keeping up their M.O., Murder Inc. continued to blur the lines between reality and entertainment with the music video Murder Reigns by Ja Rule which depicted an informant 50 Cent handing over info on Murder Inc. to a prosecutor. The highly publicized raid, satirized in the video featuring Patrick Swayze as a grim faced FBI agent, thrust the probe of Murder Inc. into the middle of a growing debate over law enforcement's scrutiny of rappers, fueling claims that the government had launched a war on rap.

"I left the set thinking the feds weren't going to find this video funny," the Southside player says.

With the raid on Murder Inc. and Preme's incarceration, it wasn't looking good for Queens most storied street hustler. The government seized all assets from Supreme's companies, Picture Perfect Films and Picture Perfect Entertainment. The assets included $350,000 of the upfront payment by Murder Inc. and all proceeds of the *Crime Partners* film. A law enforcement official said that among the company's principals were Preme's sister, Barbara McGriff and Jon "Love" Ragin. The feds seized four bank accounts at HSBC which belonged to the company tied to Supreme. Supreme's lawyer said that the money was for the production of the movie sound track, and the disbursements from the account were legitimate and overseen by a reputable entertainment management company.

"Before the raid, it was all good," Irv said. "Lyor Cohen and Russell Simmons know Preme. They knew Preme before me. Back in the 80s Preme was doing the parties, and they would bring the artists."

Russell Simmons backed this up. "I knew Supreme better than Irv," he said. "I knew him when he was a kid. I knew him and James 'Wall' Corley and Lorenzo 'Fat Cat' Nichols and all those guys from southeast Queens. I couldn't help it; they booked my acts." It was all love, but the tide was turning. Still, the worst was yet to come. Jon "Love" Ragin turned snitch and entered the Witness Protection Program. Love pleaded guilty to two felonies and decided to work off his sentence by flipping on Preme. Love told the feds that he worked for Supreme in a "widespread narcotics distribution and money laundering organization that committed homicides and other acts of violence using the *Crime Partners* DVD to launder proceeds of their criminal activities."

The probe by authorities in New York portrayed the well traveled drug path to Baltimore as a trade route that provided start up funds for Murder Inc. and said the label was secretly run by Supreme. *Cash from Baltimore's Drug Trade Helped Bankroll Murder Inc., The Baltimore Sun* headline read on May 17, 2003. While Murder Inc. fought for their lives and livelihood in New York, Preme was pleading guilty to a federal gun charge in Baltimore. Preme's attorney argued that federal prosecutors were overreacting in charging Preme after he used a loaner gun for target practice at the Select Fire range. Without elaboration, the court papers filed by government investigators insisted that Supreme had been transporting drugs "from New York to the Baltimore, Maryland area, among other locations" since the late 1990s, had jumpstarted his drug dealing career, and had overseen other violence to keep his enterprise intact. "I don't think at this point that they have established that he was involved in any recent narcotics activity at all," Preme's attorney Robert Simels said. "Everybody who went to jail in the 1980s and got out saw the entertainment field as the place to go."

Preme was sentenced to 37 months by U.S. District Court Judge Frederick Motz on June 2, 2003. The judge said there was no reason to "be anywhere near a firearm" or target practicing. "There's no reason for you to keep your skills up," the judge told Preme. Preme still faced up to seven years in prison on the state gun charge in New York, but he was trying to withdraw that plea, especially with the federal investigation into Murder Inc. and all the allegations swirling around the streets, the hip-hop industry, and in the media. Concerning the allegations being bandied about Simels said, "They're not proven. They're not charged, but they're terrible allegations."

The 37 month gun charge stemmed from a certificate of completion for a handgun training course issued to Lee Tuten, one of Preme's aliases. An ID in that name was found in the 2001 search of the Red Run Apartment stash house after the Clarrett double murder with Preme's photo affixed. Preme was eventually sentenced in Manhattan Supreme Court for the 2001 New York State gun charge by Justice Michael Correiro. Assistant District Attorney Anthony Capozzolo called Supreme "a remorseless criminal" and asked that his five year sentence be run consecutive to the 37 month term Preme was already serving, but the plea deal Preme took bound the judge to sentence him concurrently.

As Preme was taken to FCI Gilmer in West Virginia to serve his federal time, his name was fodder for media reports as journalists and writers ate up the Murder Inc./Supreme/50 Cent story and turned it into international headlines. Preme was linked to everything from 50 Cent's shooting to Jam Master Jay's murder to the double homicide of two men outside the Red Run Apartment complex. According to the media he was a one man crime wave, a super gangster who ruled the drug trade up and down the east coast, and regulated the rap world through his ownership of Murder Inc. His fearsome reputation was legendary as was his mythical entrance into hip-hop lore through the lyrics of raps biggest stars. Preme claimed he was the victim of a "vindictive investigation" by "overzealous and politically ambitious individuals," and his supporters echoed this sentiment.

"From my point of view they trying to judge him from his past. Every article talking about the Supreme Team. That shit was 20 years ago," Choke says. But a story emerged of Preme's air travel and hotel stays across the country, two way text messaging pagers, drugs, and murder. Prosecutors also introduced evidence of other violent acts by Supreme. Some of the evidence included an incident where a man was thrown through a barbershop window and an incident where Supreme allegedly ordered a man killed for bumping into him at a nightclub. It was a gangster story straight out of a Hollywood movie. From the heights of hip-hop celebrity to the gutters of South Jamaica, Queens, and inner-city Baltimore, Preme was the man to see for whatever was needed- kilo's of cocaine, a rap recording contract, murder for hire, show security, and straight to DVD movies. Preme was the man and had his hand in everything. Just like Frank White from the *King of New York*, if a dime bag was sold in Central Park, Preme wanted in. From reading all the newspaper headlines and news reports, a fearsome picture emerged. Preme was the preeminent gangster of the day, a cross between John Gotti and Puff Daddy, king of the underworld and hip-hop royalty.

As 2003 went on, the news reports intensified. Preme was on the compound at FCI Gilmer with the rumors circulating. Prisoners talked freely and Preme was what they were talking about. "He was kind of to himself," one prisoner said. "But I think it was best because his case was pending. He was a cool dude, chill and quiet, didn't bother nobody. I was in my room writing when a nigga came in and said they got Supreme on BET, saying he was facing the death penalty. The feds are always trying to assassinate a black man with power. I saw Preme the next day; he wasn't looking worried, but he was conscious of what they was trying to do. Dudes on the pound respected Supreme. They were saying Irv Gotti was gonna rat him out but he always checked niggas, saying Irv was a man and would carry his own weight."

The feds heard a lot of the talk from prison through their informants and started shuffling Queens and New York City hustlers back to MCC New York to pump them for information on Supreme. "A lot of guys are so scared of these walls. That's why most of them tell everything," the prisoner says. "I hate snitches myself, so I know how Supreme felt. But he carried it like a real nigga supposed to." Preme walked the yard everyday and was courteous and polite to prisoners from all backgrounds. Mainly he stuck to his inner circle dudes like Tuck, T, and Choke. Every time he went to recreation dudes would try to holler at him.

"Man, we would be trying to get somewhere on the move and all these dudes would be hollering at Preme, talking about they want to spit sixteen bars and shit," Choke says. "I always told Preme, 'Why you talk to these crackheads?' Preme told me, 'You can learn a lot from a dummy.'"

Preme was getting lots of letters requesting interviews too, but he wasn't going for it. He chose to remain silent. "I think some of the big people like Supreme and Prince have been kind of holding on to their stories in hopes that they may one day get some kind of great book deal or Hollywood deal or something like that," Ethan Brown said.

But Tuck explains, "He's never gonna sit down and give an interview. The only time a gangsta is gonna sit down and talk is when it's over."

By November 2004, several staffers at Murder Inc. had been indicted on money laundering charges. Irv Gotti's bookkeeper, Cynthia Brent, was arrested for conspiring to conduct improper financial transactions involving drug cash and released on $250,000 bond. She was put under pressure by the feds to cooperate against Gotti and Supreme. "Gotti and them defended Supreme. They defied law enforcement," T says. Murder Inc. hired Guy Petrillo, who was an Assistant U.S. Attorney in Manhattan for seven years, to represent Brent at $300 to $500 an hour.

Even with the situation looking dire, Preme was still trying to regulate Murder Inc. "When Dahlu came home, Preme sent him up to Murder Inc. to get some money and they called the police on him," the Southside player says. It was getting too hot for the record label. They wanted no part of Preme's people.

Prosecutors said that between 1999 and 2002 Supreme provided Murder Inc. with drugs, muscle, and cash. Preme was also suspected of ordering at least eight drug related murders in Queens and Maryland. Ron "Gutta" Robinson, Ja Rule's manager, was arrested a week after Brent on an indictment charging he conspired with others to launder more than $1 million in drug proceeds. "It's like Supreme said, 'They could have easily not been on the indictment by saying what the cops wanted them to say,'" T says. This was the feds' first volley. As the feds circled like vultures, Ja Rule shouted out his man on his 2004 album *RULE*, *Preme, I'm sittin' under the tree and the apples about to fall in my lap, hold ya head, we'll see you soon.* Despite Ja's wishes and positive outlook, the feds investigation continued, and more evidence would come to the surface.

The surveillance video that the detectives found in the Red Run stash apartment was pivotal. It showed E-Money Bags driving around the area on 111th Street, where he was later murdered, in his Navigator in the four days before he met his demise. Detective William Courtney, a cop with the NYPD's High Intensity Drug Trafficking Task Force and a special FBI agent, filed an affidavit stating that the video was without a doubt made in preparation for the killing of E-Money Bags. "Based on my training and experience, which includes the investigation of numerous homicides, it is my opinion that this surveillance videotape was in preparation for the killing of Eric Smith," Courtney said in the affidavit. "A reliable cooperating witness has informed agents that Supreme admitted to participating in the shooting of E-Money Bags for the killing of Colbert 'Black Just' Johnson on December 11, 1999."

A Queens couple, Dennis "Divine" Crosby and Nicole Brown, were indicted in the slaying of E-Money Bags that Supreme allegedly ordered. "Crosby and Brown videotaped E-Money Bags before the killing from their apartment," a police spokesman said. Nicole Brown told police that a few days prior to E-Money Bags' murder, Divine brought a videotape recorder to Brown's house. Divine videotaped the victim as he congregated with his friends on Brown's street. Divine called Brown on a daily basis to have her arrange three way calls between Divine and Preme. They were also charged with participating in a drug-trafficking enterprise run by Supreme. This was the first of many indictments and superceding indictments the feds would file against Preme, Murder Inc. and their associates.

CHAPTER 12
SUPREME GETS LIFE

"Anytime your name is ringing bells the way Supreme's was, it should be expected that police would not be far behind."
— **Don Diva, Issue 23**

"So on ya' grave it's gon' read/here lies Fifty who snitched on many."
— **Ja Rule, Loose Change**

As Preme was waiting for his release date to arrive at FCI Gilmer in the summer of 2005, the feds were busy gathering evidence to prepare their indictment. They fought their battle through the media with *The New York Daily News* airing the prosecution's sound bites, *Hip-Hop Mogul Gotti Linked to Drug Kingpin*. In reality Preme knew he wasn't going home. He knew he wouldn't see the streets again, but that didn't mean he wouldn't fight. If anything, he was going out like a gangster. "All is well, as can be expected under the circumstances," Preme said. "The fix is in; the government is sparing no expense to eliminate me. But I remain undaunted and resolute in my stance, head up and chest out. I am in the box and have been for several months. The captain told me I will remain here indefinitely. It only strengthens my resolve. I am more focused."

With his name omnipresent in the news media, things weren't looking good. The press had already tried him and convicted him. The feds told the media that Supreme was responsible for multiple homicides and the sale of vast quantities of narcotics in Queens, Baltimore, and elsewhere. They said he carried out Mafia style murders while moving multiple kilos of cocaine. They maintained that when he emerged from prison in the mid-90s he became involved in illegal activity that generated substantial proceeds and restarted a criminal organization whose members and associates engaged in acts of murder, narcotics trafficking, and money laundering. In effect the feds said that Supreme reformed the Supreme Team and carried on where Prince left off.

While the feds were busy getting ready to indict the so called new Supreme Team, the members on the RICO act case with Prince were either wilding in prison or getting ready to go home. "C-Just was in ADX," the Southside player says. "He allegedly had an issue with an Aryan Brotherhood guy whom the Muslims were beefing with. C-Just became Muslim in prison. His Muslim name is Sadiq. He still goes hard."

Prince, C-Just, and the others with life sentences were still fighting their case. "Many of us remain striving to regain our feedom," C-Just says. "And the families of those that have fallen don't deserve to have their children, husband, wife, father or mothers' name being connected to vicious rumors. Some of us remain incarcerated with pending appeals, and we don't need anyone trying to glorify or rekindle rumors and fables that may far exceed our true legacy. The Assistant U.S. Attorneys do enough of that already."

In the penitentiary it was a constant battle for Prince and his crew, but some of Prince's men like Tuck, Teddy, and Bing were waiting to go home after completing their sentences. After many years, Puerto Rican Righteous showed up on the radar again. A team member's sister saw him in Virginia Beach pushing a Mercedes during beach week. "Tell Teddy, Tuck, and them that wasn't meant for them," Righteous said, meaning that his testimony was for Prince, who allegedly slept with Righteous' wife when he got locked up before the big bust. Still, the collateral damage was done. As Tuck, Teddy, and Bing readied themselves to go home, Preme was facing the music.

"I've seen him in the streets, and I've shared a cell with him in prison," Tuck says. "No one is infallable, but I don't think the Supreme of 2005 is the same man the media portrays him to be."

To them Supreme and Murder Inc. were public enemies number one and treated as such. "They painted this picture themselves," Antoine Clark said. "There's something that comes behind bringing in a kingpin to sit and ride with you. There's a certain ghetto pride and ghetto respect, but there's also a police investigation into the ties." On January 26, 2005, Supreme, Murder Inc., and others were charged in an indictment with laundering more than $1 million in drug proceeds through their control of the rap music label Murder Inc. and a straight to video film. Nine individuals and two corporations were charged with an array of offenses including racketeering, trafficking in cocaine, heroin, and crack, money laundering, and homicides.

"They don't call it gangsta rap for nothing," sneered FBI agent Fred

Snelling. "The thug image is not accidental."

The sprawling 37 page indictment detailed a wide variety of criminal activity, including racketeering, drug trafficking, illegal use of firearms, money laundering, and most ominously for Supreme, multiple murders. These murders included the August 20, 2001 homicides of Karon Clarrett and Dwayne Thomas in Owings Mill, Maryland, the July 16, 2001 homicide of Eric Smith, the aforementioned E-Money Bags in New York City, and the Troy Singleton murder. Informants told authorities that Supreme bragged about the slaying of the wannabe rapper and street thug who was shot ten times in his SUV. For more than two years law enforcement officers and agents from the NYPD, IRS, FBI, and ATF investigated what they called "the new Supreme Team."

"The feds put charts up in the courtroom and said that Murder Inc. Records is now the Supreme Team," Irv said. It was a very Hollywood prosecution by the feds. Like a script straight out of a gangster movie.

The investigation revealed that upon Supreme's release from prison, he rebuilt a far reaching and violent organization with several new members, since many of his former Supreme Team members were incarcerated as a result of earlier convictions. Against a backdrop of a massive poster of the *Crime Partners* DVD cover and a flow chart titled *Laundering of Drug Proceeds of the McGriff Enterprise Through Murder Inc.*, U.S. Attorney Rosalynn Mauskopf announced the indictment of Preme and the Gottis. She claimed, "In Irv and Chris Gotti, Supreme's friends and executives in control of the record company Murder Inc., Supreme found two willing allies and a network of businesses at the ready. The Gottis and Supreme became partners- crime partners- and together they laundered over $1 million in illicit drug proceeds through Murder Inc."

The feds alleged that Supreme's new organization, referred to in superceding indictments as the McGriff Enterprise, became involved in a wide variety of criminal conduct, including racketeering, drug trafficking, illegal use of firearms, money laundering, and homicide. "It is easy to go before a grand jury and tell them anything. It is very easy to paint a picture for the government," Teddy said. This time, however, instead of a retail operation focused on a Queens housing project, the feds said Preme's wholesale narcotics trafficking reached out from New York through a wide corridor on the East Coast, into Maryland and North Carolina. In contrast to the Supreme Team's street level operations, between 1997 and 2003 the new Supreme Team trafficked in wholesale quantities of narcotics, distributing over 30 kilograms of heroin, 150 kilograms of cocaine, and 1.5 kilograms of cocaine base.

"We will not tolerate violent drug organizations and those that help them prosper by laundering their illicit proceeds," U.S. Attorney Rosalynn Mauskopf said. She maintained that Murder Inc. was part of a murderous criminal enterprise that protected its interstate crack and heroin operation with calculated street assassinations.

"In Supreme's situation, he is the perfect target," T says. "Because of his past and because the hip-hop generation accepted him and put him on a pedestal as an example of what a gangster or hustler should be, the feds wanted to bring him down. You got overzealous prosecutors who aren't looking for a crime. They're looking for victims to put something on.

"Supreme was targeted from the word go. Any man of substance who stands out in a crowd can become a target. The jury has got to see that this guy was being set up to fail before he got out of jail. The feds have become so astute at creating situations where they bring indictments against people with no validity. If you're not going to lie on somebody or try to put somebody in jail or comply with the government, they're gonna come after you," T says, implying that the feds twisted the evidence to their purposes, which is not unheard of, and was very true in this case.

"Armed criminals, whether street thugs or businessmen, are still armed criminals," ATF Agent McMahon said. "Hiding behind a record label does not shield anyone from the law. Guns in the wrong hands have proven to be deadly." Charged in the indictment were Kenneth "Supreme" McGriff, Dennis "Divine" Crosby, Victor Wright, Nicole Brown, Irving "Gotti" Lorenzo, Chris "Gotti" Lorenzo, Ronald "Gutta" Robinson, Cynthia Brent, Vash-Ti Paylor, and two corporations associated with Murder Inc.

"McGriff and company represented a triple threat to the movies and music world: drugs, money laundering, and murder. No more, thanks to the inspired work of our detectives, agents and prosecutors," Raymond J. Kelly, the New York City Police Commissioner said. "If you're going to be involved in money laundering, drug dealing, or murder, we're going to be coming after you. That's our business."

To the world at large and hip-hop in particular, it looked like a war on rap. And a war on rap was a war on blacks. "It's stressful to know this shit is bogus, but this is how they stop these black companies from making money; put a federal investigation on them," Ja Rule said. Real or imagined, conspiracy or not, Preme and Murder Inc. were in the cross hairs.

"Men change over the years, but with the feds it's like once a drug dealer always a drug dealer. These days being a drug dealer is worse than being a rapist. Once you have that stigma, you're hit," Tuck says.

Feeling the sting of media criticism, the feds denied it was an attack on hip-hop. "This case was never about investigating rap music. It was about investigating guns, drugs, murder and money laundering," FBI agent Pasquale D'Amuro said. "Whether their tastes ran to rap, rock, or classical, those who launder drug money and engage in violent criminal acts will face the music of aggressive law enforcement scrutiny and lengthy prison sentences."

The Gottis' attorney Gerald Lefcourt disagreed, accusing the feds of targeting the rap record label. "They hated the name; they hated the nicknames; they hated the music, and they hated the way they talked on pagers," he said. To him it was clear what the feds were doing.

On the day of the indictment Irv Gotti and his brother Chris surrendered to authorities. Four other people associated with Murder Inc. were charged with money laundering in the indictment. The indictment charged that Irv Gotti wrote $281,000 in checks from his own account and that of Murder Inc. to "various entities for McGriff's benefit." It also said that Gotti and his brother used their positions to press Def Jam executives to pay tens of thousands of dollars to cover Preme's travel expenses. "I never wrote phony checks to Preme," Irv said. "I did pay for some trips. During his last days of freedom, he comes to me and says, 'Yo, Gotti, I want to go see my nephew. I'm going into prison, and I may never come out.' I paid for the trip. Plus I took him with us to video shoots and other places to show him a good time before he went back in."

The indictment also charged that Gotti persuaded Def Jam to finance production of the *Crime Partners* soundtrack by providing a $500,000 guarantee that was secretly backed by drug money. Based on that guarantee, Def Jam put up $500,000 for the project. "They went through a great deal by refusing to denounce me," Preme said. "I've had to check a great deal of people who don't know how to gauge a real man. The government at one point offered the brothers six months, and they refused. I know a lot of tough guys who can mean mug all day who would have folded under that kind of pressure. These guys did nothing illegal, but because they supported me on my dream, they chose to make an example of them. But unlike my self, the feds had no background to paint Irv and Chris with. Through it all Irv and Chris stood up. The whole indictment was a charade that I owned Murder Inc., and I gave them start up money, and I laundered a million dollars. All that information came from the government's supposed creditable informants." One of which was said to be 50 Cent.

"I think it's sad about Irv Gotti's situation," 50 Cent said. "He's the guy who allowed his blessings to turn into something negative. Anybody that's in the street is trying to get out. You can't blame anyone but Irv.

When Preme blows trial and they send him to Texas and he hits the max, they gonna eat him alive. He's a buffon. Are you an organized crime boss or were you a nigga from Baisley that sold crack?"

Prosecutors believed that Preme and Irv Gotti funneled hundreds of thousands of dollars in drug profits through Murder Inc. "Money laundering through Murder Inc. is ridiculous. A couple of hundred thousand ain't a lot of money. This is a multimillion dollar company," T says. "And to accuse Preme of murder? He's never been in that part of the game. It's clear he's a negotiator. To kill someone is to create a problem, and a negotiator would never do this." By attaching Murder Inc. and Preme to the murders, they were trying to paint them with a broad brush.

"It's just unfortunate that this investigation has constantly been dragging Irv through the mud," Gerald Lefcourt said. "Ultimately he will be vindicated."

Preme's lawyer, Robert Simels, accused the government of pushing cooperating witnesses to falsely implicate the ultimate targets of the investigation. "I'll be curious to see which one of these creative geniuses have been able to weave a tale that the prosecutors want to hear," he said. "I feel it's a case that can be won; there were many people who had a motivation to kill E-Money Bags and Troy Singleton."

The feds contention that Supreme brought bags of dirty drug money to clean through Murder Inc. was outlandish also. "I never saw Supreme with no bags of cash," Irv said. "I can't say he never sold drugs after he got out of prison, but if he did, he wasn't doing it very good because he was always broke."

Dudes on the street blamed 50 for the indictment. "That nigga 50 got a nigga looking at a life sentence in prison because of that sucker ass shit he rapping about," the Queens hustler says.

The feds were trying to give Supreme the death penalty in the case. They were constantly adding new allegations and superseding indictments. On January 18, 2005, the grand jury handed down the first superseding indictment charging Preme with the E-Money Bags murder. On June 23, 2005, the grand jury handed down a second superseding indictment which charged Preme and Divine with the Singleton murder. Emanual "Manny Dog" Mosely from Harlem was indicted on murder charges in the third superseding indictment for having drafted the hitmen who took the lives of E-Money Bags and Troy Singleton in separate shootings.

"Kenneth McGriff wanted these people dead and needed Mosley's help in hiring the shooters," Assistant U.S. Attorney Carolyn Pokorny said.

While prosecutors contended that Manny Dog was a member of the Supreme Team, Paul Brenner, his lawyer, portrayed his client as a loving father and husband. "He's taking care of the baby, changing diapers- Mr. Mom, so to speak," Brenner said at a bail hearing. But Brooklyn Federal Magistrate Joan Azrack ordered that Manny Dog remain behind bars until his trial.

"What you describe is a person who lives a storybook life," Judge Azrack said. "There couldn't be any more serious charges than what he's charged with. To me it's not even close."

According to legal sources, the prosecution of Supreme wouldn't be easy. "Supreme is being charged with murders that will be hard to prove," the source said. "There are no witnesses, no physical evidence, no forensics, no confessions, no weapons, nothing." But the feds forged ahead and hit Preme with another attempted murder charge. Their police intelligence told them that Supreme was a ruthless and calculating crook who was willing to murder at any provocation. In a fourth superseding indictment he was accused of conspiring to murder a woman identified only as "Jane Doe" after he learned she was pregnant with his unborn child. "The charge is related to an incident in which Supreme is alleged to have attempted to murder a woman who was pregnant with his child because she refused to have an abortion," Ethan Brown said. And his old Supreme Team cohort Dahlu was involved.

"They got Dahlu on the phone for conspiring to murder the pregnant girl," the Southside player says. With all the allegations stacking up, it didn't look good for Supreme.

"The dark outlook for Supreme- he is also charged with two murders- just got darker," Ethan Brown said, foreshadowing the outcome of the events. "All I know is that they ain't letting no black man win no federal trial, no murder case; especially a dude like him with his history," Bing says. "He got more shit against him than we did in the RICO act case. I don't think he can beat that. I hope he does for his sake."

Despite his fearsome rep, Supreme was far from the typical thug. "He'd talk to anyone if they pulled him up." Choke says. "You wouldn't even know who he was. He didn't ever deny nobody nothing. He'll take the shirt off his back for somebody. I've been doing time for 20 years and most dudes I meet that be high profile try to act like they like that. They look down on people, but Preme don't. He respect men." In prison, at FCI Gilmer and then MDC Brooklyn where the feds took him when he got indicted, Preme was a celebrity in high demand. All the prisoners clamored around him, just wanting to know him, some for case jumping reasons. The feds were known to plant informants. It was probably hard for Preme to differentiate between the prisoners trying to get at him and those who just wanted to meet him.

"Preme gets a lot of mail everyday. He got photos with Jay-Z, J-Prince, Irv, and Chris Gotti. Magazines were writing him for interviews. When that shit was on BET, everybody wanted to watch it," Choke says.

Tony Yayo, from 50 Cent's G-Unit, was in MDC Brooklyn when Supreme was there. "He was on a different floor so I never saw him," Tony Yayo said. "But to me he was really nobody. He's a person who's living in the past. I had messages sent to me, 'Fuck you, fuck 50.' I sent messages back like, 'Suck my dick.'" But Yayo was fronting because Preme doesn't get down like that.

In reality at MDC Brooklyn, when they moved Preme for a visit or lawyer meeting, they would have to shut down all movement in the prison because there were so many inmates that had separations on Preme. The whole building was ready to testify on him it seemed. The feds even reached out to Preme's old friend Fat Cat, who was in the Witsec program in the Bureau of Prisons in the cheese factory at FCI Marianna in Florida. "I know they wanted Cat to speak on Supreme," a Witsec prisoner, who was there with Cat, says. "But he told them to kick rocks, never. The feds were pissed. That was the reason he was kicked out of the Witsec program. They were done with him and mad about him not helping prosecutors with Supreme's Murder Inc. case." The feds promptly shipped Cat back to the New York State prison system.

Besides all this the case would take an even more unusual twist. It was already media saturated, but Ethan Brown, a writer for New York Magazine, came out with a very controversial and informative book before the trial that cast more doubt on the prosecutor's case and made Supreme look more like a regular person than the legendary gangster he was in the streets of New York and hip-hop circles. *Queens Reigns Supreme* was the book, and it added more intrigue to the already interesting case. "I was stunned that the investigation into Murder Inc. was built almost entirely on falsehoods promulgated by informants and cooperations," Ethan Brown said.

The book put Preme, Murder Inc., and 50 Cent squarely back in the spotlight of the public's eye, especially with 50's skyrocket to stardom and accumulation of movie deals, video games, books, a vitamin water company, clothing line and more which were directly attributed to and marketed with his gangster thug image. Brown's piece by piece breakdown of the rise and fall of the organized crime families of Queens in the 1980s was exhaustive and compelling. While the mythology of these gangs had filtered down through the years in the lyrics of popular rap songs, movies like *New Jack City* and even in the co-opted names rappers christened themselves with, Brown took the time to lay out how each family came to be, and what ultimately brought them down. In the process Brown drew clear lines between the real life drug dealers and killers and the men who would later sing their songs. The book showed how the culture of Queens was infecting popular culture once again just as it had in the late 1980s when hip-hop crashed the party.

"That book was just more of the same shit," Irv said. "I was kind of numb to everything. I didn't hide the fact that Preme is my man. The book was nothing to me. It was stuff my lawyers was already talking about. You opened the book to Irv Gotti and Supreme. That's the shit with me and Preme; no one gets us. Let people tell it and Preme is a criminal mastermind, mass murderer. They give you stories of extortion, that he was muscleing me. No one ever knew he was kind hearted, a problem solver, never looks to have problems with people. But if you wanted problems with him, he knew how to deal with you." The author of the book, Ethan Brown, became a celebrity overnight in hip-hop circles for his work and became the go to reporter on the case.

"Supreme's in a tough situation," Ethan Brown said. "He's facing the death penalty, and the feds keep adding superseding indictments to his case. He's also facing a number of uncharged allegations including the shooting of 50 Cent. It's going to be a long, complicated trial, that's for sure." In his book Brown offered an engaging tale of the confluence of hustling and hip-hop in Queens. He articulated how the combustible careers of the 1980s Queens drug kingpins like Supreme were transformed into hip-hop folklore by contemporary rap artists. "Supreme's myth was fed by the outsized nature of the Supreme Team, the matching uniforms, the tricked out cars, the army of members, as well as the many rap songs about him. He's probably the most mythologized hustler of the 1980s, which is why his story is so fascinating and continues to reverberate today," Ethan Brown said.

As street legends like Supreme were mythologized in lyrical lore, rappers and record labels discovered that the marriage of hustling and hip-hop brought increased record sales. But Ethan's book, contemplating the Preme/Murder Inc. federal indictment, asked hard questions: was playing hustler and gangster, complete with real hustlers and real guns, worth the demise of a legitimate multimillionaire business such as Murder Inc.? Supreme knew all too well the difference between a federal prison and being in a music video. Even so, he got caught up in the glitz and glamour of the entertainment world, while at the same time digging a hole for himself by trying to live up his gangster reputation.

The allure of most gangsta rap for the middle-class white kids who listened to it was that for four minutes at a time they could feel like the gangsters and hustlers alluded to in the music. Just as *The Sopranos* was an escape for middle-class suburban adults, so is hip-hop for the youngsters. What separated *Queens Reigns Supreme* from other books on hip-hop was that Brown's writing didn't fall prey to the romance of guns and money. Instead he painted a world of Shakespearean tragedy, one that stars like 50 Cent formed into an entirely new form of hustle which capitalized on the long held outlaw hero myth that American consumers purchase by the millions. The collateral damage left in 50's wake though was Preme and Murder Inc.'s ordeal and their descent into the American criminal justice machine.

"I met Supreme soon after *Queens Reigns Supreme* was published," Ethan said. "I was scared to death when I met him because QRS really broke down his mythology. I think he understood why I wrote the book the way I did. I was surprised by his incredible intelligence. He's self educated but in really surprising ways. He has great taste in literature, and he is a very astute observer of politics." Ethan's book humanized Supreme and questioned the government's vendetta against him. In his own way, Ethan Brown was Supreme's biggest defender, advocate, and supporter. Instead of promoting the government line, which was based on rumor and hearsay, he investigated the facts and came to his own conclusions. His book was a thorough accounting of the era and in no way did he have a prior connection to Supreme.

"I didn't know who Supreme was back then, so I did some research and thought it was really interesting. It started in 2003 when I was researching a cover story for New York Magazine about the Murder Inc. investigation," Ethan said. "And when I was researching, going back through all the newspaper articles from the 80s, it blew my mind what was going on back then and how much of the crack epidemic was centered in one area. I realized there weren't many articles on these guys beyond 1988, the year when rookie cop Edward Byrne was murdered by one of Fat Cat's hit men. I went to the U.S. District Court in Brooklyn and requested all the case files for Fat Cat, Supreme, and Prince. Out of everyone, whether it be Fat Cat or Pappy, Supreme kind of had the worst luck in terms of constantly being arrested, being told on by informants. Supreme had this reputation as this guy who is like a Teflon kind of hustler. The actual truth of the matter is pretty far from that." Ethan's book found the streets up close and personal, but he didn't do it alone.

"I came up with the idea to put all the guys in Queens in one book and then to connect it to hip-hop," Curtis Scoon said. "Most people appreciate more about the first half, the street guys than anything else in the book. If you are going to do a story, the biggest names come out of

Queens."

With the book out and the trial looming, it was a surreal moment made even more surreal with 50's continued media bombardment of Supreme, Murder Inc., and also Ethan's book. "The reason 50 Cent is in big bold letters on the cover is for marketing purposes," 50 said. To 50 it was all about him, but Supreme's legend found a whole new relevance in pop culture through the book at the exact time when he was going through his most trying challenge. The book came in for a lot of criticism.

"Certain people began writing books and articles about the Supreme Team, my uncle, the Southside and my self," Prince said. "These books caught the attention of my daughter. From time to time she would question me about my past and the Supreme Team in general. The things she was reading were inconsistent with what I shared with her. This made her upset."

Another hustler from the era tried to discredit Brown also. "He ain't talk to me," Spoon said. "He mainly went through the court and got documents. In the federal indictment I'm not in there, so I don't exist to Ethan Brown. His talking to a dude directly involved? He ain't do that."

The book was big news in the hip-hop world, everybody was sounding off about it. "The thing about people writing about us, you see it's a bunch of bullshit," Bimmy says. "No concrete to it. We're not giving no one shit. My brothers still fight for their life." But even bigger news was coming.

On September 7, 2005, *The New York Post* reported that after 50 Cent survived the initial shooting in 2000, Preme and various members of Murder Inc. kept tabs on the rapper in an ongoing plot to kill the by then multiplatnium phenom. The feds came to that conclusion after intercepting a series of two way pages like the one that Preme recieved from Chris Gotti on August 17, 2002, which simply said, "50 is in the hood Guy R. Brewer." Fifty even saw the release of court papers detailing the plot by Preme to have him killed as a means of trafficking on his notoriety. "Regardless where they pick a juror from, the juror knows 50 Cent," he said. "And they'll understand this is the kind of person they need to keep off the street." These were not very gangster comments from the supposedly gangster 50.

The World Entertainment News Network reported shortly thereafter that 50 Cent was calling for the release of the incarcerated Supreme so that he could die on the streets. "They should let him out so he can die in the streets like he's supposed to," 50 said. "If he could touch down in the street and find out what the difference between 50 Cent without finances is and the new me. In my neighborhood you can get somebody killed for $5,000. If I showed you my bank account, you know I could really create Vietnam there at $5,000 a body." Some believed that Supreme was responsible for the murder of 50 Cent's mother, Sabrina, who allegedly worked for the Supreme Team in the 80s and was caught stealing to support her crack addiction. This fueled the belief that 50 had been on a life long mission to get revenge on Supreme. Others said that Majestic in 50's movie, *Get Rich or Die Tryin'* was based on Supreme.

In the film, Majestic was connected to the death of the mother of 50's character, and there's a suggestion that Supreme could be 50's father. "He's not my father," 50 said. "I can't stand that nigga. I wasn't accusing him of fucking killing my mother." On the eve of the trial 50 Cent was front and center, his super thug persona that he ripped off from Supreme ever present. "Fifty makes his entire movie, which should be this puffy bio pic about himself. But it's about Supreme." *Get Rich or Die Tryin'* was not just a reflection of real life but a revenge fantasy for 50 as well. He couldn't get Preme in real life, at least not how a gangster would, but in his movie he could. His shooting, the most critical chapter in 50's mythology oeuvre, was the crux of the biopic. The movie allowed 50 to act out his long nurtured fantasy of a gangster style vengeance.

"I don't think there will be any fallout from the movie. Preme is really immobilized at this point. He's got a death penalty case. Everyone, including his closest friends and associates, believe he's never coming home. The 50/Supreme beef is really strange," Ethan Brown continued. "I don't even know what to say about it at this point particularly because I am suddenly drawn into the beef because of 50's new cover story with XXL where he goes after me and Supreme. This is perhaps the weirdest moment related to the book." In reality, the whole case, book, and scenario seemed much more reality TV than real life with all the twists and turns of *The Jersey Shore*. But where did the reality end and the entertainment start? The feds' case seemed to be prosecuted off of 50's lyrics and grandstanding in magazines. But how much truth existed in those? Apparently a lot because the defense would introduce 50 Cent's lyrics to *Many Men*, interviews conducted by 50 Cent, and Ethan Brown's book as evidence at the trial.

"The game has been over for a long time," Supreme said. "It's in a sad state of affairs. It is now designed so that the only one who can flourish is a rat. As long as he is willing to sleep with the government, he can operate without penalty. The feds always create monsters they can no longer control. These snitches are no different. The government has a history for adding dots as opposed to connecting the dots. If you examine the indictment in 2005, the initial premise was a criminal enterprise consisting of me and Murder Inc. Now all of the egregious assertions articulated in the first indictment, the exhaustive and extensive investigations for five years were a charade. The entire case against me was inconsistent. I was convenient in nature and my past put me in a precarious position. The case was about some prosecutor's lofty ambitions and closing a chapter." But in hip-hop it was about slamming the door shut on Murder Inc. while 50 used the beef to catapult to stardom.

"I've discovered that 50 is an incredibly shrewd, almost Machiavellian character," Ethan Brown said. "Supreme was very unhappy with 50 for a long time over various things. You probably heard about him being upset about *Ghetto Qur'an*. It's true. At one time I think he was trying to manage Ja Rule, and he was unhappy with 50's non-stop attacking of Ja. He said Ja was like his son, a young kid, very talented. Preme had a lot of reasons to be upset with 50. He did take action about these feelings. He made 50 very aware of how upset he was. But I don't believe he put him under surveillance. I don't believe Irv or Chris was working to put 50 under surveillance. That's what the feds are intimating; they're saying there were text messages between Irv and Preme. I just think they were talking shit back and forth about 50, not surveillance. Fifty's amazing at sizing people up. He sized up Preme perfectly. He sized Murder Inc. up incredibly."

With the trial looming, Supreme told Chris Gotti that he planned to "reach out to Jay and Puff about some shorts for my investigators. Both of them is situated really well. Wouldn't be nothing but peanuts to them." Gotti told Preme that both rap moguls had "asked about you individually." Supreme said he would write a note to the rappers and have his defense team hand deliver them. They also talked about how 50 was "staging shootings, creating these things." Preme called 50's newest album, *The Massacre*, "garbage" and told Chris Gotti that 50 would be doing Kentucky Fried Chicken commercials. Preme wanted to reach out to Russell Simmons, his old friend, but Simmons shut him down. "I'm not standing up for Preme," he said. "I can't stand up for Supreme. I hope he's innocent. I hope he didn't hurt anyone."

Irv Gotti, charged with money laundering, wanted a separate trial from Preme and the others who faced the death penalty. In court papers his attorney sanitized their client's past, dropping the Gotti nickname adopted by Irv and his brother Chris. And their Murder Inc. record label founded in 1999 was referred to simply as M.I. Records. "When you go through a federal investigation like Irv did, it's like having an atomic bomb dropped on you," the Southside player says. Murder Inc. was being tried under RICO laws, and after the Gotti's posted $1 million bail each, they forfeited their passports and were prohibited from leaving the New York area.

"They offered me six months, and I said no," Irv said. "We didn't want a guilty plea on us, so they could talk about that shit in Supreme's case." The Gottis stood up like soldiers even though they were innocent. "I was speaking to Irv on the phone, and I told him 'We did nothing wrong. When you stand on the side of right, when you know you're right, you die for that,'" Preme said. "I am proud of them. That is why I was in total agreement with severing our trials. I didn't want them painted with my brush. I am the usual suspect. The charges were all lies. Throughout our history when any member of society becomes an agent of the government, chaos ensues. It's neighbor against neighbor, brother against brother. People are using this to settle old scores. A rat is the lowest life form known to man. They serve no purpose on this planet. That is just a glimpse of how they operate. I'll never get that image out of my mind, that Sambo prosecutor up there- the only black saying, 'They don't call it Murder Inc. for nothing.'" Preme knew the only way the feds could convict the Gottis was by association.

Assistant Brooklyn U.S. Attorney Carolyn Pokorny opposed the severance motion, charging that the Lorenzo's not only sought to benefit financially by allegedly laundering Supreme's drug cash through Murder Inc., but had other motives as well. "Indeed, far from being harmed by the McGriff enterprise's murderous reputation, the Lorenzo's alignment with McGriff afforded a level of protection. Would be robbers and criminals, who extort those in the music industry, knew that if they targeted Murder Inc., its employees or executives, they would suffer retribution from the McGriff enterprise," she said.

"These young men are not charged with any violence," said Gerald Shargel, the Gottis' lawyer. "I don't think repeating the name is terribly helpful." The Murder Inc. crew feared they couldn't get a fair trial if they had to sit through evidence of gruesome crime scene photographs, autopsy reports, and testimony about drugs and guns. "The Lorenzo defendants seek a speedy trial at which they will be able to clear their names and business reputations," Shargel wrote in court papers. As the feds tried to merge the blurred lines Murder Inc. had created between entertainment and reality, the Gotti brothers quickly shed the image they'd worked so hard to establish.

"In the rap world everybody gets their turn," Supreme once said talking about the vagaries of fame and fortune. On October 24, 2005, Murder Inc. got its turn in a Brooklyn federal court, but there was more than fame and fortune on the line, the members faced a maximum of 20 years if convicted. *Life Imitates Art in NY Hip-Hop Trial, The New York Times* headline read. The drug and homicide charges related to Supreme's suspected East Coast narcotics empire didn't involve Murder Inc., but prosecutors charged that they used a variety of deals and cash transactions to launder more than $1 million in drug cash. To avoid the possibility that allegations against Supreme would prejudice the case against Murder Inc., Judge Edward Korman severed the brothers' money laundering trial from that of the more violent charges facing Supreme and his associates.

"Preme wanted that. He didn't want me dragged into the bullshit that they were draggin' him through," Irv Gotti said. "The whole time Preme felt bad, he was like, 'Yo, they fuckin' with you just because you're my man.' The two major things that the government was trying to prove was one, if you're a criminal stay a criminal, and two, if you come from the hood and you make it out and you're successful, leave them niggas there and don't help no niggas." Association made Murder Inc. guilty in the eyes of the feds. In truth, though, it was an association that Murder Inc. wanted and ran wild with, as the feds did with the case where they couldn't separate fact from fiction. "Rather than inquire with Universal or Def Jam as to the true origins of Murder Inc., the feds chose to rely on a confidential witness whose own knowledge that Murder Inc. was founded with drug money appears to have been based on street gossip and rumor," Gerald Shargel said. With the tide turning against them, the feds pressed on.

"You launder our money, we take care of you," was Supreme's bargain with Murder Inc., prosecutor Sean Haran said in court. Prosecutors contended that Supreme ordered shootings, including that of rapper 50 Cent, as a way of helping Murder Inc.'s music empire. The defense contested this vehemently, deeming it had no bearing on the case. At one point Shargel could be heard yelling from the judge's chambers, "Hommo did it, Hommo did it, Hommo did it. Even 50 Cent says it." Shargel emphasized to Judge Korman that allowing evidence related to 50's shooting would have a nuclear effect on the trial akin to revealing "a plot to assassinate Bob Dylan." Haran also alleged that Supreme's associates strong armed radio station officials to get more airtime for Murder Inc.'s artists. When they saw all the felons on Murder Inc.'s payroll, it scared the feds to death. Murder Inc.'s office looked like a probation office waiting room with all of the parolees.

"I probably got like 20, 25 niggas on parole," Irv said. "I think from a federal standpoint, they may look at it like, this nigga got an army of criminals." But in reality it wasn't like that. It was more about street cred and image than real violence.

"Our position is Supreme provided street credibility in a very rough and violent world of rap, a method of protection so to speak," Shargel told the court. "He was a legend in Queens and provided a certain aura and image. It's all about show business." The government's case consisted of Skytel pager records, copies of checks ranging from $38,000 to $100,000 to Supreme, and prison phone records from Supreme. Their chief premise was that Irv Gotti used proceeds from drug trafficking in New York and Maryland as start up money for Murder Inc. The feds contended that Gotti was the public face of the label while Supreme was the true owner.

"I'm going to make a chart," Shargel said sarcastically in the courtroom after prosecutors had made opening statements featuring a flow chart that tried to show how Murder Inc. laundered cash from Supreme. Shargel held a poster board and wrote, "Says Who?" on the poster board in capital letters. "Says who?" Shargel said. "Who says they're laundering money? I'm going to make a promise to you. I'm going to show you by the end of the trial that the government's witnesses are shameless liars who have lied about every situation they've been in." The defense said the government had no evidence to corroborate their money laundering charges against Murder Inc. and worse, federal investigators had trolled the streets and prison system looking for cooperators.

"The feds were listening to any nigga from New York who said he had info on Preme. These niggas was case jumping like crazy," the Southside player says. Dudes who didn't even know Supreme or the Gottis were signing up to testify against him.

"Do you know that after you were selected as jurors in the case the government is still out looking for witnesses?" Shargel told the jury. During the three week trial, Shargel's initial assertions proved to be true. Not only did the credibility of the cooperators in the case implode on the witness stand, but the prosecutors offered little evidence to support their charges. During testimony to jurors, Love stated that he routinely saw bags and shoe boxes of cash delivered to Murder Inc.'s offices. He testified that checks cut from Murder Inc. were reimbursed with drug money. Phillip "Dahlu" Banks testified that he would gladly commit perjury if it would help him receive leniency from prosecutors at sentencing. After a series of critical setbacks, including 50 Cent's shooting being dismissed, federal prosecutors rested their case against Murder Inc.

Def Jam cofounder Russell Simmons, Def Jam president Jay-Z, artists Ja Rule and Ahsanti sat together, while Terror Squads Fat Joe grabbed a seat in the back of the court to watch the proceedings. The trial attracted a Who's Who of the hip-hop community. Lyor Cohen, Dame Dash and

Minister Benjamin Chavis also attended. Russell Simmons dismissed accusations that Murder Inc. was funded with Preme's drug money. "Irv was the best thing to happen to Def Jam," he said. "I funded his company, and he has been a constant source of strength for Def Jam. I am just praying that we spend money reforming or convicting the criminals that are in our communities and less time and resources chasing the poets and artists who are conscious of and speak about the suffering of the masses."

During closing arguments Assistant U.S. Attorney Carolyn Pokorny labeled Supreme one of the "baddest, most dangerous drug lords in New York City." She then asked if it would be possible for Murder Inc. to be unaware what their "close friend did for a living." She then held up a gun, bags of crack, and pointed to a chart that listed numerous checks written to Supreme and expenses Supreme incurred that were paid for by Murder Inc. She also stated that Supreme's drug dealing gang invaded Murder Inc. and afforded the label protection. The government claimed Supreme had an unreported salary and a corporate charge card.

"They are interpreting all of this through dirty glasses," Shargel told the jury. Shargel said the prosecutors despised the relationship between Supreme and Murder Inc., but "that doesn't make it a criminal relationship." Shargel pointed out several inconsistencies between statements given by government witnesses Dahlu and Donnell Nichols. He noted Dahlu was a former Supreme Team member and convicted perjurer, who had been incarcerated from 1997 until 2004. Shargel claimed Dahlu didn't have firsthand knowledge of Preme and Irv's relationship because he wasn't around. When Dahlu was arrested on February 17, 2005, on charges ranging from credit card fraud to assault with a gun he told officers, "I want to talk to you about Supreme." The feds had no concrete evidence in the case, only snitches' stories.

"They were desperate to prove what they announced to the world," Shargel said. "The publicity was a casting call for the government to make their case." He told the jury that the government's case was based on guess work. "We don't destroy young lives based on guess work," he yelled to the jury. After two days of deliberations that cast Murder Inc.'s fate in doubt, jurors sided with the defense and acquitted them on all charges. *Gangsta Rap Label Executive Acquitted, The Los Angeles Times* headline ran on December 3, 2005. "This is a great victory for the entire culture of hip-hop," Minister Chavis said of the verdict. "Hip-hop profiling in the case of Irv and Chris Gotti exposes why the government should not attempt to censor or harass poets, lyricists, and music producers. Irv and Chris Gotti will emerge from this episode even stronger." Rapturous applause followed the not guilty verdicts. Outside of the Brooklyn courthouse, the scene was more striking.

"One of the jurors said 'this case was so weak,'" Ethan Brown said. "Some people were pretty appalled by the government's behavior at trial. The prosecution brought no evidence to support their theories like Supreme founded Murder Inc. This has a huge impact on the Supreme trial. I think the government is going to make a redoubled effort to make sure Supreme gets the harshest punishment imaginable." Murder Inc. beat the feds, but Preme was next, and he was facing much more serious charges.

"It's hard to explain what Preme's dealin' with," Chris Gotti said. "I'm gonna use the line from *Crime Partners*, Clifton Powel said it and he said, 'History will record his greatness.' Preme's a stand up dude. I don't know how many men could take what he's getting dealt, cause they are really tryin' to crush that dude. They got him charged with murders, and here's a guy who has never been a violent felon in his life. He used to sell drugs, okay. That's Supreme from the Supreme Team, but he's never been a violent dude. I've never seen him do a violent act."

The feds thought by indicting Murder Inc. they could get them to turn on the ultimate target of their probe, the one that they felt got away, Supreme. But it didn't work, Murder Inc. stood fast. "The government, with a renewed vigor, used my criminal history to discredit and vilify me as a monster with no conscience," Supreme said. "The deck is stacked, but I am prepared, still standing tall. You can put the death penalty on me. I've lived my life already. I've done everything I wanted to do. I'm going to stick to my values and face certain death. Every shooting, they point the finger at me, the bad guy. It's like a desperate grab. I've never been known as a murderer, and all of a sudden I'm this psychotic killer." Supreme was ready to fight all the charges. His whole life had prepared him for this moment. He was ready to face it like the legend he was, like the man he had always been.

"From day one the feds wanted us to cooperate with them to try and help them build a case against Supreme. But that's not in our make up," Chris Gotti said and his brother echoed that sentiment. "I stood up and I'm going to continue to stand up and I stand up for Preme," Irv Gotti said. "I love Preme. That nigga is my heart. My nigga Preme said it best, 'Irv always be on the side of right. Nothin' bad can come to you if you're on the side of right.'" The Gottis didn't snitch; they rode with their man, but some of Supreme's other associates sold him out as the government tried to bury Murder Inc. "A snitch is a person who agrees verbally or by his actions to participate in a situation, and once things start looking bad, he betrays that trust," T says.

"Donell Nichols is the worst scum bag on the face of the earth," Irv Gotti said. "He's worse than Jon 'Love' Ragin and worse than Phillip 'Dahlu' Banks. He went to the government just to tell them a story. And Love was a credit card scammer, but he don't wanna do his time, so he gonna talk so he don't have to do any time. A funny thing happened with him and Dahlu. I call it snitches' pride. They get up there and lie, but when the defense get at them, they hang themselves. My lawyer said, 'Jon Ragin, it's clear to say that you'll lie on Irv to save your own ass?' And he answers, 'Yes, I will lie.' He's on the stand, and he just said that he'll lie. The lawyer asked, 'Do you even know Irv Gotti?' He answers, 'Not really.' He just starts blurtin' out lil' shit like, 'I don't give a fuck about Irv. I don't give a fuck about the prosecution. I don't give a fuck about the defense.' He said this on the stand. They would rather turn these convicted criminals free to convict me." That's how the feds play, especially in the Murder Inc./Supreme case. They were actively hunting snitches to testify and make their case come together.

"After that big search was executed in January 2003, almost three years ago, the news stories were like casting calls for snitches," Gerald Lefcourt said. "The news stories said we're investigating Supreme's connection to Murder Inc. and money laundering, and there you have these snitches out there that raise their hands and volunteer in order to help themselves out of their predicaments. A guy like Phillip Banks; he's been in jail sixteen out of the last 24 years, and he is now facing life, and he wanted to get out. So he made up stories that Supreme was giving money to Irv."

And during the whole trial 50 Cent loomed large. "I know that his name, for some reason, was mentioned a hell of a lot in our trial and case," Chris Gotti said. "You're talkin' about a money laundering case and a lot of things didn't make sense. Whether the government was making things up or not, I dunno. I just know a lot of stuff didn't make sense."

To Murder Inc. it seemed the feds whole case was based on 50's lyrics. "It's outrageous really," Gerald Lefcourt said. "People write lyrics because they rhyme. You can't take this stuff literally. I don't think that lyrics should be taken out of context. What happened in our case was the government wanted to introduce lyrics, and then we said how about these lyrics which countered them. It got into the kind of situation where the judge realized the whole thing was absurd, and he wasn't going to allow any of it." The lines between reality and entertainment blurred, but one thing was certain, Murder Inc. and Preme thought 50 was a rat.

"In the affidavit they have these things called CI's and CW's. CI's are confidential informants, and CI's don't testify; they just give information," Irv said. "So much that I read in the affidavit it could only be this nigga. When it says 'CI #5 said this, this and that,' and you go back and recollect that situation in your head, it could only be one or two people saying shit like this. Who else knows about the intricacies of the Hit Factory beat down? Who knows about Atlanta when him and Ja had altercations? Why is this same CI saying, 'Preme is the seed money, Preme is extorting them.' It's all the shit he used to say. If you ask me, this dude been working with the police for a minute because I think he's a CI. When he got shot, I'm pretty sure he had police around him crazy, and I think he sold his soul right then and there. Let's go back to the studio beat down, that order of protection is real. That nigga went to the police, and he did sue us for $250,000 for whooping his ass. So is it so hard to believe that he is in cohorts with the police?"

As Preme approached trial the papers reported that 50 Cent was ready to testify for the prosecution against him, but it never happened. Fifty kept talking in the press. "We married til' death do us part," 50 said of Supreme. "They compare him to John Gotti, but John Gotti never had a problem getting his lawyers fees paid."

As the trial loomed Supreme was being represented by a public pretender. "Robert Simels was gonna represent him. Irv was gonna pay, but they froze his money," the Southside player says. "People always wonder why Ja Rule didn't pay. His money wasn't froze."

Preme did an interview with Vibe magazine about the case also, and 50 fired off, "He's fucking on trial. He shouldn't be talking. He should be keeping his fucking mouth shut. Preme destroyed what he was in the minds of so many people with this article. He was a nigga you would look at and say, he the real deal. But the nigga is broken at this point."

Preme wasn't broken, but he might have been broke. "He's broke; he has a court appointed lawyer," Ethan Brown said. "He's totally off the street forever. I don't think he's really a force at all anymore."

The feds backed off on the seed money theory also and went right for the jugular trying to prove a murder for hire case. "The investigation was started trying to link Murder Inc.'s start up to drug money," T says. "Now it's turned into something else."

The feds produced a remixed racketeering case. "That man is a drug dealer and murderer," Assistant U.S. Attorney Jason Jones said. They had flipped more of Preme's co-defendants, and with his case severed from all the others, he stood alone to face the death penalty, alone but undaunted, a true and certified gangster to the end staring death in the face with the charisma and integrity that made him the legend he was.

As Preme's trial opened, the feds still seemed intent on portraying his legal business ventures, the *Black Gangster* soundtrack and *Crime Partners*

DVD, as merely fronts for his illegal activities. But both were clearly legit as a rep from Holloway House, the publishing house that owned the rights to Donald Goines books, testified in court that Supreme's production company Picture Perfect did option the book. The Murder Inc. trial proved that *Crime Partners* was not a front for money laundering but a low budget, straight to DVD movie that had a promising soundtrack set to be released by Def Jam. *Former NYC Drug Kingpin Had Movie Dreams*, *The New York Post* headline read. The prosecution's efforts to discredit Supreme's business ventures didn't work in the Murder Inc. trial, so it was obvious they were stumbling around and grasping for a new angle.

"I provided tangible proof of my efforts," Preme said. "All my years of hard work to put together a legitimate project- a movie and soundtrack. All of my witnesses were hard working tax paying legitimate people. Government workers, hospital, police, concert clubs owners, the owner of Holloway House Publishing, DMX's manager- they all testified under oath for me, and the jury dismissed them totally and accepted the words of a bunch of rats whom in the next five to ten years, they or their family members may have to encounter them when they are set free in the streets."

Supreme was facing charges ranging from murder to drug conspiracy. Money laundering wasn't even among the thirteen counts in his new indictment handed down on March 31, 2006. In the fifth superseding indictment that Preme faced, prosecutors announced they were pursuing capital cases against five defendants including Preme, Emmanuel "Manny Dog" Mosley, Barry Broughton, Alvin Derek Smiley, and Russell Allen. Less than two weeks later, the prosecutors reversed themselves without explanation saying Supreme alone would face death. On April 13, 2006, Preme's co-defendants were Mosley, Dennis Crosby, Victor Wright, Nicole Brown, and Vash-Ti Paylor. After all the superseding indictments and government defections, his co-defendants on January 8, 2007, were Dennis Crosby, Alvin Derek Smiley, Barry Broughton, and Russell Allen. After more defections and severances, Preme stood alone.

"The shooters were Alvin, Rus, and Barry," the Southside player says. "They was all killing, all from Harlem. They'd ride bikes. Do tricks." Federal prosecutors wouldn't explain the rational behind the reversals, but what drove the decision to drop the death penalty against some of Supreme's co-defendants seemed pretty clear. Soon after Manny Dog's case was death authorized in the spring of 2006, he began cooperating with the government in their case against Supreme. The government also dropped their death notices against Broughton and Smiley, two of the men who were accused of working under Manny Dog in the hit squad that carried out the E-Money Bags and Troy Singleton slayings. They both worked out deals to sell out Supreme just as their boss Manny Dog had.

After all the guilty pleas and cooperation agreements, the main thrust of the government's case was that Preme paid 50 grand to have two rivals gunned down in 2001.

The case against Supreme was "about a man with the power and will to get people murdered," prosecutor Jason Jones told jurors in his opening statements in Brooklyn. In 2001, prosecutors said Supreme met Manny Dog, who was a Harlem based hitman and paid Manny Dog to kill E-Money Bags in retaliation for the slaying of Black Just.

"Preme met Manny Dog through Wayne Davis who he was locked up with," the Southside player says. According to Manny Dog he took the payment from Supreme at a pita shop in downtown Manhattan.

Prosecutors said that after the killing Supreme sent a text message to Irv Gotti reading, "You missed the party." Love testified that Preme told him that the gunfire from the E-Money Bags murder was like "the fourth of July," a quote that unsurprisingly was picked up nearly everywhere in the media coverage of Supreme's trial. Manny Dog testified that Supreme approached him again during the summer of 2001 about the Troy Singleton job. Supreme wanted him killed for fucking with Murder Inc. Love also testified that Preme feared Singleton because he was an associate of E-Money Bags and might be seeking revenge.

Manny Dog put the same hit squad together, but this time allegedly included Eric "E-Bay'" Moore to do the hit. Prosecutors said that Supreme sent a text message, "I'm on these guys; there is no stopping me. Four dogs, we're going to turn it up."

On October 28, 2001 Manny Dog sent a text message to Supreme at 1 a.m., "I'm at this club called Doobies." Preme replied at 1:25 a.m. that Manny Dog should "go to Liberty, take a left, go all the way to the Van Wyck." Just after 3 a.m. Singleton was slain, cut down in a hail of bullets outside a sports bar.

The next morning Supreme received the text message, "Big news, Troy is a wrap." To the feds these text messages were paramount to a confession.

"The shooting happened right off the Van Wyck on Liberty," prosecutor Pokorny said. "There is no innocent explanation I can submit to you for this conversation, and all these messages came from the pager unit itself. It didn't come from a phone call. And you know that when you look at the source of them, there is no innocent explanation for why he is telling a hitman to go to a sports bar, and then an hour and forty minutes later the hitman kills Troy Singleton. The only reason is that he was helping him, and he wanted him to kill Troy Singleton for him. The man sitting in the courtroom is one of the most dangerous, feared, and ruthless gangsters in all Queens, and when Supreme gets in a fight with somebody, he doesn't go to the cops. He doesn't hire lawyers. He hires a hit team to assassinate them, to blow them away, so that their mom can barely recognize them when they go down to the morgue."

The prosecutions whole case was built on a combination of text messages and cooperator testimony and Preme's attorney, David Ruhnke, pointed this out to the jurors.

"What we don't have on these murders is wiretaps," he said. "We don't have anyone discussing murder over a wiretap; we don't have fingerprints associated with the murder at all. We don't have an eyewitness that saw Supreme sitting in a car with Manny Dog. They don't have DNA, firearm matches. It's just a complete non-event as far as ballistics are concerned." But none of it mattered. David Ruhnke tried to convince the jury that "the government in this case is prosecuting somebody who just doesn't exist anymore." But they didn't listen.

"The jury came in with a predisposed notion of who I was based on how I was depicted," Preme said. "A lot of these jurors were secretly going on the Internet. The judge had to get rid of the ones that spoke truthfully about it. Throughout the trial the jury was more concerned with who was in my support section, as if the Supreme Team existed and was in the courtroom. There wasn't a case to prove. There was no enterprise, and I never paid anyone $50,000 to kill two street corner hustlers. The feds initial premise was recalibrated numerous times. I was superseded four times. They formulated their case as they went along."

Actually, the trial was bizarre as prosecutors kept speaking about the Supreme Team in the present tense when in truth Supreme was indicted by the feds in 1987, and the rest of the Supreme Team including Prince went down in the early 1990s. There was no more Supreme Team, but the media coverage of Supreme's case gave the public the impression that the Supreme Team was still in existence. Michael Todd Harvey told the jury how he was involved in selling heroin and cocaine to Supreme in the 90s. Others testified of his narcotics conspiracy, but the main thrust was the murder for hire charges. Prosecutor Porkony even defended her snitches to the jury.

"Now, a word about Emmanual Mosley, completely repulsive," she said. "We fully expected that you would be disgusted by him, and what he does for a living. The issue is not whether you like him. He has done terrible things. We told you that in the opening statement. We brought it out on direct. It's not whether you like him; it's whether he's credible."

Love proved to be the star witness against Supreme. The one time pimp and credit card fraudster's testimony was consistently convincing.

"He had an incredible capacity for recalling events and even entire conversations while adding dramatic flourishes to his testimony," Ethan Brown said.

A Brooklyn jury deliberated for five days before finding Supreme guilty of murder for hire and drug dealing. The court found that there was sufficient evidence to convict him of racketeering and conspiracy offenses including drug distribution and murder for hire, where multiple witnesses testified about their roles in his drug distribution trade, and the record contained direct testimony that Preme ordered two murders to maintain the reputation of his enterprise. The court found that Preme ordered two murders not simply for revenge or personal self aggrandizement but to re-establish and maintain the reputation of his enterprise after the two individuals disrespected him.

"The feds gave out eleven deals, and six of these snitches testified at my trial," Preme said. "I had only actually met two of them- Emanuel 'Manny Dog' Mosley and Jon Ragin. Then there was Climent 'CJ' Jordan, Barry Trip, Mongo Broughton, Alvin Smiley, Michael Harvey, Terrance 'Tony' Terrall, Eddie 'Divine Knowledge' Oliver, Juan Romano, and Phillip 'Dahlu' Banks. Climente 'CJ' Jordan was the catalyst. He was doing fifteen years in Delaware and decided to cut his sentence at my expense. I had never met him. He told on Manny Dog and his crew. All the rats had numerous murders. They testified under oath that they would lie. The government is willing to tolerate any type of behavior when it serves their interest."

Supreme, who was acquitted on lesser drugs and weapons charges, looked back and smiled at his supporters when the verdict was issued on February 1, 2007. As the proceedings moved into the death penalty phase, Preme's lawyer said, "We're pretty confident this jury will spare his life."

The mother of one of the victims told reporters that she opposed the death sentence for Supreme. "Death is not the answer," she said. And the judge on the case warned prosecutors that pursuing a death sentence would be a waste of time and money.

"There's no chance in the world there would be a death penalty verdict in this case," U.S. District Court Judge Frederick Black said. "If I'm wrong, I will have egg on my face, but I will not be incorrect. Theres no chance that twelve jurors will vote for the death penalty in this case, and I think it is good for us to save money if we can do that and judicial resources."

The prosecutors pressed on with the death notice. "We think these are sham notices," David Ruhnke said.

The prosecution countered. "The notices are real," prosecutor Pokorny said. "It's something that got a real close look in Washington."

Fourteen-year-old Troy Singleton, Jr. tearfully testified how much he missed his father. The paper reported that Supreme didn't have the stomach to look the slain man's son in the eyes. The feds pulled out all the stops even though the judge was against the death penalty. "Even the judge in my case, after hearing all the evidence, had serious concerns on why they were seeking the death penalty. The poltical nuances at play were highly sophisticated," Preme said. The feds had an agenda, and they were trying to keep it, but they didn't account for the jury's take on Supreme.

The defense had humanized Supreme. Ruhnke told jurors that both victims were known thugs who were armed when killed. Though Supreme's name was huge on the street and in the hip-hop business, the defense argued he was suprisingly vulnerable to attacks from all sorts of street guys. "While researching *Queens Reigns Supreme,*" Ethan Brown said. "I spoke with a number of people close to Supreme who said there were constant attempts on his life. And Supreme's former accountant told me that Supreme feared for his life and that he felt young street guys could earn their stripes if they harmed him."

The jurors believed this angle, which was very close to the truth. "Remember the government claimed my actions were to prevent these guys from killing me. All the jury had to say to the judge is, 'We're not going to believe these snitches,'" Preme said.

"There's no way he deserves to get his life taken," Joanne McGriff, Preme's sister, who broke down on the stand said. "He's not that type of person." She was the final witness, and her cries echoed though the courtroom as she was led back to the where the spectators sat. There was sympathy for Supreme but not in the prosecution's eyes.

"Kenneth McGriff has not earned your mercy," prosecutor Jones said in his final argument. "He has not earned your sorrow. He has earned the penalty of death." The feds were determined to put Preme to death.

Eleven jurors found that Smith and Singleton's willing participation in dangerous and illegal activity contributed to their unfortunate deaths, Newsday reported. Seven jurors also said Supreme seriously believed the victims and others were out to kill him. With all the anti-death penalty sentiment, the prosecutors dropped the death penalty in Supreme's case. *Death Penalty Dropped, The New York Daily News* headline read and *The New York Post* declared, *Supreme Escapes Execution*. Still, he was sentenced to life.

"I know Supreme pretty good," Chaz Williams said. "We are all from Queens. I didn't get to talk to him when he was going through his court case because he was locked up. I went to support him on the death penalty phase. He got life, but I will never say he won't get out. He might win on appeal." *Ex-Druglord McGriff Gets Life in Prison, The New York Times* read on February 10, 2007. Preme had cheated death in the courtroom, but he still had lost his freedom.

Preme sat impassively as the jury declined to order his death. He swiveled slowly in his chair and stared away from the jurors as they announced their verdict after barely two and half hours of deliberations. Before the U.S. Marshals led Preme back to jail, he waved to three rows of his friends and family and gently tapped his chest about his heart. "The client feels relieved and we feel relieved to have gotten to death's door and not have to open it," David Ruhnke said. Preme was vanquished, but his legend remained as did his legacy. For an ex-convict to produce a film was "an achievement," Preme's lawyer said. "They will never take that away from him." With Preme being convicted and sentenced to life, it seemed the story was over, but in the world of hip-hop and the streets, the legend and controversy never dies. Like the Energizer Bunny it just keeps going and going and going.

CHAPTER 13

THE AFTERMATH

"He is one of the only renowned drug kingpins of the 80s to outlast the crack era and law enforcement legal assault. By standing up and never cooperating with the government Kenneth 'Supreme' McGriff secured his position as one of the most notorious men to ever walk the streets of New York."
— **Don Diva, Issue 30**

"Many emcees have put the McGriff myth into verse."
— **New York Magazine**

"To both law enforcement and a generation of rappers and hustlers, Supreme is a black John Gotti, a larger than life figure whose underworld reach seems limitless."
— **Vibe Magazine**

To both the NYPD and the feds Supreme was a black John Gotti, a larger than life figure whose underworld exploits endeared him to a generation of rappers and hustlers. He was a legendary druglord with ties to both the hip-hop industry and a notoriously profitable and ruthless drug crew that became iconic on the same Queens streets that produced rap stars like LL Cool J, 50 Cent, Ja Rule, and Run DMC. "Dudes might stare at him like he's Michael Jordan or something and he always downplays the attention," the Southside player says. "If you call him famous, he'll correct you in a minute, 'Nah, the infamous.' He'll say. He was never anyone else than Supreme. I believe Preme can go home right now and ask to borrow a million dollars." Supreme's reputation as a man and a gangster is forever intact. Through Nas, Fat Joe, Ghost Face, and other rappers, Preme's crime boss lore of bravado and fearlessness is secure.

"By taking the storm and not flipping, Preme secured his spot as one of the baddest guys to ever walk the streets of New York City," Ethan Brown said. By standing up and never cooperating with the government, Supreme has gone down as one of the most notorious men to ever grace the chroncles of gangster lore.

"Preme is that guy for real. A true O.G.," the Southside player says. In the aftermath of his conviction and life sentence, Supreme was shipped off to ADX Florence, the Bureau of Prisons supermax prison in the Rockies. Even though he had not ever been in high security level prisons before, only mediums and lows, the feds pushed the BOP to incarcerate him at ADX where the worst of the worst were housed. With limited outside contact, Supreme is disconnected from the outside world, but his name still made international headlines, usually in connection with superstar rapper 50 Cent.

50 Cent Fears Supreme's Revenge, The World Entertainment News Network headline read on Febraury 18, 2007. The news network reported that 50 feared for his life after Supreme was spared a death sentence. They said 50 mobilized an extensive team of minders to protect himself, as he was convinced Supreme would seek revenge on him for spilling secrets about his activities in his music. This was reality, but in 50's fantasy gangster paradise he still talked mad shit. "I find enjoyment in things I probably shouldn't enjoy," 50 said. "Like seeing Supreme broken because he's weak. Sometimes you think someone's strong, but it's because everyone is standing in front of them. He's not strong himself. Irv Gotti's on the radio talking about how he wanted it to be over cause Preme got life in jail. You supposed to ride all the way out baby." Fifty was always at his best distorting matters.

Irv Gotti sets the record straight.

"Preme ain't want to end nothing," Irv said. "He was like, 'I'm facing the death penalty. If my life is to end in jail, it's all good, the only thing I'm asking is that you win.' Fifty don't understand that because he's a faggot, he's going to make fun of that? He would never stand up to 20 years for his man. It amazes me how much he's on my dick. He's like, 'Irv got on a Supreme Team shirt in the new video. He's from Hollis, Supreme Team is Southside' I'm not even thinking about this nigga." And neither are the streets. A 30 foot billboard in Jamaica, Queens, summed up the overall view of 50 Cent and his reputation on the Southside- G-Unot. And one time G-Unit member, The Game, put out a *Stop Snitching / Stop Lying* DVD, which pointed to 50's complicity.

"You need to stop telling on people. That's not cool," The Game said. Fifty laid it on thick too. After Preme was sentenced, 50 was on the radio laughing and telling prisoners at MDC Brooklyn to go wake Supreme up, so he could listen to 50 clowning him on the radio.

The reality of it was that Supreme rejected 50 and if you believe 50, Supreme was the one who tried to kill him. Fifty grew up idolizing the Supreme Team and Supreme. He wanted to be them. He emulated them in every aspect of his life, and when it came down to it, Supreme rejected him and embraced some dudes from Hollis. In the end, though, 50 got his revenge. But despite that revenge Supreme and the Supreme Team will live on in legend. While Supreme, C-Just, Prince, and the others are doing life in federal prison, their stories are still reverberating in the streets and hip-hop, in the media, and in entertainment. Other members like Bimmy and Tuck are working on documentaries and books to put out reliving their experiences with the team. And still others like Babywise and Bing are just trying to live their lives out peacefully. They were the best to ever do it on the Southside, and they spawned a legion of imitators who tried to bite their style- in the streets and in hip-hop, making their lifestyle fodder for movies, documentaries, rap videos, and popular culture as a whole. And the story isn't over.

"When Manny Dog and them get out, they're gonna recant their testimony, get Preme back in court," S says. But if they're going to do that, they never should have snitched in the first place.

Still the rumors fly, and Tuck breaks it down like it is. "It is what it is. I'm not receiving a pension or endorsements for the shit I did," Tuck says. "I never wanted to be a famous nigga living the street life. If I could turn back the hands of time, I would have made different choices. Coming up in the hood is rough. You see all types of shit, and it's not pretty. I would never in a million years do what I've done all over again. I don't give a fuck how much money you have. No amount of money is worth a life sentence. When you're young, you make decisions that affect the rest of your life. You have to pay the consequences of your actions. You can't say, 'I got to find a way out of this.' Dudes want to play Monopoly all day, but nobody wants to go to jail. Be willing to handle this jail shit just like you handle that street shit."

Life in prison for neverending infamy is a high price to pay. But for some that is the cost they pay to be the boss. That's the lure of the drug game, to live fast and go down in flames. In the drug game it's real, and choices must be made. The team made theirs. They stuck to their principles, their ideals, and their loyalty to their comrades.

"Crime is a cancer that eats away at our communities," Ving Rhames, the host of BET's *American Gangster* series said. "But for a generation that grew up thinking greed is good, they're not quite so sure whether crime pays or not. I grew up around a lot of criminals, thugs, dope dealers, and gangbangers. But in life with the hood gangster, the hood legend, some things turn out negative. They eventually wind up destroying themselves." This holds true for Supreme, but his myth is still celebrated. BET showed that about his celebrity with their series *American Gangster*, which featured Preme. With the litany of magazine articles and books on the Supreme Team, *American Gangster* cashed in, but was their portrayal accurate?

"From quite a few things that I've read in a number of different publications, there are a lot of people out there telling lies and fabricating truths," the Queens insider says. "The guys who did most of the narrating on the *American Gangster* episode were guys that Preme didn't really know. His name is Wakim and the other guy's name is Prince Rasheem. Wakim was down with Cat. Prince Rasheem is Tony Fuertado's first cousin. The only persons that have had something to say thus far that I respect and know what he said as being the truth and not a fabrication of the truth is Prince and Supreme, and we know Preme don't do a lot of unnecessary talking."

Preme was and is a monsterous legend worthy of honor as are all the team members. Their legend has survived intact and unblemished. "I feel I didn't portray Supreme correctly in QRS," Ethan Brown says. "It's not like anything in his past was misrepresented. But I didn't capture how charismatic he is. I hadn't met him in person until after the book came out. It was a mind-blowing experience to see how charismatic he actually is." Preme affects everyone the same way. He is a gentleman gangster, an icon in the streets, in prison, and in hip-hop, a true ladies' man who knows how to carry himself.

"Preme is my brother to the end," Irv Gotti said. "You know they got him in one of the worst jails in the country in solitary confinement-basically a hole, 23 hours a day. They limit his visitation rights, and they limit his phone privileges; it's just hard. People are always asking me, 'Why do you still speak about Supreme?' It is because my man is in the hole, yo. So when that word gets back to him from the other inmates that I'm still riding, it makes my nigga smile."

SOURCES

The Almighty Latin King and Queen Nation by David Brotherton
Vibe Magazine
www.smokingsection.net
New York Magazine
Queens Reigns Supreme by Ethan Brown
Cop Shot by Mike McAlary
As Is Magazine
Don Diva Magazine
F.E.D.S. Magazine
Dead on Delivery by Robert M. Stutman and Richard Esposito
Pieces of Weight by 50 Cent
www.gorillaconvict.com
XXL Magazine
www.VH1.com
New York Daily News
The New York Times
New York Newsday
King Magazine
www.allhiphop.com
Court Records
www.thesmokinggun.com
www.rapmusic.com
www.rapbasement.com
www.sixshot.com
www.sohh.com
www.rapnews.net
www.vibe.com
King of Kings DVD
Five Percenters by Michale Muhammad Knight
Hustle and Win by Supreme Understanding
Street Legends Vol. 1 by Seth Ferranti
www.wikipedia.com
Notorious Cop by Derek Parker
BET's *American Gangster* series

* Also I have talked to numerous Supreme Team members, Supreme, other convicts and dudes from New York and Queens who have helped me to put this story together.

ABOUT THE AUTHOR

Seth Ferranti exists, writes, and resides in the Federal Bureau of Prisons. He has been in the belly of the beast almost nineteen years with his current release date in 2015. The people and subjects he writes about are those that he knows extremely well, being in close confinement with them. He just is not only interested in what he writes about, he lives it, as he is serving a 304 month sentence for a drug conspiracy charge. He is the real deal- the Gorilla Convict Writer- penning articles since 1999. His work has appeared in Don Diva, Out of the Gutter, King, F.E.D.S., Vice, FHM, Street Elements, Elemental, 4Front, Get Money, Urban Celebrity and many other magazines and websites. Check out his archived published articles on www.gorillaconvict.com on the publications section along with all the interviews, profiles, and reviews of him and his work on the media section. His published books include Prison Stories and Street Legends Vol. 1 and 2. He also wrote a short story for Nikki Turner's Christmas in the Hood, his writing appears in The Baddest of the Bad from Gutter Books, and The Prison Writing of Seth Ferranti from Strategic Media Books. To order his books and read his blog go to www.gorillaconvict.com

For more on the Supreme Team check out *Team Player: Truths of a Southside Ambassador* by Ronald "Tuck" Tucker from Manumit Publishing

COMING SOON

"A compelling and thought provoking true-crime account of one man's life in the drug game. Discover the inner workings of the Supreme Team from a man who lived the life, walked among legends, went through the chaos, and came out alive. This story is a must read. It had to be told, and Ronald 'Tuck' Tucker is the only one who can tell it." — Seth Ferranti

FEDERAL PRISONERS

If you would like to get the Gorilla Convict newsletter and be updated on future Gorilla Convict releases or if you have a story to tell email us at diane@gorillaconvict.com on Corrlinks and we will accept and add you to our email mailing list.

Gorilla Convict Publications now offers all our titles in all ebook formats. Download them now at www.gorillaconvict.com.

Prison Stories	978-0-9800687-2-6	$9.99
Street Legends Vol. 1	978-0-9800687-3-3	$9.99
Street Legends Vol. 2	978-0-9800687-6-4	$9.99
The Supreme Team	978-0-9800687-5-7	$12.99

Also look out for Infamous Gangsters: Rayful, Fat Cat and Alpo, Legendary figures in the Black Underworld and Hip-Hop Lore. It will be on sale as an ebook soon.

The Don Diva Bestselling Author

SETH FERRANTI

PRISON STORIES

"Seth Ferranti writes with the bluntness and slangy-ness of street lit but with a much more penetrating gaze into the world of prison." – Ethan Brown, author of Queen's Reigns Supreme: Fat Cat, 50 Cent and the Rise of the Hip-Hop Hustler

"Prison Stories outlaw rawness mixes well with hip-hop's street essence. Fans of Iceberg Slim's pimp tales or HBO's 'Oz' series will really dig this" – Elemental Magazine

"Prison Stories is very real. I love Seth Ferranti's writing" – Wahida Clark, Esscence best selling author of Payback is a Mutha

"Don't expect a heartwarming story of redemption; expect an unbelievable addictive take of how things really operate in prison." – Giant Magazine

"Plenty of blood is shed in this intense record of the harsh realities of the penal system." – Smooth Magazine

"An episode of 'Oz' couldn't capture prison drama the way Seth Ferranti does in Prison Stories." – Don Diva Magazine

"Prison Stories is what 'Oz' and 'Prison Break' weren't real enough to be." – Kwame Teague, author of Ghetto Sam and the Dutch series

"Prison Stories reveals a world of fearless convicts, inconspicuous snitches and deadly gang rivalry" – The Ave Magazine

"With Prison Stories, Seth Ferranti now finds himself among urban fiction's top writers." – urbanbooksource.com

ISBN 978-0-615-12685-2

9 780615 126852

GORILLA CONVICT PUBLICATIONS
B 28
SUPREME TEAM
VOL 1
STREET LEGENDS
SETH FERRANTI
DON DIVA BEST SELLING AUTHOR

Kenneth "Supreme" McGriff

Wayne "Silk" Perry

Anthony Jones

Aaron Jones

Peter "Pistol Pete" Rollack

George "Boy George" Rivera

DEATH BEFORE DISHONOR

In a time where the world is infatuated by the streets, learn firsthand what a true hustler is— and the price they pay for the crown. This book profiles some of the streets most feared and respected gangsters of the late 20th century. They invented "Ball 'til you fall." Read their stories and see if it was worth it.

Death before Dishonor is their creed and omerta their code. The six gangsters featured here epitomize the definition of a street legend. They were down with the stop snitching movement from the jump. And they are serving life sentences for holding their weight. This book profiles the street legends of the crack era like never before.

Kilo's of cocaine and heroin, millions of dollars of drug money, luxury customized cars, dime pieces galore, bling bling to shine, multitudes of violence and vicious murder— these dudes were street stars and their lifestyles are what gangsta rap represents. Read their stories and ride shotgun with a hood legend.

ISBN 978-0-9800687-0-2

5 1 5 0 0

9 780980 068702

www.gorillaconvict.com

GORILLA CONVICT PUBLICATIONS

STREET LEGENDS
VOL. 2
OG's

SETH FERRANTI
DON DIVA BEST SELLING AUTHOR

ORIGINAL GANGSTERS

Frank Matthews

Maurice "Peanut" King

Michael "Fray" Salters

The Boobie Boys

Short North Posse

New World

Ice-T spit, "Gangsters don't die, they multiply" and to keep it all the way official read about the street's real legends. The Original Gangsters that inspired BET's American Gangster series, all those Hollywood gangsta flicks, the litany of true crime street documentaries and gangsta rappers galore. The Black Gangster is in effect. Taking over where the Italian mobsters and Colombian cocaine cartels left off. **Street Legends** gives you their stories. Read about the black John Gotti's and Pablo Escobars. True to life and hood to hood. Real recognizes real. And this book will give you the truth.

Let recognized prison journalist and gangster chronicler Seth Ferranti aka Soul Man take you on a journey to the criminal underworld. Where real O.G.'s go hard and suckers get exposed. In **Street Legends, Vol. 1**, he mesmerized readers with the exploits of the Death Before Dishonor six— Supreme, Wayne Perry, Anthony Jones, Aaron Jones, Pistol Pete and Boy George. Now in Street Legends, Vol. 2, he introduces the Original Gangsters. Men of honor, respect and violence. Street stars and hood icons.

The Black Caesar, Frank Matthews, Original King of New York. Peanut King, Lord of B-More's heroin trade. Michael Fray, the Ambassador of Chocolate City. The Boobie Boys of Miami and rapper Rick Ross fame. Short North Posse, the Columbus, Ohio crew that Triple Crown publisher Vickie Stringer snitched on, and The New World, Islamic bank robbers from Newark, New Jersey. Read these tales of chaos, murder and mayhem that embody elements of cash money, debonair style, brutal diplomacy, unchecked violence, vicious betrayal and brotherly unity.

ISBN 978-0-9800687-1-9

9 780980 068719   51500

www.gorillaconvict.com

Michael G. Santos Foundation

Are you facing a lengthy prison term? If you are, consider signing up for the Straight-A Guide. It is a free, self-directed program designed to prepare prisoners for success upon release. To the extent that individuals participate in the Straight-A Guide, they emerge with values, skills, and resources that help them conquer the negative influences of imprisonment. Signing up is simple.

Send an email invite to the following address: enroll@Straight-A-Guide.com. Within seven days of receipt of your invite, representatives from the Straight-A Guide will send a copy of the book *Triumph! Conquering Imprisonment and Preparing for Reentry* along with a question to which you should respond through email:

How would you define success upon release?

Upon receipt of your question, representatives of the Straight-A Guide will send the entire program, free of charge. The literature is written by long-term prisoners like Seth Ferranti, men who make a habit of conquering imprisonment. Be a man, not an inmate—Sign up for the Straight-A Guide today!

The Straight-A Guide is a prisoner reentry program sponsored by The Michael G. Santos Foundation.
Non-profit Tax ID # 27-1904346

Justin Paperny
Executive Director
PO Box 261908
Los Angeles, CA 91426
www.Straight-A-Guide.com
enroll@Straight-A-Guide.com

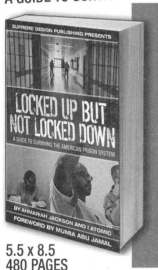

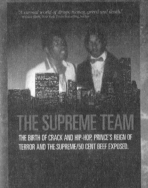

THOROUGHBRED PUBLICATIONS

PRESENTS

CHI LIFE, MY LIFE

DON'T GET IT TWISTED

MR. WILLIE BOUNCEBACK